Altruism in Private Law

Liability for Nonfeasance
and
Negotiorum Gestio

Altruism in Private Law

Liability for Nonfeasance
and
Negotiorum Gestio

JEROEN KORTMANN

OXFORD
UNIVERSITY PRESS

OXFORD
UNIVERSITY PRESS

Great Clarendon Street, Oxford OX2 6DP

Oxford University Press is a department of the University of Oxford.
It furthers the University's objective of excellence in research, scholarship,
and education by publishing worldwide in

Oxford New York

Auckland Cape Town Dar es Salaam Hong Kong Karachi
Kuala Lumpur Madrid Melbourne Mexico City Nairobi
New Delhi Shanghai Taipei Toronto

With offices in

Argentina Austria Brazil Chile Czech Republic France Greece
Guatemala Hungary Italy Japan South Korea Poland Portugal
Singapore Switzerland Thailand Turkey Ukraine Vietnam

Oxford is a registered trade mark of Oxford University Press
in the UK and in certain other countries

Published in the United States
by Oxford University Press Inc., New York

First published 2005

British Library Cataloguing in Publication Data

(Data available)

Library of Congress Cataloging-in-Publication Data

Kortmann, Jeroen.
Altruism in private law : liability for nonfeasance and negotiorum gestio / Jeroen Kortmann.
p. cm.
Includes bibliographical references and index.
ISBN 0-19-928005-3 (hard cover : alk. paper) 1. Negotiorum gestio—Europe. 2. Assistance in emergencies—Europe. I. Title.
KJC1083. K67 2005
346. 03—dc22

2004025248

ISBN 0-19-928005-3 (hbk)

10 9 8 7 6 5 4 3 2 1

Typeset by Newgen Imaging Systems (P) Ltd., Chennai, India
Printed on acid-free paper by
Biddles Ltd., King's Lynn

Preface

In *Altruism in Private Law* I discuss two issues that are raised by the parable of the good Samaritan. The first falls mainly within the area of tort law and is generally referred to as the issue of 'liability for nonfeasance' or 'the duty to act'. The second and, in my view, related issue concerns the intervener's right to recover expenses made, loss suffered, or perhaps even to be remunerated and/or rewarded for his or her intervention. Discussions of this second issue are commonly found in books on the law of restitution. While *Altruism in Private Law* includes two chapters with brief accounts of the ways in which the Roman, French, and German legal systems approach the two respective issues, these chapters are not – in the strict sense of the word – 'comparative'. My main objective in writing this book has been to explore the position of English private law on the two issues raised by the parable of the good Samaritan. The purpose of also including two chapters on the continental position was to draw inspiration and to demonstrate the viability of some of the alternative solutions to the issues discussed, not to give any form of detailed comparative analysis.

Altruism in Private Law is the result of four years of research at the University of Oxford. It is an adaptation of my doctoral thesis, submitted for the degree of Doctor of Philosophy on 31 August 2002. I owe a debt of gratitude first and foremost to my thesis supervisors, Mr Robert Stevens and Dr Gerhard Dannemann for the enthusiasm with which they guided me through this project. I would also like to thank, in alphabetical order, Prof. John Bell, the late Prof. Peter Birks, Prof. Frits Brandsma, Dr Duncan Fairgrieve, Prof. David Ibbetson, Prof. Corjo Jansen, Dr Michael Macnair, Prof. Ewan McKendrick, Prof. Jason Neyers, Prof. Francis Reynolds, Prof. Francis Rose, and Dr Simon Whittaker for helping me understand various issues relating to their respective areas of expertise. Their comments and suggestions were of great assistance.

Mr Softley, of Surrey Breakdown Ltd, kindly sent me all the materials relating to his case against Mr Knight. Many thanks also to Nick Smith and my wife, Shannon McBriar, for proof-reading earlier drafts of this book and helping me assemble the tables.

I am very grateful to Professor Herman Schoordijk whose *De verbintenis uit en de verplichting tot altruisme* (1987) inspired my decision to write a thesis on this subject.

Finally, I would like to take this opportunity to thank the many institutions that have so generously supported me: the European Commission through the TMR (Training and Mobility in Research) Programme; the *Radboudstichting* for granting me a '*stimuleringssubsidie*'; the Art and Humanities Research Board for awarding me a studentship; Merton College for awarding me a *Domus* Graduate Scholarship; and my current employer *Stibbe* for allowing me the time to prepare this book for publication.

Jeroen Kortmann

Amsterdam,
July 2004

Table of Contents

Abbreviations

ABGB	*Allgemeines Bürgerliches Gesetzbuch*
AC	Law Reports, Appeal Cases
AcP	Archiv für die civilistische Praxis
A.D.	*Anno Domini*
Adel LR	Adelaide Law Review
A & E	Adolphus and Ellis, King's Bench reports
A-G	Attorney-General
Ala.	Alabama Reports
Aleyn	Aleyn, King's Bench reports
ALJR	Australian Law Journal Reports
All ER	All England Law Reports
ALR	Australian Law Reports
Am Dec	American Decisions
Am.J.Comp.L.	American Journal of Comparative Law
Am Rep	American Reports
Anm	*Anmerkung*
Anst	Anstruther, Exchequer reports
App Cas	Law Reports, Appeal Cases (1875–1890)
art., artt.	article, articles
Atl	Atlantic Reporter (American Law Reports)
Barbour	*Barbour's Supreme Court Reports, State of New York*
B & C	Barnewall and Cresswell, King's Bench reports
Beav	Beavan, Rolls court reports
BGB	*Bürgerliches Gesetzbuch*
BGH	*Bundesgerichtshof*
BGHZ	*Entscheidungen des Bundesgerichtshofes in Zivilsachen*
Bing	Bingham, Common Pleas reports
Black W	W. Blackstone, King's Bench reports
BMLR	Butterworth's Medico-Legal Reports
Build LR	Building Law reports
Bulstr	Bulstrode, King's Bench reports
BW	*Burgerlijk Wetboek*
C.	*Codex Iustinianus*
CA	Court of Appeal
Cal LR	California Law Review
Camp	Campbell, Nisi Prius reports
cap.	*caput*
Car & P	Carrington and Payne, Nisi Prius reports
CB	Common Bench reports
CBNS	Common Bench reports, new series
CC	City Council
C. civ.	*Code Civil*

cf.	confer
Ch D	Law Reports, Chancery Division (1875–1890)
ch.	chapter
Ch	Law Reports, Chancery Division
CILSA	The Comparative and International Law Journal of Southern Africa
Civ.	*Cour de Cassation, Chambre Civile*
CJ	Chief Justice
CLJ	Cambridge Law Journal
CLP	Current Legal Problems
CLR	Commonwealth Law Reports
CLY	Current Law Yearbook
C & M	Carrington and Marshman, Nisi Prius reports
Co.	Company
Coll.	*Mosaicarum et Romanarum legum collatio*
Com.	*Cour de Cassation, Chambre Commerciale*
Co Rep	Coke, King's Bench reports
Corp.	*Corporation*
Cox CC	Cox's Criminal Law Cases
C. pén.	*Code pénal*
Crim.	*Cour de Cassation, Chambre Criminelle*
C Rob	C. Robinson, Admiralty reports
Cro Eliz	Croke's reports, vol. 1, Queen's Bench reports
Cro Car	Croke's reports, vol. 3, King's Bench reports
Cro Jac	Croke's reports, vol. 2, King's Bench reports
D.	*Digesta* (Justinian's Digest)
D	*Receuil Dalloz*
Dana	Dana's Court of Appeals Reports, Kentucky
DC	District Council
DC	*Receuil Dalloz Critique*
Den	Denison, Crown cases
De G F & J	De Gex, Fisher and Jones, Chancery reports
DH	*Receuil hebdomadaire de jurisprudence Dalloz*
DLR	Dominion Law Reports
Dods	Dodson, Admiralty reports
DR	*Deutsches Recht*
ed., eds	editor, editors
edn	edition
e.g.	*exempli gratia* (for example)
Eq Ca Abr	Equity cases abridged
ER	English Reports
etc.	*etcetera*
esp.	especially
Esp.	Espinasse, *Nisi Prius* reports
EWCA Civ	England and Wales Court of Appeal, Civil Division
Ex	Exchequer Reports
ff.	and following pages
F & F	Foster and Finlason, *Nisi Prius* reports

fo.	folio
Fort	Fortescue, King's Bench reports
G.	*Gai Institutiones* (Gaius' Institutes)
Godb	Godbolt, King's Bench reports
Hagg	Haggard, Admiralty reports
H Bl	H. Blackstone, Common Pleas reports
Hil	Hilary term
Hob	Hobart, King's Bench reports
HoL	House of Lords (Appellate Committee)
Holt KB	Holt, King's Bench reports
I.	*Iustiniani Institutiones* (Justinian's Institutes)
ibid.	*ibidem*
ICA	Iowa Code Annotated
i.e.	*id est*
Ill LR	Illinois Law Review
J	Justice
JCP	*Juris-classeur périodique (La Semaine Juridique)*
J.Leg.Stud.	The Journal of Legal Studies
JO	Journal officiel
Johns	Johnson, New York Supreme Court Reports
Jones W	Les Reports de Sir William Jones
JP	Justice of the Peace
JR	*Juristische Rundschau*
KB	Law Reports, King's Bench Division
Keb	Keble, King's Bench reports
Kan.	Kansas Reports
KB	Law Reports, King's Bench Division
Ld Raym	Lord Raymond, King's Bench reports
Leon	Leonard, King's Bench reports
lib.	*liber*
LG	*Landesgericht*
LJ	Lord Justice
LJ	Law Journal
Lloyd's Rep	Lloyd's Law Reports
Lloyd's Rep Med	Lloyd's Law Reports Medical
LMCLQ	Lloyd's Maritime and Commercial Law Quarterly
LQR	Law Quarterly Review
LR	Law Review, Law Reports
LR CP	Law Reports, Common Pleas cases
LR PC	Law Reports, Privy Council cases
LT	Law Times Reports
Ltd	Limited
Mass	Massachusetts Reports
MDR	*Monatsschrift für Deutsches Recht*
M & S	Maule and Selwyn, King's Bench reports
M & W	Meeson and Welsby, Exchequer reports
Mich	Michaelmas term

MLR	Modern Law Review
Mod.	Modern Reports
Moore NS	E. F. Moore, Privy Council reports, new series
Moore PC	E. F. Moore, Privy Council reports
MR	Master of the Rolls
NE	North Eastern Reporter (American Law Reports)
NJW	*Neue Juristische Wochenschrift*
NJW-RR	*Neue Juristische Wochenschrift, Rechtsprechungs-Report Zivilrecht*
NoC	Notes of Cases in the Ecclesiastical and Maritime Courts
NW	North Western Reporter (American Law Reports)
Noy	Noy, King's Bench reports
nr, nrs	number, numbers
NZLR	New Zealand Law Reports
OJLS	Oxford Journal of Legal Studies
OLG	*Oberlandesgericht*
ORS	Oregon Revised Statutes
OUCLF	Oxford University Comparative Law Forum
OUCLJ	Oxford University Commonwealth Law Journal
p., pp.	page, pages
P	Law Reports, Probate Division
Pac.	Pacific Reporter (American Law Reports)
Palmer	The reports of Sir Jeffrey Palmer
par.	paragraph
Pas	*Pascha* (Easter term)
PC	Privy Council
PD	Law Reports, Probate division (1875–1890)
PIQR	Personal Injuries and Quantum Reports
Plc.	Public limited company
PN	Professional negligence
pr.	*principium*
PrALR	*Preussisches Allgemeines Landrecht*
P Wms	Peere Wiliams, Chancery reports
QB	Law Reports, Queen's Bench Division, or Queen's Bench Reports, by Adolphus and Ellis
QBD	Law Reports, Queen's Bench Division (1875–1890)
rev.	revised
Rev.trim.dr.civ.	*Revue trimestrielle de droit civil*
RG	Reichsgericht
RGZ	*Entscheidungen des Reichsgerichts in Zivilsachen*
Rly	Railway
Roll Abr	H. Rolle, Abridgement des plusieurs cases
RS	Rolls Series; editions of YBs of Edw I and 11–20 Edw III
RTR	Road traffic reports
s., ss.	section, sections
Salk	Salkeld, King's Bench reports, 1689–1712
SE	South Eastern Reporter (American Law Reports)
SLT	Scottish Law Times Reports

SS	Publications of the Selden Society
So.	Southern Reporter (American Law Reports)
Sp Ecc & Add	Spinks, Ecclesiastical and Admiralty Reports
St	Saint
Stark	Starkie, Nisi Prius reports
StGB	*Strafgesetzbuch*
Strange	Strange, King's Bench reports
Swab	Swabey, Ecclesiastical reports
Syd LR	Sydney Law Review
THRHR	Tydskrif vir hedendaagse romeins-hollandse reg
TLJ	Torts Law Journal
TLR	The Times Law Reports
Tort L Rev	The Tort Law Review
TR	Term Reports
T Raym	Sir T. Raymond, King's Bench reports
Trin	Trinity
T.S.F.	*Télégraphie sans fil*
U.Pa.LR	University of Pennsylvania Law Review
V-C	Vice-Chancellor
VersR	*Versicherungsrecht*
Ves Jun	Vesey, junior, Chancery reports
Ves Sen	Vesey, senior, Chancery reports
Vol.	volume
WLR	Weekly Law Reports
W Rob	W. Robinson, Admiralty reports
WSA	Wisconsin Statutes Annotated
Y & J	Younge and Jervis, Exchequer reports
YB	Year books
Yelv	Yelverton, King's Bench reports
ZSS	*Zeitschrift der Savigny-stiftung. Romanistische Abteilung*

Table of Cases

ENGLISH CASES

FRENCH CASES (IN CHRONOLOGICAL ORDER)

GERMAN CASES (IN CHRONOLOGICAL ORDER)

CASES FROM OTHER JURISDICTIONS

Table of Legislation (in alphabetical order)

PART I

LIABILITY FOR NONFEASANCE

1
Introduction

'But he, willing to justify himself, said unto Jesus, And who is my neighbour?

And Jesus answering said, A certain man went down from Jerusalem to Jericho, and fell among thieves, which stripped him of his raiment, and wounded him, and departed, leaving him half dead.

And by chance there came down a certain priest that way: and when he saw him, he passed by on the other side.

And likewise a Levite, when he was at the place, came and looked on him, and passed by on the other side.

But a certain Samaritan, as he journeyed, came where he was: and when he saw him, he had compassion on him.

And went to him, and bound up his wounds, pouring in oil and wine, and set him on his own beast, and brought him to an inn, and took care of him.

And on the morrow when he departed, he took out two pence, and gave them to the host, and said unto him, Take care of him; and whatsoever thou spendest more, when I come again, I will repay thee.

Which now of these three, thinkest thou, was neighbour unto him that fell among thieves?

And he said, He that shewed mercy on him. Then said Jesus unto him, Go, and do thou likewise.'

(Luke, 10:29–37)[1]

From a private law point of view, the parable of the good Samaritan raises two questions:

(1) Do we have a legal duty to give aid to our fellow human beings? In particular: can we be held liable for damages if we fail to do so? This question falls mainly in the area of tort law.

(2) If we do come to the rescue, like the Samaritan did, will we have any claim for the expenses that we incurred, for the losses we suffered, or perhaps even for remuneration or a reward? As we shall see, such claims could arise under many different headings.

[1] *The Holy Bible*, authorized King James version. See also Exodus 23:4–5 and Deuteronomy 22:1–4.

This book will address both questions in turn, commencing with the first: do we have a duty to give aid to our fellow human beings? Or: can we be held liable if we omit to intervene where a reasonable person would have intervened? Lord Atkin's speech in *Donoghue v Stevenson*[2] gives reason to believe that the answer is affirmative under English law:[3]

> The rule that you are to love your neighbour becomes in law, you must not injure your neighbour; (. . .) Who, then, in law is my neighbour? The answer seems to be – persons who are so closely affected by my act that I ought reasonably to have them in contemplation as being so affected when I am directing my mind to the acts *or omissions* which are called in question.[4]

However, in *Home Office v Dorset Yacht Co. Ltd*[5] Lord Diplock criticized Lord Atkin's test in *Donoghue*. In the view of Lord Diplock, omissions give rise to no legal liability:

> The very parable of the Good Samaritan which was evoked by Lord Atkin in *Donoghue v Stevenson* illustrates, in the conduct of the priest and of the Levite who passed by on the other side, an omission which was likely to have as its reasonable and probable consequence damage to the health of the victim of the thieves, but for which the priest and the Levite would have incurred no civil liability in English law.[6]

It has been confirmed in later judgments that English law does not in principle recognize an affirmative duty to act,[7] and thus in general does not require us to give aid to our neighbours in need. In this respect English law differs from most legal systems in Continental Europe. The delictual provisions in the civil codes of, for example, Germany and France do not distinguish between acts and inaction.

In Part I the theoretical justifications for distinguishing between acts (or 'feasance') and inaction (or 'nonfeasance') will be set out in Chapter 3. Chapter 4 will proceed with a brief examination of the law in two Continental European countries, Germany and France. In Chapter 5 the position in English law will be subjected to a closer analysis. The final aim of this Part I is to investigate if and, if so, to what extent the position of English law on liability for nonfeasance should be reconsidered. However, before we can start a more detailed investigation into 'liability for nonfeasance', it is necessary to decide what definition of 'nonfeasance' will be used.

2 [1932] AC 562.

3 *Contra*: J.C. Smith and P. Burns, 'Donoghue v. Stevenson – The Not So Golden Anniversary' (1983) 46 MLR 147 at 155–156. Smith and Burns suggest that the neighbour principle was never intended to cover 'pure' omissions. Yet, Lord Atkin drew directly upon the biblical parable of the good Samaritan, itself unquestionably a case of 'pure' omissions.

4 *Ibid.* at 580 (emphasis added).

5 [1970] AC 1004.

6 *Ibid.* at 1060. Cf. *Hargrave v Goldman* (1963) 110 CLR 40 at 65–66, *per* Windeyer J.

7 See below, Part I, Section 5.2 with further references.

2

What is Nonfeasance?

When dealing with liability for nonfeasance, other terms that are generally used to indicate a lack of feasance are 'inaction', 'omission', or 'failure to act'. There is a subtle difference between these terms. On the one hand we have 'nonfeasance' and 'inaction', which are both neutral terms.[1] 'Omission' and 'failure to act', however, presuppose the existence of a duty, be it legal or moral. To say that a person has 'omitted' or 'failed to act', is to say that he or she really should have done what he or she omitted or failed to do.[2] In the following, the terms 'omission' and 'failure to act' will therefore only be used in cases in which the existence of a duty to act is indisputable.

So what is nonfeasance? An answer such as 'the opposite of feasance' does not really help us much. In truth, there are many situations in which it is very difficult to draw any logical distinction between feasance and nonfeasance.[3] Part of the problem is caused by the complications that lie in a sophisticated language. Many words that are grammatically active connote inactive behaviour: sleeping, starving, fasting *etc*. Moreover, with double negations, the English language creates the possibility to describe every positive conduct with a negative equivalent: shooting is equivalent to not refraining from shooting and shouting a warning is equivalent to not forbearing to shout a warning.[4] And is 'making an incorrect diagnosis' not the same as 'not making the correct diagnosis'? [5] A hard rule that is always able to make the proper distinction is impossible to give. [6] Yet, some guidance can be had from Bentham, who in his *Introduction to the Principles of Morals and Legislation* drew a distinction between 'positive' and 'negative' acts, that is, feasance and nonfeasance.[7] In the view of Bentham, positive acts always involve bodily movement. Negative acts, therefore, must be the absence of such bodily movement. Not the absence of all bodily movement – after all, while we are alive at least our lungs and

[1] *Contra*: L.B. Curzon, *Dictionary of Law* (6th edn 2002), p. 288, where it is suggested that the term 'nonfeasance', like 'omission', presupposes the existence of a duty.

[2] J. Austin, *Lectures on Jurisprudence*, Vol. II (1863), p. 101 (Lecture XX) and A.M. Honoré, 'Are Omissions Less Culpable?' in P. Cane and J. Stapleton (eds), *Essays for Patrick Atiyah* (1991), pp. 33 and 36–37.

[3] P. Cane, *Atiyah's Accidents, Compensation and the Law* (6th edn 1999), p. 60.

[4] Cf. A.M. Honoré, 'Are Omissions Less Culpable?' in P. Cane and J. Stapleton (eds), *Essays for Patrick Atiyah* (1991), pp. 37–38

[5] *Harnett v Bond* [1924] 2 KB 517 at 541, *per* Bankes LJ.

[6] See Honoré's description of and comments on Bennett's theory; A.M. Honoré, *ibid.*, pp. 39–41.

[7] J. Bentham, *An Introduction to the Principles of Morals and Legislation* (J.H. Burns and H.L.A. Hart, eds, 1970), p. 75.

heart are moving – but the absence of a particular bodily movement: a positive act.[8] When we say that we are 'fasting', for example, this does not imply that we are not doing anything at all, but it does mean that we are not eating. 'Eating' requires bodily movement, hence fasting is (one of) the inactive opposite(s) of eating. And, despite the fact that the grammatical structure of these phrases suggests otherwise, 'not refraining from shooting' is the active opposite of 'refraining from shooting' (inactive). For 'not refraining from shooting' requires bodily movement, whereas 'refraining from shooting' connotes the absence of exactly that movement.

In practice, however, cases are often more complicated, especially if they include instances of both feasance and nonfeasance. A car driver who does not brake in time to avoid hitting a pedestrian can be said to have 'driven' negligently. Yet, can it not equally be argued that his negligence did not consist of an act, but rather of a failure to act? Fleming's answer is negative:

> What superficially looks like non-feasance is often, upon correct analysis, a case of misfeasance. A motorist's failure to brake in time to prevent a collision is not an example of supine inaction: an omission is involved, but it is merely the element that makes his *active* conduct – driving – negligent.[9]

In other words: although the failure to brake, in isolation, is nonfeasance, it is part of a larger activity, driving, which has to be qualified as feasance. The problem with this view is that although it helps in answering one question – 'are we dealing with feasance or nonfeasance?' – it also gives rise to two new questions:

(I) 'Is there a larger activity?', and
(II) 'Is the isolated nonfeasance part of this larger activity?'

The answer to the first question is often arbitrary. Fleming does not hesitate to regard 'driving' as a larger activity. Yet, when railways fail to provide signals at a level crossing, he regards this as inaction.[10] Does this mean that 'running a railway company' does not qualify as a larger activity? Similarly, 'supervising your children' and 'babysitting' are apparently not to be regarded as larger activities, for Fleming treats 'losing control over children' as (isolated) inaction.[11]

If we have identified a larger activity, the second question will prove at least as high a hurdle as the first one. Why is it that we regard a motorist's failure to brake as part of the larger activity of driving? Let us consider the following example: a motorist drives his car down a country road. Suddenly he sees a severely wounded man 'stripped of his raiment', beckoning for help. He decides not to brake. The man continues his journey and a little while later he is confronted with a pedestrian crossing the road. Again he fails to brake, and the pedestrian is killed in the

[8] *Ibid.* See also D. Birnbacher, *Tun und Unterlassen* (1995), pp. 34–35.
[9] J.G. Fleming, *The Law of Torts* (9th edn 1998), p. 163. See also *Kelly v Metropolitan Rly Co.* [1895] 1 QB 944 at 947, *per* Rigby LJ and *Stovin v Wise* [1996] 3 All ER 801 at 820, *per* Lord Hoffmann.
[10] J.G. Fleming, *The Law of Torts* (9th edn 1998), p. 167.
[11] *Ibid.*, p. 171. Cf. D. Howarth, *Textbook on Tort* (1995), p. 180.

collision. [12] Now we have two instances of failure to brake. Yet, Fleming would probably only regard the second failure to brake as being part of the larger activity 'driving'. The most likely reason for this is that the traffic regulations require the motorist to stop in the second case, but not in the first. In other words, he regards only the second instance of inaction – not braking for a crossing pedestrian – as part of the larger activity – driving – because only in the second instance the motorist has a *duty* to act. Thus, it appears that to Fleming the mere existence of a duty to act can make the difference between inaction and action. For obvious reasons, Fleming's way of distinguishing between feasance and nonfeasance cannot be adopted here: by qualifying inaction as part of a larger act, he unwittingly obscures from our view the very duty to act that we are trying to investigate. Instead, we will look at nonfeasance itself, isolating it from the acts that may accompany it. Hence, we will regard both 'not stopping your car to help a man in need' and 'not stopping your car to avoid collision' as instances of nonfeasance. [13] This is of course not to say that similar liability will arise in both cases, because the existence of a duty to act is not at all certain in the first case, whereas it almost certainly is in the second. [14]

The courts however, do not adopt one uniform definition of nonfeasance. As a result it will sometimes prove difficult to establish in individual cases whether the court has made its decision on the presumption that the behaviour complained of is misfeasance or nonfeasance. In those cases close attention should be paid to the court's reasoning. Most importantly, we must try to establish what particular part of the defendant's behaviour prompted the court to conclude that he had been negligent. For example, was it the fact that he hit a cricket ball over the fence or that he had failed to build a higher fence? Some of the judgments in the famous cricket case of *Bolton v Stone* indeed give reason to believe that this case was concerned with liability for nonfeasance, rather than feasance. [15] In much the same way we approach the fictitious example by Bankes LJ of the medical man who diagnoses a case of measles as one of scarlet fever:

> [he] may be said to have omitted to make a correct diagnosis; he may equally well be said to have made an incorrect diagnosis. [16]

While the medical man's conduct clearly includes both an active and an inactive element, it is incorrect to assume that they are two sides of the same coin. This will become apparent if we look at the consequences that may follow from the active

[12] Example taken from H. Mazeaud, L. Mazeaud and A. Tunc, *Traité Théorique et Pratique de la Responsabilité Civile* (6th edn 1965), nr 525.

[13] See also C. von Bar, *The Common European Law of Torts*, Vol. 2 (2000), pp. 222–223.

[14] Cf. A.M. Honoré, 'Are Omissions Less Culpable?' in P. Cane and J. Stapleton (eds), *Essays for Patrick Atiyah* (1991), pp. 43–44; P. Cane, 'Negligent Solicitors and Disappointed Beneficiaries' (1980) 96 LQR 182–185 at 184 and H. Mazeaud, L. Mazeaud and A. Tunc, *Traité Théorique et Pratique de la Responsabilité Civile* (6th edn 1965), nr 525.

[15] *Bolton v Stone* [1951] 1 All ER 1078 at 1078, *per* Lord Porter, at 1083, *per* Lord Normand and at 1087, *per* Lord Radcliffe.

[16] *Harnett v Bond* [1924] 2 KB 517 at 541, *per* Bankes LJ.

and the inactive elements of his conduct. The physician's failure to diagnose measles will probably mean that the patient does not receive treatment against measles. If this is the patient's only complaint, we are dealing with a claim for loss caused by negligent nonfeasance. The active misdiagnosis of scarlet fever, however, may result in different loss. This is most clearly so, if the patient is prescribed medicines or receives treatment for his supposed scarlet fever, which in turn has an adverse effect on his health. In this respect the plaintiff's claim must then be for loss caused by active misfeasance. After all, this part of his loss followed *not* from the physician's failure to diagnose measles, but from his misdiagnosis of scarlet fever. [17]

Thus, while it probably remains impossible to provide a rule that always correctly distinguishes feasance from nonfeasance, the following three guidelines shall be applied here:

(1) Close attention will be paid to the court's reasoning as to which part of the defendant's behaviour prompted the court to conclude that he or she had been negligent.

(2) In answering that question, all action and inaction that is part of the defendant's behaviour will be regarded in isolation. No inaction is 'part of an act' and vice versa.

(3) Once a particular element of conduct has been identified, it will be regarded as active if it requires bodily movement, and inactive if it does not.

[17] See also D. Birnbacher, *Tun und Unterlassen* (1995), pp. 54–55.

3

Theoretical Justifications for Distinguishing between Feasance and Nonfeasance

3.1 Introduction

Assuming that it does not recognize a general affirmative duty to act, English law does not encourage members of the public to give aid to those in need of help. Quite the reverse, English law in fact *dis*courages giving aid, for once someone has started to give aid, he or she can be held liable for mistakes he or she makes in doing so. The advice Gregory gave in 1966 – 'Don't ever "fease" unless you have to'[1] – is still valid in modern English law. Nevertheless, there are apparently enough justifications for the House of Lords to uphold the distinction between feasance and nonfeasance, and to deny the existence of a general duty to act. In *Stovin v Wise*, Lord Hoffmann explained:

There are sound reasons why omissions require different treatment from positive conduct. (. . .) One can put the matter in political, moral or economic terms. In political terms it is less of an invasion of an individual's freedom for the law to require him to consider the safety of others in his actions than to impose upon him a duty to rescue or protect. A moral version of this point may be called the 'Why pick on me?' argument. A duty to prevent harm to others or to render assistance to a person in danger or distress may apply to a large and indeterminate class of people who happen to be able to do something. Why should one be held liable rather than the other? In economic terms, the efficient allocation of resources usually requires an activity should bear its own costs. If it benefits from being able to impose some of its costs on other people (what economists call 'externalities') the market is distorted because the activity appears cheaper than it really is. So liability to pay compensation for loss caused by negligent conduct acts as a deterrent against increasing the cost of the activity to the community and reduces externalities. But there is no similar justification for requiring a person who is not doing anything to spend money on behalf of someone else. Except in special cases (such as marine salvage) English law does not reward someone who voluntarily confers a benefit on another. So there must be some special reason why he should have to put his hand in his pocket.[2]

1 Ch.O. Gregory, 'The Good Samaritan and the Bad' in J.M. Ratcliffe (ed.), *The Good Samaritan and the Law* (1966), pp. 23–41 at p. 28.

2 [1996] 3 All ER 801 at 819.

Each of the justifications given by Lord Hoffmann will be examined in the following, together with two additional justifications that have been put forward in academic writings.

3.2 A Positive Duty to act would be too much of an Invasion of an Individual's Freedom

In academic debates a mere reference to the sanctity of freedom is often treated as irrefutable and conclusive to the outcome of the debate. We seem satisfied that invasion of an individual's freedom cannot be tolerated, and often regard an argument to that effect as self-evident and self-justifying, thus rendering additional reasons unnecessary.[3] Yet, what an individual's freedom actually consists of is a question that has hardly been answered by two ages or two countries alike.[4] Hence, Lord Hoffmann is not being very informative when he tells us that omissions require different treatment from positive conduct because 'it is less of an invasion of an individual's freedom for the law to require him to consider the safety of others in his actions, than to impose upon him a duty to rescue or protect'.[5] At the most we can deduce from this statement that Lord Hoffmann's understanding of 'freedom' includes the right to refrain from acting. Regrettably, Lord Hoffmann fails to give us his definition of 'freedom', nor does he tell us why one kind of 'invasion of an individual's freedom', the imposition of liability for wrongful inaction, would be illegitimate where another, the existing liability for wrongful acts, apparently is legitimate.

Freedom or liberty (both words shall here be regarded as synonymous) is normally said to be the absence of interference by others, or indeed the state, with an individual's activity. If I am prevented by others from doing what I could otherwise do, I am to that degree unfree.[6] This is not to say that interference is necessarily a bad thing. If we want to guarantee everyone a minimum degree of freedom, we will have to restrain everyone from interfering with others' freedom. Thus, the freedom of one individual finds its limits where it collides with the freedom of others.[7] The difficulty lies in finding the proper standard of interference to apportion a fair share of freedom to each individual. Lawyers and philosophers alike have made numerous attempts to define such a standard of interference. This is

[3] E. Lucas, 'Mill on Liberty' (1869) 13 NS *The Dublin Review* 62, reprinted in A. Pyle (ed.), *Liberty* (1994), pp. 255 ff. at p. 255.

[4] J.S. Mill, *On Liberty* (G. Himmelfarb, ed., 1974), p. 64.

[5] Cf. J. Kohler, *'Die Menschenhülfe im Privatrecht'*, (1887) 25 *Jahrbücher für die Dogmatik des heutigen römischen und deutschen Privatrechts* 1–141 at 2.

[6] I. Berlin, 'Two Concepts of Liberty' (1958), Inaugural Lecture delivered before the University of Oxford, reprinted in I. Berlin, *Four Essays on Liberty* (1969), pp. 118 ff. at p. 122. I shall continue to adopt a 'negative' definition of freedom, as I regard this definition to be sufficiently accurate for the purposes of this book. For a description of the difference between the notions of 'negative' and 'positive' freedom see Berlin, *ibid.*, pp. 122–134.

[7] A.T. Denning, *The Family Story* (1981), p. 179.

not the place for a detailed survey of the different standards that have been suggested through the centuries. For present purposes we will have to content ourselves with a summary of the philosophical views that are most often referred to by supporters and adversaries of the rule of no liability for nonfeasance.[8]

Supporters of the no-liability rule most often refer to the works of Kant for confirmation of their views.[9] In his *The Metaphysics of Morals*, first published in 1797, Kant made a distinction between the doctrine of right on the one hand, and the doctrine of virtue on the other. Regarding the doctrine of right he wrote:

> The concept of Right, insofar as it is related to an obligation corresponding to it (i.e., the moral concept of Right), has to do, *first*, only with the external and indeed practical relation of one person to another, insofar as their actions, as facts, can have (direct or indirect) influence on each other.[10]

Because the doctrine of right only deals with external actions, Kant is said to have been of the view that the law should not require any particular affirmative actions.[11] An individual's choice whether or not to act was an internal affair, which was governed by the doctrine of virtue, rather than of right. Accordingly, a duty to aid others was an ethical, not a legal duty:

> (. . .) duties of benevolence, even though they are external duties (obligations to external actions), are still assigned to ethics because their lawgiving can be only internal.[12]

Thus, the Kantian idea appears to be, as Howarth puts it, 'that the state has no business telling people that they are bad people, that they are immoral or wicked'.[13] However, Kant himself may not have been as opposed to state interference as is often assumed. *The Metaphysics of Morals* included a section on the rights of a state, in which Kant wrote that a government was authorized to 'constrain the wealthy to provide the means of sustenance to those who are unable to provide for even their most necessary natural needs', for example by imposing taxes to that effect.[14] One could argue that the imposition of taxes is different from the imposition of liability in that the former does not involve casting a judgment on an individual's character: after all, everyone has to pay taxes regardless of one's (internal) virtue. Yet, Kant's suggested solution for the maintenance of abandoned children does appear to involve a straightforward judgment on the taxpayers' virtue:

> (. . .) the state has a right to charge the people with the duty of not knowingly letting them die, even though they are an unwelcome addition to the resources of the state. Whether

[8] See for a more detailed investigation E.J. Weinrib, 'The Case for a Duty to Rescue', (1980) 90 Yale LJ 247–293.

[9] *Ibid.* at 266–267 and N. Gray and J. Edelman, 'Developing the law of omissions: a common law duty to rescue?' (1998) 6 TLJ 240–259 at 1–2 with further references.

[10] I. Kant, *The Metaphysics of Morals*, translated by M. Gregor (1991), p. 56. (Footnotes omitted).

[11] E.J. Weinrib, 'Law as a Kantian Idea of Reason' (1987) 87 Columbia LR 472–508 at 489 and *idem*, 'The Case for a Duty to Rescue', (1980) 90 Yale LJ 247–293 at 266.

[12] I. Kant, *The Metaphysics of Morals*, translated by M. Gregor (1991), p. 47.

[13] D. Howarth, *Textbook on Tort* (1995), p. 184.

[14] I. Kant, *The Metaphysics of Morals*, translated by M. Gregor (1991), p. 136.

this should be done by taxing elderly unmarried people of both sexes generally (by which I mean *wealthy* unmarried people), *since they are in part to blame for there being abandoned children*, in order to establish foundling homes, or whether it can be done rightly in another way (it would be hard to find another means for preventing this) is a problem which has not yet been solved (. . .).[15]

Adversaries of the no-liability rule tend to refer to the works of Bentham and Mill.[16] Bentham appears to have agreed with Kant that 'the rules of beneficence' generally belonged to the 'jurisdiction of private ethics'.[17] However, in cases involving danger to others, he thought that the law ought to interfere:

(. . .) why should it not be made the duty of every man to save another from mischief, when it can be done without prejudicing himself, as well as to abstain from bringing it on him?[18]

Unfortunately, Bentham did not proceed to reveal his arguments in favour of imposing such a duty to rescue.[19] Mill's views are more helpful in this respect. In his *On Liberty*,[20] Mill made an attempt to define the proper standard of state interference:

(. . .) the sole end for which mankind are warranted, individually or collectively, in interfering with the liberty of action of any of their number, is self-protection. That the only purpose for which power can be rightfully exercised over any member of a civilised community, against his will, is to prevent harm to others. His own good, either physical or moral, is not a sufficient warrant. He cannot rightfully be compelled to do or forbear because it will be better for him to do so, because it will make him happier, because, in the opinions of others, to do so would be wise, or even right. (. . .) Over himself, over his own body and mind, the individual is sovereign.[21]

[15] I. Kant, *The Metaphysics of Morals*, translated by M. Gregor (1991), at 136–137 (second emphasis added).

[16] E.J. Weinrib, 'The Case for a Duty to Rescue', (1980) 90 Yale LJ 247–293 at 266, and C.K. Allen, 'Legal Duties' (1931) 40 Yale LJ 331–380 at 368. Professor Weinrib later became a proponent of the no-liability rule, because in his view it is a necessary feature of tort law, the systematic absence of which would mean 'the loss of our entire mental representation of tort law'. Central to our conception of tort law, he argues, are 'the bipolar procedure that links plaintiff and defendant' and 'the causation of harm'. Elaborating on the latter notion, Weinrib states that causation of harm requires an act that results in suffering: 'suffering by the plaintiff that is independent of the defendant's doing has no significance for tort law. Accordingly, no liability lies for failure to prevent or alleviate suffering.' This is not the place to investigate generally the viability of Weinrib's theory of legal formalism. However, in as far as the centrality of the nonfeasance rule is concerned, Weinrib's submissions are highly subjective. It is difficult to see how without this rule we would lose 'our entire mental representation of tort law'. Moreover, as we shall see in Part I, Chapter 5, it is by no means certain for how long and to what extent the supposed rule of no liability for nonfeasance has been part of English private law. See E.J. Weinrib, *The Idea of Private Law* (1995), pp. 12–14 and *idem*, 'Understanding Tort Law' (1989) 23 Valparaiso ULR 485–526 at 493–494 and 517.

[17] J. Bentham, *An Introduction to the Principles of Morals and Legislation* (J.H. Burns and H.L.A. Hart, eds, 1970), p. 292. (First published in 1789).

[18] *Ibid.*, p. 293.

[19] E.J. Weinrib, 'The Case for a Duty to Rescue', (1980) 90 Yale LJ 247–293 at 280.

[20] J.S. Mill, *On Liberty* (1859).

[21] J.S. Mill, *On Liberty* (G. Himmelfarb, ed., 1974), pp. 68–69 (footnotes omitted).

The proper standard according to Mill was what we now know as the 'harm principle'; the community is only permitted to restrain the behaviour of its members, insofar as this behaviour causes harm to others.[22] Consequently we, as individuals, should in principle[23] be free to do what we want as long as we do not cause harm to others. From the very moment of its publication, *On Liberty* has been lauded by some,[24] while denounced by others.[25] The main objection to the harm principle seems to be its apparent vagueness. If 'harm to others' is to be the standard of legitimate interference, what must 'harm' be understood to mean? In a chapter devoted to applications of his harm principle, Mill wrote that a man should be free to be drunk if he wants to, provided that he does not harm others in doing so.[26] Many of Mill's contemporaries however, regarded the mere state of drunkenness as in itself harmful to others, because in any case it would set a bad example for the rest of the community.[27] Thus interpreted, application of Mill's harm principle could justify (state) interference with nearly every type of human behaviour. However, such interpretation does not do justice to Mill's theory. Mill used a common-sense concept of harm, which did not include mere offences,[28] nor the kind of negative effects that can be attributed to the free will and consent of the 'harmed' person. Thus, one cannot stop a drunkard from being drunk or forbid an atheist preacher from leading his audience astray, because those who may be negatively affected are free to ignore the drunkard and the atheist priest and have themselves to blame if they do not.[29]

Although Mill's critics reject the harm principle as the general standard of (state) interference, most of them accept that 'harm to others' can be a sufficient reason (though not the only reason) to justify such interference. The reviewer of *The Athenaeum* predicted as much in 1859:

> We doubt if anyone, in modern times, will venture to dispute the principle. Some will take it as their guiding rule *on principle*: others will aver that, whatever other principles they may also allow to act, there is no proper case of application in which this principle does not *also* apply.[30]

[22] See for a more detailed account of Mill's harm principle C.L. Ten, *Mill On Liberty* (1980), pp. 52–67.

[23] There are exceptions: *ibid.* pp. 40–41.

[24] *E.g.* the review in (1859) 1635 *The Athenaeum* 281–282, reprinted in A. Pyle (ed.), *Liberty* (1994), pp. 1 ff. and J. Morley, 'Mr. Mill's Doctrine of Liberty' (1873) 20 *The Fortnightly Review* 234–256, reprinted in A. Pyle (ed.), *Liberty* (1994), pp. 271 ff.

[25] Most vehemently by E. Lucas in 'Mill on Liberty' (1869) 13 NS *The Dublin Review* 62, reprinted in A. Pyle (ed.), *Liberty* (1994), pp. 255 ff. and J.F. Stephen in *Liberty, Equality, Fraternity* (1873).

[26] J.S. Mill, *On Liberty* (G. Himmelfarb, ed., 1974), pp. 167–168.

[27] *E.g.* the review of *On Liberty* in (1859) 1635 *The Athenaeum* 282, reprinted in A. Pyle (ed.), *Liberty* (1994), pp. 1 ff. at pp. 4–5, and R.W. Church, 'Mill on Liberty' [1860] 2 *Bentley's Quarterly Review* 434–473, reprinted in A. Pyle (ed.), *Liberty* (1994), pp. 210 ff. at pp. 246–247. On the harmfulness of setting bad examples in another context see J.F. Stephen in *Liberty, Equality, Fraternity* (1873), p. 131 and especially the second edition of this work (1874), p. 144, footnote.

[28] J. Morley, 'Mr. Mill's Doctrine of Liberty' (1873) 20 *The Fortnightly Review* 234–256, reprinted in A. Pyle (ed.), *Liberty* (1994), pp. 271 ff. at pp. 293–294.

[29] J.S. Mill, *On Liberty* (G. Himmelfarb, ed., 1974), pp. 145–149 and A. Pyle, 'Introduction' in A. Pyle (ed.), *Liberty* (1994), p. xvi.

[30] Review of *On Liberty* in (1859) 1635 *The Athenaeum*, pp. 281–282, reprinted in A. Pyle (ed.), *Liberty* (1994), pp. 1 ff. at pp. 1–2.

It has been argued that even Kantian ethics are not altogether inconsistent with the harm principle.[31] Thus, the predominant opinion appears to be that if a certain type of behaviour causes harm (in Mill's narrow sense of the word) to others, there is a *prima facie* case for state interference. We must then ask ourselves whether nonfeasance is or can be the kind of behaviour that causes harm to others. This question will be dealt with in more detail below, Part I, Section 3.6. For the moment we will content ourselves with Mill's response:

> A person may cause evil to others not only by his actions but by his inaction, and in either case he is justly accountable to them for the injury. The latter case, it is true, requires a much more cautious exercise of compulsion than the former. To make anyone answerable for doing evil to others is the rule; to make him answerable for not preventing evil is, comparatively speaking, the exception. Yet there are many cases clear enough and grave enough to justify that exception.[32]

Accordingly if we assume, as Mill does, that nonfeasance can cause harm, there appears to be a *prima facie* case for interference. Nonetheless, there may be good reasons '*secunda facie*', 'at second sight', to support Lord Hoffmann's argument that liability for nonfeasance would be too much of an invasion of an individual's freedom. Regrettably however, Lord Hoffmann does not advance such reasons.

One reason that has been suggested is that we may consider positive duties to be more burdensome than negative duties. This argument is easily met by Professor Atiyah.[33] For although positive duties can indeed be quite burdensome, we deny liability even in those cases where there would hardly be any burden. Atiyah gives the example of a person who sees a neighbour's house on fire. 'How burdensome would it be to require that person to telephone for the fire brigade?'[34] We should also remember that negative duties can sometimes be very burdensome. For although the imperative 'not to act uncarefully' may seem to be an easy instruction to follow, acting thus will become more difficult the more we raise the standard of care. The behaviour of learner-drivers, for example, is measured against the standards of experienced drivers.[35] As a result, the learner driver will either have to drive as carefully as an experienced driver, which to him or her is nearly impossible, or not drive at all. And if anyone were to suggest that the latter option, 'not driving at all', is hardly burdensome, they are mistaken. Where the use of a car may have been a luxury in the past, it is now to many people an indispensable tool of transportation.[36]

Also, it should be noted that the 'burdensomeness' of a duty is a factor that the courts can take into account at another stage of their judgment, namely when deciding whether the defendant was at fault. If the court finds the performance of

[31] D.A.J. Richards, 'Kantian Ethics and the Harm Principle: a Reply to John Finnis' (1987) 87 Columbia LR 457–471.

[32] J.S. Mill, *On Liberty* (G. Himmelfarb, ed., 1974), p. 70.

[33] P. Cane, *Atiyah's Accidents, Compensation and the Law* (6th edn 1999), pp. 62–63.

[34] *Ibid.*, p. 63.

[35] *Nettleship v Weston* [1971] 2 QB 691.

[36] B.S. Markesinis, *The German Law of Obligations*, Volume II (3rd edn 1997), pp. 471–472.

a duty too burdensome, it can decide that in the specific case before the court, the defendant has behaved like a reasonable person. Take for example the case of *Latimer v AEC Ltd.*,[37] where the defendant was held not to be at fault for failing to prevent an accident that happened when an employee slipped on the wet factory floor after a flooding. The court was of the opinion that the only possible way of preventing the accident from occurring would have been to close the whole factory altogether until the floor was cleaned. But it regarded this remedy as too burdensome, and concluded that the defendant had behaved like a reasonable person. Hence, the 'burdensomeness' of a duty does not have to prevent the imposition of liability in a whole category of cases, but can be taken into account when deciding in specific cases whether the behaviour complained of was reasonable.[38] Thus, if Lord Hoffmann's 'freedom-argument' relies on the presumption that the imposition of liability for nonfeasance would be too burdensome, it is difficult to support his view. More potent, however, is the reasoning found in Lord Nicholls's speech in *Stovin v Wise.*

A. Lord Nicholls and the 'freedom of choice'

In his speech in *Stovin v Wise*, Lord Nicholls articulated what is perhaps the strongest basis for distinction between feasance and nonfeasance. It focuses on the limited choice offered by affirmative duties to potential defendants, and owes much to the so-called 'will-theory':[39]

> Liability for omissions gives rise to a problem not present with liability for careless acts. He who wishes to act must act carefully or not at all. (. . .) With liability for omissions, however, a person is not offered a choice. The law compels him to act when left to himself he might do nothing.[40]

It must not be doubted that every duty that the law imposes – whether positive or negative – restricts to a certain extent our freedom to choose. Yet, Lord Nicholls argues, positive duties are more restrictive because they deny us the option to avoid being subjected to them. In general, negative duties do offer us this option. If we do not feel competent enough to meet a specific negative duty, we can avoid being subjected to it by not acting at all. Thus, if I feel I cannot live up to the standard of the reasonable driver, I can decide not to drive at all. However, if the law were to require a witness of an accident to act as the reasonable rescuer would do, he would not have an alternative option that would allow him to avoid being subjected to this duty to rescue.

37 [1953] AC 643.

38 P. Cane, *Atiyah's Accidents, Compensation and the Law* (6th edn 1999), p. 63 and K.J. Kemp, 'The duty to rescue – compulsion or laissez faire?', (1985) XVIII CILSA 163–186 at 168.

39 Cf. S. von Pufendorf, *De Jure Naturae et Gentium* (edn 1688), *lib.* I, *cap.* IV.

40 *Stovin v Wise* [1996] 3 All ER 801 at 809. Cf. K.J. Kemp, *Delictual Liability for Omissions* (1978) (Unpublished thesis, University of Port Elizabeth, South Africa), p. 386.

Lord Nicholls's justification of the feasance–nonfeasance distinction bears some resemblance to the so-called 'cab-rank' argument, used in the past to justify the immunity of barristers from certain claims in negligence. The fact that barristers were in principle not allowed to refuse clients meant that if a duty of care were imposed, they would have no option to avoid being subjected to this duty. In *Rondel v Worsley*,[41] this was cited as one of the arguments for protecting barristers against liability altogether.

There are however some objections to this type of argument. Firstly, the law already imposes liability in some cases in which the defendant does not have a choice in the sense here discussed. If I blamelessly become the source of a danger, the law imposes on me a duty to prevent this danger from culminating in harm.[42] Thus, if through no fault of my own I fall on the road (*e.g.* I was pushed by a stranger), it appears that I do have a duty to stand up and clear the road in order to avoid endangering other road-users, even though I had no choice which would have allowed me to avoid being subjected to this duty. Therefore, if the law recognizes Lord Nicholls's version of 'freedom of choice', it does not consistently apply it.

Secondly, it is not entirely true to say that we do not have an option that allows us to avoid being subjected to affirmative duties. For in theory, we could lock ourselves in our houses in an attempt to avoid witnessing accidents or other occasions that could require our positive action. The same goes for the duty of care imposed upon barristers: barristers could avoid being subjected to this duty by changing careers. True, few people would regard these as realistic options, but the same can be said in some cases involving negative duties. For example, 'not driving at all' in order to avoid being subjected to the relatively high standard of care required of car drivers is to many of us not a realistic option either. Hence, the distinction between cases of feasance and of nonfeasance, as it is drawn here, appears to be one of degree, not of principle. Imposing positive duties does not leave us *without* an option to avoid being subjected to these duties, but rather with *less* of an option than is commonly the case in respect of negative duties. And because the distinction is one of degree, the more obvious response is to adjust the measure of care that is required, not deny a duty altogether. To deny a duty would be, as Lord Hoffmann put it in the decision that finally abolished the immunity of barristers, 'burning down the house to roast the pig'.[43]

3.3 'Why Pick on Me?'

When caught red-handed with his or her pockets full of sweets, a child may try to avoid punishment by pointing at the bolder sibling who did the actual stealing. Parents are rarely impressed by this 'why pick on me?' argument. After all,

[41] [1967] 3 All ER 993. [42] Cf. below, Part I, Section 5.3.
[43] *Arthur JS Hall & Co. v Simons* [2000] 3 All ER 673 at 702.

one child's fault is not erased by the fact that another child was equally or even more at fault. Though essentially still the same argument, the 'why pick on me?' argument may seem more convincing in complex situations involving nonfeasance. Let us for example recall the (in)famous case of Kitty Genovese who was raped and murdered in broad daylight. Dozens of people watched from their windows and ignored her cries for help. Nobody called the police.[44] Why would we allow Kitty's family to 'pick' on one of these people, by bringing a claim in negligence? After all, were the other spectators not equally to blame? And, is it not true that the rapist/murderer was the 'real' culprit? As with the sweets-stealing siblings, the answer is fairly straightforward: the question is not whether others were equally or even more culpable, but whether this individual defendant was at fault.[45] In this respect there is no reason to differentiate between feasance and nonfeasance.[46]

This is not to say that the presence of other people has no bearing whatsoever on the duty of an individual. Depending on the circumstances, a reasonable person may sometimes refrain from acting or limit his/her actions because there are other people who are in a better position to intervene than he/she is. The passer-by in the street who witnesses Kitty's ordeal may be required to run to a phone box and call the police if he or she is the only one there. However, another conclusion may be reached if he notices that there are dozens of people witnessing the crime from their windows. Under such circumstances it can be argued that the passer-by may legitimately believe that his intervention is unnecessary, relying on one of the other witnesses to make the phone call. Thus, the presence of other people – especially if they are in a better position to intervene – can be taken into account when we decide whether the defendant's behaviour was reasonable. However, if and when we decide that his or her behaviour was unreasonable, there is no (good) reason to deny a claim against him or her merely because someone else was equally or even more culpable. Thus, we allow a plaintiff to single out, or 'pick on' the defendant of his choice. Any unfairness that might arise from this system ought to be overcome by the Civil Liability (Contribution) Act 1978, which allows the defendant to bring an action against anyone else 'liable in respect of the same damage' to recover a contribution from them.[47]

[44] J.M. Ratcliffe in his introduction to J.M. Ratcliffe, (ed.), *The Good Samaritan and the Law* (1966), pp. IX–X, and Ch.O. Gregory, 'The Good Samaritan and the Bad', in J.M. Ratcliffe, (ed.), *The Good Samaritan and the Law* (1966), pp. 23–41 at 33 with further references in footnotes 30 and 31.

[45] P. Cane, *Atiyah's Accidents, Compensation and the Law* (6th edn 1999), p. 63 and K. Williams, 'Medical Samaritans: Is There a Duty to Treat?' (2001) 21 OJLS 393–413 at 398.

[46] E.J. Weinrib, 'The Case for a Duty to Rescue', (1980) 90 Yale LJ 247 ff. at 262. Of course, the other requirements of liability in negligence would also have to be met. In the case of Kitty Genovese, there are indications that calling the police would not have prevented Kitty's death, because the police would either have come too late or not at all. Hence, it is doubtful whether the failure to call the police *caused* Kitty's death.

[47] Civil Liability (Contribution) Act 1978, s. 1(1).

3.4 Economic Arguments

In the second half of the twentieth century, the law of torts has increasingly been subjected to economic analyses. Terms like 'wealth maximization', 'price deterrence', 'internalization of externalities' and 'the cheapest cost avoider' have become commonplace in textbooks on the law of torts. This is not the right place to examine the various economic theories that have been developed.[48] However, the concept of 'price deterrence' requires some attention, if only because Lord Hoffmann directly refers to this concept in his speech in *Stovin v Wise*. Price deterrence has been put forward as an economic justification for the imposition of tort liability on the person who causes loss to others. Essential to the concept of price deterrence is the presumption that if we hold a person liable for the losses his behaviour causes, he will eventually be unable to afford to continue or repeat his harmful behaviour. Take for example two factories that produce a similar type of car. Factory A causes no harm in doing so. Factory B, however, uses a production method that has a negative effect on others; say, it causes pollution to the neighbouring land. If the social costs represented by the pollution are not transferred to factory B, there are 'externalities'. If we 'internalize' these externalities to the activity of factory B, the price of the cars of factory B will rise to a level reflecting the 'true social costs' of the product. As a consequence, some consumers will buy the cars of factory A instead of B, and eventually factory B will go out of business and the pollution will stop.[49] Thus, imposition of tort liability removes externalities and consequently enhances efficiency. As is the case with the general argument of deterrence, the argument of price deterrence is open to considerable criticism.[50] Let us however presume that it has some merit in justifying the imposition of liability. Then, why is it that Lord Hoffmann alleges that this theory does not provide a 'similar justification for requiring a person who is not doing anything to spend money on behalf of someone else'?[51] If it is true that to accomplish efficiency the externalities caused by actions need to be internalized, then why is this not similarly true for the externalities caused by inaction?

Inaction, like action, can cause externalities. An example can be drawn from the Australian case of *Modbury Triangle Shopping v Anzil*.[52] There, an employee of a store that was part of a shopping centre was brutally attacked in the centre's car park. This attack took place in the dark, because the owner of the premises had,

[48] See for a comprehensive summary of the various economic theories on the law of torts D. Howarth, *Textbook on Tort* (1995), pp. 15 ff.

[49] J. Stapleton, *Product Liability* (1994), p. 102. Cf. also A. Pigou, *The Economics of Welfare* (4th edn 1932), p. 183 and G. Calabresi, 'Some Thoughts on Risk Distribution and the Law Of Torts' (1961) 70 Yale LJ 499.

[50] J. Stapleton, *Product Liability* (1994), pp. 108 ff. and pp. 118 ff. and P. Cane, *Atiyah's Accidents, Compensation and the Law* (6th edn 1999), pp. 361 ff.

[51] *Stovin v Wise* [1996] 3 All ER 801 at 819, quoted above in the opening of Chapter 3.

[52] (2000) 176 ALR 411 (High Ct of Australia).

despite earlier complaints, failed to switch on the car park lights. The employee sued the owner of the shopping centre, but his claim was eventually dismissed by the High Court. However, this decision has been criticized, *inter alia* on the basis that the defendant's omission resulted in externalities.[53] Indeed, there is no (good) reason why the economic reasons to put factory B out of business do not equally apply to the shopping centre. The cost of refusing to ensure safety for both employees and customers, it could be argued, should be reflected in the price of the products sold and services rendered at the shopping centre.

Perhaps what lies at the heart of Lord Hoffmann's argument, is an assumption that inaction does not *cause* loss, and therefore does not *cause* externalities. In Part I, Section 3.6, we shall see that this point of view is not easy to maintain.

A rather different economic argument has been put forward by Professor Honoré in a 1991 tribute to Atiyah:[54]

> The most plausible arguments for sanctioning acts more severely than omissions have so far been economic. One can refrain from a great many harmful acts, like poisoning, at the same time, while it is difficult or impossible to combine more than one helpful act, like providing food. The benefit of abstention is also widely distributed, in that if I abstain from doing harm no one is harmed, while the benefit of helpful acts is confined to the few who get the food I can provide.[55]

In other words, the performance of a negative duty involves a *smaller effort* than the performance of an affirmative duty, because one can 'refrain from a great many harmful acts (. . .) at the same time'. Moreover, the performance of a negative duty has a *more widespread effect*, because 'if I abstain from doing harm no one is harmed'. However, both submissions are debatable. As for the effort required, *for the individual* the performance of a negative duty often requires less effort than the performance of an affirmative duty. However, the performance of a negative duty is not always without effort. Sometimes one cannot perform a negative duty other than by taking affirmative action. When confronted with a traffic sign that tells you not to turn left on a T-junction, you will either have to stop your car or turn right. Moreover, for a negative duty to have its required effect, it needs to be performed by *all the members of the public* who are in the vicinity of the protected interest. The cumulative effort of these members of the public in performing the negative duty can very well exceed the individual effort that is required for the performance of the corresponding affirmative duty. An example can clarify: during a stormy night an unlucky pedestrian is knocked unconscious by a falling branch and falls down in the middle of a street. During the morning rush hour the unconscious man creates a considerable obstacle. To protect the man from being hurt, we can either impose a negative duty not to drive into the man or an affirmative

[53] H. Luntz, 'Torts Turnaround Downunder' (2001) 1 OUCLJ 95–106 at 101–102. Cf. *Modbury Triangle Shopping v Anzil* (2000) 176 ALR 411 at 434, *per* Kirby J.

[54] A.M. Honoré, 'Are Omissions Less Culpable?' in P. Cane and J. Stapleton (eds), *Essays for Patrick Atiyah* (1991), pp. 31 ff.

[55] *Ibid.*, pp. 31–32 (footnotes omitted).

duty to remove the man from the street and/or revive him. For the individual car driver the negative duty requires less effort. It is easier to manoeuvre his car around the unconscious man than to have to stop his car, get out and help him. But to avoid the man being hurt, it is not just this car driver who has to guide his car around the man. Every single car driver who passes through this street will have to do the same. By contrast, it only takes one car driver's effort to reach the same result by performing the affirmative duty. The cumulative effort of the car drivers in performing the negative duty may in this case very well exceed the individual effort in performing the corresponding affirmative duty, reaching the same effect.

The example of the unconscious man also shows that the performance of a negative duty does not always have a more 'widely distributed' benefit; it is only the unconscious man who benefits from the car drivers' abstention from driving into him. Yet, affirmative action – e.g. taking the man off the street – will not only benefit the unconscious man, but also all the car drivers who will be passing through the street; they will no longer have to manoeuvre their cars around the unconscious man.

Even in cases where the benefit of the performance of a negative duty is more 'widely distributed' than the benefit of the performance of an affirmative duty, this does not force us to the conclusion that imposition of the negative duty is necessarily more efficient. For the 'output' of a positive act depends on more than just its 'distribution'. The example given by Honoré provides a good illustration:[56] although everybody in my vicinity enjoys the benefit of my abstention to poison them, this is relatively only a very small benefit. For the fact that I abstain from poisoning a hungry man by no means protects him from being poisoned by somebody else. And even if we all abstain from poisoning this hungry man, he may still die of starvation. If I actively feed him, he will survive. Thus, the benefit of a positive act may often be less 'widely distributed', but also larger than the benefit of inaction.

The most elaborate attempt to give an economic justification of the general denial of liability in cases of nonfeasance was made by the influential American legal economists Landes and Posner. In 1973, Posner had voiced the opinion that – at least in rescue cases – there are sound economic reasons for imposing affirmative duties.[57] In rescue cases, Posner argued, transaction costs are so high that we cannot rely on the free market principle for efficiency. We must therefore create an incentive for potential rescuers to come to the rescue when such intervention is efficient, by introducing liability for failure to rescue. When the costs of rescue are lower than its benefits, potential rescuers will feel compelled to come to the rescue in order to avoid liability. When the rescue costs are higher than the benefits, the

[56] A.M. Honoré, 'Are Omissions Less Culpable?', pp. 31 ff. (quoted above).

[57] R.A. Posner, 'Strict Liability: a Comment', (1973) 2 J.Leg.Stud. 205–221 at 218–219. Cf. J.G. Fleming, *The Law of Torts* (9th edn 1998), p. 164, footnote 102.

'reasonable man standard' allows potential rescuers to abstain from intervention. By 1978 however, Posner's views had radically changed. After a detailed study into the economic aspects of altruism, carried out with Landes, Posner came to the conclusion that introduction of a positive duty to rescue would not necessarily promote efficiency.[58] In individual cases, Posner and Landes argued, the view that the presence of a duty to rescue would promote efficiency is broadly sound. As a general rule, however, liability for failure to rescue would have negative side effects that might lead to inefficiency. Landes and Posner had the following negative side effects in mind:

1) Potential rescuers would avoid liability by 'substituting away' from activities that give rise to rescue opportunities.[59] For example, good swimmers would avoid crowded beaches.[60] Hence, there would be fewer potential rescuers on the beach, and those remaining would be more likely to be called upon.
2) Even if imposition of a legal duty to rescue would lead to a rise in successful rescues, this would encourage potential victims to disregard their own safety. Moreover, the number of potential victims would increase, as hazardous activities would become more attractive.[61]
3) Under the present Common Law regime, rescuers enjoy public recognition as altruists. Under a regime of liability for failure to rescue, it would be impossible for a rescuer to prove that he was motivated by altruism. This could again discourage potential rescuers from going to places where there is a relatively high likelihood that they will be called upon (e.g. crowded beaches).[62]
4) The costs of administering a liability rule are high. 'Legal error costs in particular might be high because of the difficulty, in many settings (e.g., on a crowded beach), of identifying potential rescuers.'[63]

It must be seriously doubted whether these predicted side effects are likely to occur. The prediction of the first side effect overlooks two important points. Firstly, we learn from experience that imposition of liability rarely dissuades people from partaking in activities that may give rise to such liability. Rather, they take more careful precautions or insure themselves against the increased risk of liability.[64] Moreover, there are so many activities that may give rise to rescue opportunities that it is virtually impossible for potential rescuers to substitute away from them. Not only will they have to avoid crowded beaches, but also sporting grounds, industrial sites, busy roads and areas with a relatively high crime rate.

58 W.M. Landes and R.A. Posner, 'Salvors, Finders, Good Samaritans, and Other Rescuers: an Economic Study of Law and Altruism', (1978) 7 J.Leg.Stud. 83–128.

59 *Ibid.*, p. 120.

60 R.A. Posner, *Economic Analysis of Law* (4th edn 1992), p. 190.

61 W.M. Landes and R.A. Posner, 'Salvors, Finders, Good Samaritans, and Other Rescuers: an Economic Study of Law and Altruism', (1978) 7 J.Leg.Stud. 124.

62 *Ibid.*, p. 124. Cf. R.A. Posner, *Economic Analysis of Law* (4th edn 1992), p. 190.

63 *Ibid.*, p. 124.

64 P. Cane, *Atiyah's Accidents, Compensation and the Law* (6th edn 1999), p. 364.

The suggested second side effect must be met with similar scepticism. People do not risk their own safety just because they know that other people will have a legal duty to rescue them if an accident occurs. In fact, there are clear indications that their own safety is one of the few considerations that keep people from acting hazardously.[65] Moreover, most legal systems accept that by taking unreasonable risks, one may incur liability in negligence towards the person who comes to the rescue.[66] Thus, liability in negligence provides an additional deterrent against hazardous behaviour.

When Posner and Landes predicted the third side effect, that rescuers would no longer enjoy public recognition for their altruism, we must wonder what kind of liability rule they had in mind. Thus far, not a single proposal for a legal duty to rescue entails a standard of care that is higher than that of the 'reasonable person'. A rule of liability for nonfeasance would at the most require a person to take affirmative action if it would be unreasonable not to do so. It would not require acts that are beyond the call of moral duty, acts of heroism or acts of sacrifice.[67] In other words, it would not require the kind of acts that deserve special praise and public recognition for being truly altruistic. Hence, the public recognition for jumping into a sea with treacherous tidal currents in order to rescue someone, for going into a burning house to save a cat, and for giving large donations to charities will remain unchanged, because these acts are, and would remain, 'beyond the call of duty'.

As for the fourth and last side effect, it is conceivable that imposition of liability in cases of nonfeasance would bring with it an increase in administrative costs, especially in cases of multiple potential defendants. The reason for this increase in costs is not, as Posner and Landes seem to suggest, that it would be difficult for the victim to identify a defendant. In cases with multiple potential defendants (e.g. the case of the crowded beach) it is relatively easy for the victim to identify a defendant, since there are so many of them. However, for the defendant bringing an action under the Civil Liability (Contribution) Act 1978, it would indeed be difficult to identify all the other potential defendants, as well as to establish the contribution that each of them would have to pay. Yet, this is not a side effect that is particular to cases of nonfeasance. The same problems, and similar costs, occur in cases of feasance involving multiple potential defendants.[68]

We must therefore conclude that the economic arguments put forward by Lord Hoffmann, by Honoré, and by Posner and Landes amount to very little. It is here submitted that in general the imposition of affirmative duties would promote efficiency as much[69] (or as little) as the existing negative duties do.

[65] P. Cane, *Atiyah's Accidents, Compensation and the Law* (6th edn 1999), pp. 364–365.

[66] Cf. for English law *Baker v T.E. Hopkins & Son Ltd* [1959] 3 All ER 225 and *Ogwo v Taylor* [1987] 3 All ER 961. See also below, Part II, Section 5.6a.

[67] E.J. Weinrib, 'The Case for a Duty to Rescue', (1980) 90 Yale LJ 247 ff. at 261.

[68] *Ibid.* at 262.

[69] Fleming states that by failing to impose liability for nonfeasance in cases of easy rescue, the law 'clearly abjures the economic standard of efficiency': J.G. Fleming, *The Law of Torts* (9th edn 1998), p. 164, footnote 102.

Thus, economic analysis does not offer a valid argument for a general denial of liability for nonfeasance.

3.5 The Law does not Reward the Performance of Affirmative Duties

'Binding obligations', it has been observed by Friedmann, 'usually have a "built-in" element that justifies their imposition'.[70] This built-in element, it is here suggested, is most often a *quid pro quo*. Generally, the law is reluctant to impose duties without providing something in return, be it monetary or otherwise. This is most obviously so in the law of contract, where in principle no duty is imposed without consideration. Likewise, it must be assumed that we receive something in return for the performance of our duty to pay taxes. When it comes to duties in tort law there is usually a benefit, too, although not always easy to discern. Sometimes it is the benefit of the protected enjoyment of property that justifies the imposition of a duty. This is one of the reasons underlying the affirmative duties imposed on owners and occupiers of land.[71] In other cases, it is the act of the defendant itself that constitutes the *quid pro quo*. Those who make a profit from the exercise of a profession or the running of a business must accept the duty to do so with reasonable care. Similarly, the benefit of being allowed to drive cars on our public roads justifies the imposition of more severe duties on car drivers. Anyone who thinks that this benefit is not worth the burden that comes with it, Lord Nicholls would say, should not partake in the activity in the first place.

If, however, we were to impose an affirmative duty to intervene on the priest and the Levite, where is the *quid pro quo*? Is it not true that, as Lord Hoffmann stated, 'English law does not reward someone who voluntarily confers a benefit to another'?[72] And if so, is this not a good reason to reject the imposition of such affirmative duties? As was indicated in the introduction, the law relating to the claim of the intervener will be discussed in the second part of this book.

Hence, Lord Hoffmann's statement will here remain unchallenged. However, even if we assume this statement to be correct, we need not accept it as an argument against the imposition of affirmative duties. The mere absence of a remedy in one area of the law does not necessarily provide sufficient justification for the absence of a remedy in another area of the law; it may be that *both* areas of the law need to be reconsidered.

[70] D. Friedmann, 'Valid, Voidable, Qualified and Non-existing Obligations: An Alternative Perspective on the Law of Restitution' in A. Burrows (ed.), *Essays on the Law of Restitution* (1991), pp. 247–278 at 253.

[71] P. Cane, *Atiyah's Accidents, Compensation and the Law* (6th edn 1999), p. 68.

[72] *Stovin v Wise* [1996] 3 All ER 801 at 819, quoted above, Section 3.1.

3.6 Nonfeasance does not 'Cause' Harm

Another argument that has been used to exclude liability for nonfeasance is that it is difficult to see how nonfeasance can be the *cause* of any loss.[73] In the case of positive action the defendant has made the position of the plaintiff worse. By contrast, in the case of inaction the defendant has merely failed to confer a benefit to the plaintiff.[74]

Yet, there are also instances of *positive* action in which the defendant merely prevents a benefit from being conferred to the plaintiff.[75] In these cases we do not seem to have any problem with regarding the defendant's behaviour as a 'cause' of the plaintiff's loss. Let us presume that the priest and the Levite did not walk by, but waited for the Samaritan and convinced him not to help the victim. It is hardly debatable that the actions of the priest and the Levite would constitute a 'cause' of the victim's loss. But is it not true that the priest and the Levite merely prevented a benefit from coming the victim's way? The opposite view would be that 'convincing somebody to abstain from helping a victim' actually makes the position of the victim worse. But if this is true, why should 'convincing *oneself* to abstain from giving aid' be regarded as any different?[76]

The problem that has often been felt with regarding nonfeasance as a 'cause', originates in our understanding of the word 'cause' as implying a positive interference, not a mere inaction. Historically, the notion of 'movement' has been central to our concept of causation.[77] Honoré explains:

> (. . .) the reason why movements feature so prominently in our assessment of responsibility is that we have a picture of a world as a matrix into which, by our movements and especially our manipulation of objects, we introduce changes. By moving their bodies people change the world, though they may not know or foresee exactly what changes will come about. It is inherent in this world-picture that positive acts count as interventions and attract at least a minimal responsibility for their outcomes. On the other hand, non-movement is prima facie not an intervention in the world, so that the agent is not responsible for its consequences.[78] [Footnotes omitted.]

These days, the legal concept of causation is no longer completely governed by the notion of 'movement'. If and when we find that the defendant had an affirmative

[73] This seems to be the main argument relied on by Epstein, when defending the no-liability rule: R.A. Epstein, 'A Theory of Strict Liability', (1973) 2 J.Leg.Stud. 151–204, at 201. See also the writings discussed in D. Birnbacher, *Tun und Unterlassen* (1995), ch. 3.

[74] F.H. Bohlen, 'The Moral duty to aid Others as a Basis of Liability' [1908] 56 U.Pa.LR 217–244 and 316–338 at pp. 220–221; L.H. Eldredge, *Modern Tort Problems* (1941), p. 13 and J.G. Fleming, *The Law of Torts* (9th edn 1998), p. 163.

[75] J. Stapleton, 'The Normal Expectancies Measure in Tort Damages' (1997) 113 LQR 257–293 at 281–282.

[76] H.L.A. Hart and A.M. Honoré, *Causation in the Law* (2nd edn 1985), p. 448.

[77] *Ibid.*, p. 29.

[78] A.M. Honoré, 'Are Omissions Less Culpable?' in P. Cane and J. Stapleton (eds), *Essays for Patrick Atiyah* (1991), p. 41.

duty to act, we have, at least in England, no special difficulty with regarding the defendant's omission as the 'cause' of the loss.[79] Thus, a wounded man's refusal to see a doctor must be regarded as a cause of his death.[80] Likewise, a Borstal officer's failure to supervise some Borstal trainees is treated as a cause of the damage that the escaped trainees inflict on someone's yacht.[81] Honoré continues his explanation:

(. . .) superimposed on this picture of the world is a refinement of it, which treats disruptions of the normal course of events as similar to interventions which bring about change, though the change is not now a change in the existing state of affairs but rather in the normal or expected sequence of events. The regular course of things may take the form not only of recurrent natural events, but of regular human conduct such as clearing the street when the snow stops falling. If this regular or expected conduct fails to occur, the failure then counts not, as the first world-view would suggest, as a non-intervention but rather, on a wider view of what amounts to change, as a sort of intervention in the world.[82]

Thus, if the local government suddenly stops cleaning the streets and collecting the garbage, there can be no doubt that the refusal to do so is a legal cause of the resulting chaos. However, the decision of the House of Lords in *East Suffolk Rivers Catchment Board v Kent*[83] has been the source of some confusion. Owing to a very high tide, a breach was made in a sea wall, as a consequence of which the respondent's land was flooded. The appellants exercised their statutory powers to repair the wall but did the work so carelessly that the flooding continued for 178 days. It appeared from the evidence that by the exercise of reasonable skill the breach in the wall might have been repaired in 14 days. If Honoré's understanding of causation had been applied in this case, the appellants' failure to repair the wall properly would doubtlessly have been regarded as the cause of the continued flooding. Honoré would have regarded the 164 extra days of flooding as a 'change in the normal or expected sequence of events'. However, the House of Lords by a majority rejected the respondent's claim for damages. Some of the judgments in this case seem to suggest that the reason why the respondent's claim was rejected was because his loss was not *caused* by the appellants' incompetence. Viscount Simon argued:

In the present case, the damage done by the flooding was not due to the exercise of the appellant's statutory powers at all. It was due to the forces of nature, which the defendants, albeit unskillfully, were endeavouring to counteract.[84]

Similarly, Lord Thankerton's judgment read:

(. . .) I have felt throughout that the only real question in this appeal relates to causation, and the difficulty arises from the fact that, prior to the intervention of the appellants, a

[79] H.L.A. Hart and A.M. Honoré, *Causation in the Law* (2nd edn 1985), p. 139.

[80] *Ibid.*, p. 447 and *Targett v Torfaen BC* [1992] 3 All ER 27 at 37, *per* Sir Donald Nicholls V-C with further references.

[81] *Home Office v Dorset Yacht Co. Ltd* [1970] AC 1004.

[82] A.M. Honoré, 'Are Omissions Less Culpable?' in P. Cane and J. Stapleton (eds), *Essays for Patrick Atiyah* (1991), p. 41.

[83] [1940] 4 All ER 527.

[84] *Ibid.* at 531.

source of damage had been already created by the action of the flood waters (. . .) The point on which admittedly the success or failure of the appeal depends is whether the failure of the appellants to close the breach sooner by an efficient method can be held as the *causa causans* of the damage which accrued during these extra days, to the exclusion of the flood breach as a cause of the damage. However, it was in fact still the action of the water, rendered possible by the original breach, which caused the damage during these days, and failure to stop such action of the water cannot alter the fact that it is the water coming through the breach which causes the damage.[85]

If these judgments were correct, failures to remove an already present source of damage would not constitute a legal cause. A wounded man's refusal to see a doctor would not be a cause of his death, the local government's failure to clean the streets would not constitute a cause of the resulting mess, and a doctor's failure to diagnose poisoning would not be regarded as a cause of the patient's death.[86] These implications are unacceptable, and the conclusion that *East Suffolk Rivers Catchment Board v Kent* cannot be supported on the grounds put forward by Viscount Simon and Lord Thankerton is unavoidable. The question in this case was *not* whether the appellant's incompetence had caused the damage resulting from the 164 extra days of flooding. The causal connection was undeniable.[87] The real question was whether the appellant had an affirmative *duty* to abate the flooding or merely a negative duty not to make it worse.[88] The recent judgment of the Court of Appeal in *Capital and Counties v Hampshire CC*[89] must be understood in the same way. In one of three separate cases a fire brigade arrived at the scene of an explosion and satisfied itself that all the fires had been extinguished. The fire officers left the scene without inspecting the plaintiff's premises. A fire later broke out, which severely damaged the plaintiff's premises. The reason why the plaintiff's claim was rejected was *not* that the fire brigade's failure to inspect the plaintiff's premises was not a cause of the damage. The reason was that a fire brigade, in the opinion of the majority of the Court of Appeal, merely had a duty not to cause additional damage by its action, not an affirmative duty to extinguish the fire.

The confusion between issues of 'causation' on the one hand and issues of 'duty' on the other is hardly surprising. By incorporating into our 'picture of the world', as Honoré calls it, not only the 'existing state of affairs' but also 'the normal or expected sequence of events',[90] we are asking for trouble. For what we 'expect' of

[85] [1940] 4 All ER. at 539.

[86] Cf. *Barnett v Chelsea & Kensington Hospital Management Committee* [1968] 1 All ER 1068. (In this case it was found that, on the facts, no causal link existed between the defendant's wrongdoing an the plaintiff's loss)

[87] See *East Suffolk Rivers Catchment Board v Kent* [1940] 4 All ER 527, 537 *per* Lord Atkin, dissenting. Lord Atkin's speech was referred to with approval by Lord Salmon in *Anns v Merton London Borough* [1978] AC 728 at 766–767.

[88] *Ibid.* at 543, *per* Lord Romer and H.L.A. Hart and A.M. Honoré, *Causation in the Law* (2nd edn 1985), p. 140.

[89] *Capital and Counties v Hampshire CC* [1997] 2 All ER 865.

[90] A.M. Honoré, 'Are Omissions Less Culpable?' in P. Cane and J. Stapleton (eds), *Essays for Patrick Atiyah* (1991), p. 41 (quoted above).

people is often – but not always[91] – the same as their legal duty. Atiyah summarizes the issue most lucidly:

> Many people feel instinctively, if irrationally, that one can only treat nonfeasance as a 'cause' if one first starts by assuming that there was a duty to act. (. . .) the way we view the causation issue depends on whether we think that the defendant ought morally to have done something, and whether we think that this moral duty ought to be translated into a legal duty. This is a matter of legal policy and does not depend on any objective distinction between misfeasance and nonfeasance.[92]

3.7 Nonfeasance is less Culpable

In his already quoted tribute to Atiyah, Professor Honoré put forward a powerful defence of the 'acts-and-omissions doctrine'.[93] In general, contends Honoré, omissions are less culpable than acts that bring about the same or similar outcome, other things being equal. Thus, hitting someone is worse than not preventing someone from being hit.[94] However, says Honoré, omissions that violate a distinct duty that we owe to other people or associations are usually on a level with positive acts that violate those duties.[95] For a nurse it is usually just as culpable to give the wrong medicine, as it is to give no medicine at all.[96] And even if there is a distinct duty, it is sometimes worse to act than to omit:

> Take the problem of litter in the streets. If a person is employed by the local council to keep the streets clean, it can make no noticeable difference to the appearance of the streets whether he drops a wrapper in the street himself or fails to pick up a wrapper dropped by someone else. The outcome in each case is that there is one more wrapper in the street than there would otherwise have been, and the urban scene is to that extent less tidy. It is nevertheless probably worse for him to drop a wrapper than to fail to pick one up, since he is in that way adding to the very conditions he is employed to remedy.

Honoré's contentions are hardly debatable. All other things being equal, feasance is often regarded as being more culpable than nonfeasance, not least because many acts imply an additional inaction. When we say that 'dropping a wrapper is worse than not picking someone else's wrapper up', what we mean to say is that 'dropping a wrapper *and not picking it up*' is worse than 'not picking up someone else's wrapper'. And if we say that – presuming that we have a duty to protect one another – hitting someone is worse than not preventing someone from being hit,

[91] J. Stapleton, *Product Liability* (1994), p. 123.

[92] P. Cane, *Atiyah's Accidents, Compensation and the Law* (6th edn 1999), pp. 63–64 (footnotes omitted). This passage was cited with approval by Schiemann LJ in *Bellefield Computer Services Ltd v Turner & Sons Ltd* [2000] Build LR 97 at 101. See also D. Birnbacher, *Tun und Unterlassen* (1995), p. 89. and K. Williams, 'Medical Samaritans: Is there a Duty to Treat?' (2001) 21 OJLS 393–413 at 400.

[93] A.M. Honoré, 'Are Omissions Less Culpable?' in P. Cane and J. Stapleton (eds), *Essays for Patrick Atiyah* (1991), pp. 31 ff.

[94] *Ibid.*, p. 48.

[95] *Ibid.*, p. 33.

[96] *Ibid.*, p. 48.

this must be true, because by hitting we break two duties at once: the negative duty not to hit and the affirmative duty to protect.

Yet, accepting Honoré's contentions, do we also have to accept that, as he puts it, 'the acts-and-omissions doctrine is broadly sound'? Surely just the fact that nonfeasance is usually less culpable than feasance – all other things being equal – cannot justify a general denial of liability for nonfeasance? The harmful acts of a rookie doctor are usually less culpable than those of an experienced doctor. Likewise, unintentionally harmful acts are usually less culpable than acts committed with the intent to cause harm. Yet neither against the rookie doctor, nor against the unintentional wrongdoer do we deny the victim a claim.

If all other things are *not* equal, the culpability of nonfeasance can very well exceed the culpability of feasance. If inaction causes more harm than an action, the inaction is often seen as more culpable. There can be no doubt that leaving a man to drown where one could easily throw him a rope is more culpable than accidentally breaking someone's tea-pot. In rescue cases it may even happen that, although the act causes more harm than the inaction, the inaction is still regarded as more culpable than the action. Imagine that the good Samaritan, trying to do his very best to lift the wounded man 'on his beast', slipped and dropped the man, causing him to die earlier than he would have done if he had been left alone. The act of the Samaritan has caused more harm than the priest's and the Levite's inaction. However, the behaviour of the Samaritan, who after all did his very best to save a fellow human being, should probably be regarded as the less culpable. Thus, if culpability is to be the test for imposing liability, there is no (good) reason to make a general distinction between cases of feasance and cases of nonfeasance.[97]

[97] See also P. Cane, *The Anatomy of Tort Law* (1997), pp. 63–64. *Contra*: K.J. Kemp, *Delictual Liability for Omissions* (1978) (Unpublished thesis, University of Port Elizabeth, South Africa), p. 615 and *idem*, 'The duty to rescue – compulsion or laissez faire?', (1985) XVIII CILSA 163–186 at 172.

4

Liability for Nonfeasance in Continental European Private Law

This chapter contains a brief account of the continental approach towards cases of nonfeasance. After a historical introduction, the focus will be on the laws of France and Germany. It should be emphasized that it is not here intended to describe the French[1] and German systems in detail. Instead, the purpose of this chapter is merely to illustrate how these two systems operate, while their respective codes do not draw a principled distinction between cases of feasance and nonfeasance. Thus, this chapter does not contain any discussion of, for example, the specific provisions in the French and German civil codes imposing liability for loss caused by persons for whom one is responsible,[2] by the things in one's control,[3] by animals,[4] or for damage caused by the collapse of buildings.[5] Neither shall we here discuss the contract-type affirmative duties that can arise under the French doctrine of *obligations de sécurité*,[6] the German doctrine of *culpa in contrahendo*,[7] nor indeed, the fact that German law recognizes contracts may have protective effects towards third parties (*Schutzwirkung für Dritte*).[8] This chapter shall, however, include a short discussion of the affirmative duties imposed under the continental doctrine of *negotiorum gestio*. Some knowledge of these duties is required if we are to fully understand the implications of that doctrine when we investigate it in more detail in Part II of this book. The duties imposed on the *gestor* in *negotiorum gestio* are treated separately in the last section of this chapter, because they are not strictly speaking tortious.

[1] See for a detailed survey of liability for nonfeasance in French law A-F Delvilani, *La Responsabilité Civile pour Omission ou Abstention* (1978).

[2] Art. 1384 *C. civ.* and § 832 *BGB*.

[3] Art. 1384 *C. civ.*

[4] Art. 1385 *C. civ.* and §§ 833–834 *BGB*.

[5] Art. 1386 *C. civ.* and §§ 836–838 *BGB*.

[6] W. van Gerven, J. Lever and P. Larouche, *Cases, Materials and Text on National, Supranational and International Tort Law* (2000), p. 281 and 284–285.

[7] B.S. Markesinis, W. Lorenz and G. Dannemann, *The German Law of Obligations*, Vol I (1997), pp. 64–71 and C. von Bar, *The Common European Law of Torts*, Vol 1 (1998), nrs 190 and 471–477.

[8] B.S. Markesinis, W. Lorenz and G. Dannemann, *The German Law of Obligations*, Vol I (1997), pp. 276–282. The *Schutzwirkung für Dritte* has recently been codified: § 311(3) *BGB*.

4.1 Historical Background

Whether directly or indirectly, many provisions in Western European codifications have been influenced by the corresponding provisions in the laws of ancient Rome. The Romans, too, were confronted with cases of damage caused by nonfeasance. The relevant question under Roman law was whether the *Lex Aquilia*, the Roman statute establishing liability for killing slaves and cattle and for causing damage to goods, was applicable to cases of damage or death caused by nonfeasance. Through the centuries, the answer to this question has been hotly debated. The famous commentator Bartolus opined that the *actio legis Aquiliae* was granted to the owner 'for an act, not for *negligentia*'.[9] However, some three centuries later Antonius Matthaeus II reached the opposite conclusion, stating that 'it appears that the laws treat both a doing which a careful person would not do, and a not doing which a careful person would do, alike'.[10] This view was strongly criticized by Voet, who insisted that the Romans did not impose liability for omissions. After all, 'it would be too harsh for a person to be held liable on wrongdoing for the slightest fault of omission'.[11] The dispute recurred in 19th century Germany. Pernice echoed the view of Antonius Matthaeus II, stating that Roman law drew no distinction between feasance and nonfeasance.[12] The same view was held by Dernburg.[13] However, a majority of Pernice's contemporaries followed Windscheid, who thought that the Romans generally denied Aquilian liability in cases of nonfeasance.[14]

With so many distinguished scholars disagreeing,[15] any conclusion must be subject to reservation. However, the better view would appear to be that the *Lex Aquilia* did not initially apply to cases of nonfeasance.[16] A strong indication to that effect can be found in Gaius' Institutes, where it is written that there was only a direct action under the statute if the defendant had done damage with his own body, *corpore suo*.[17] If the *Lex Aquilia* required that damage be done *corpore suo*,

[9] Bartolus de Saxoferrato, *Super prima parte ff. vetus* (edn 1489) *ad D.* 7.1.13.2: '*Actio legis Aquiliae datur domino propter factum, non propter negligentiam*'. See also Baldus de Ubaldis, *Super Digesto Veteri* (edn 1540), p. 285 (*ad D.* 7.1.13.2).

[10] A. Matthaeus, De Criminibus (1644), p. 560 (*lib.* 48, *tit.* 5, *cap.* 6, *num.* 5): '*(. . .) facere quod diligens non faceret, non facere quod diligens faceret, leges juxta aestimare videntur*'. Cf. H. Grotius, *De Iure Belli ac Pacis* (1625), *lib.* II, *cap.* XVII, I.

[11] J. Voet, *Commentarius ad Pandectas*, Vol I (6th edn 1731), p. 537 (*ad* legem Aquiliam, 3).: '*(. . .) quia durum nimis foret, propter levissimam in omittendo culpam aliquem ex delicto teneri*'. Translation: P. Gane, *The Selective Voet*, Vol 2 (1955), p. 547.

[12] A. Pernice, *Zur Lehre von den Sachbeschädigungen nach Römischem Rechte* (1867), pp. 171–172.

[13] H. Dernburg, *Pandekten*, Vol 2 (7th edn 1903), p. 361, footnote 11.

[14] B. Windscheid and Th. Kipp, *Lehrbuch des Pandektenrechts*, Vol 2 (9th edn 1906), p. 974.

[15] See for a more detailed investigation; K.J. Kemp, *Delictual Liability for Omissions* (1978) (Unpublished thesis, University of Port Elizabeth, South Africa), pp. 70–74 and footnotes 44 and 45.

[16] See also Pernice, who changed his view on the subject, as far as classical law was concerned: A. Pernice, *Labeo – Römisches Privatrecht im ersten Jahrhunderte der Kaiserzeit*, Vol 2, Part 1 (2nd edn 1895), p. 128, footnote 1.

[17] *G.* III, 219. Cf. *I.* IV, III, 16.

this requirement must have blocked liability in cases of nonfeasance. After all, the very notion of nonfeasance implies the absence of direct physical contact between wrongdoer and victim.[18] Further support can be drawn from the wording of the *lex.* Liability is imposed for '*occidere*' ('killing' or 'slaying') and '*urere, frangere, rumpere*' ('burning, breaking, spoiling'). These are all verbs with a strong active connotation.[19] Finally, *D.* 7.1.13.2 (Ulpian) suggests that the *Lex Aquilia* did not in principle impose liability for nonfeasance. Julian is there cited as having stated that a usufructuary who failed to plough up an unbroken piece of land, or to plant vines, or who allowed a watercourse to fall into disrepair was not liable under the *Lex Aquilia.* If even a usufructuary was not liable for his careless nonfeasance, it would seem unlikely that a mere bystander such as the good Samaritan would have had a duty to intervene.[20]

Assuming that as a rule the *Lex Aquilia* applied only to (active) misfeasance, this rule was not without exceptions. For instance, Ulpian discussed a case in which a stoker-slave fell asleep at the furnace, as a consequence of which the house burnt down.[21] Liability would ensue, Ulpian held, regardless of whether the fire was lit by the slave himself or by a third person. Similarly, Gaius opined that a doctor could be held liable if he neglected the aftercare:

> And the law is just the same (. . .) if, having operated efficiently, the aftercare is neglected; the wrongdoer will not go free, but is deemed to be guilty of *culpa.*[22]

Interestingly, Gaius 'deemed' that the doctor's neglect amounted in law to *culpa.* '*Culpa*', it should be noted, originally denoted *active* misconduct.[23] Might Gaius have viewed the doctor's omission as part of the larger activity of 'operating'? Indeed, for this very reason Voet argued that neither of the examples given by Ulpian and Gaius involved liability for true omissions:

> (. . .) They all did wrong in taking up a duty and not fulfilling it after taking it up. It was open to them not to devote their art or labour to another, but when devoted they were bound to carry it out. By their failure in that respect (the abandonment of the curative treatment, the not putting out of the fire or the not banking it so that it could not spread

[18] J. Limpens, R.M. Kruithof and A. Meinertzhagen-Limpens, 'Liability for One's Own Act', in A. Tunc (ed.), *International Encyclopedia of Comparative Law*, Vol XI Torts (1983), ch. 2, p. 36.

[19] P.B.H. Birks, 'Doing and causing to be done' in A.D.E. Lewis and D.J. Ibbetson, *The Roman Law Tradition* (1994), pp. 32–54.

[20] Cf. however B. Beinart, '*Culpa in Omittendo*' [1949] THRHR 141–169 at 152–154 and for a survey of the various interpretations of *D.* 7.1.13.2 K.J. Kemp, *Delictual Liability for Omissions* (1978) (Unpublished thesis, University of Port Elizabeth, South Africa), pp. 75–83.

[21] *D.* 9.2.27.9 and *Coll.* 12.7.7

[22] *D.* 9.2.8 (Gaius): '*Idem iuris est si (. . .) qui bene secuerit et derelinquit curationem, securus non erit, sed culpa reus intellegitur.* '*Culpa*' is here left untranslated.

[23] L. Mitteis, *Römisches Privatrecht bis auf die Zeit Diokletians*, Vol 1 (1908), p. 322. See also W.W. Buckland, '*Diligens Paterfamilias*' in E. Albertario, P. Ciapessoni and P. De Fransisci, *Studi in Onore di Pietro Bonfante* (1930), pp. 85–108 at 102 and F.M. de Robertis, *La Responsabilita' Contrattuale nel Sistema della Grande Compilazione*, Vol 1 (1983), pp. 195–199.

while they took their nap (. . .)) they are understood to have erred alike in the undertaking the work and in not fulfilling it.[24]

It has been explained in Chapter 2, above, that the use of this fiction must be rejected.[25] The acts of operating, or indeed of lighting the fire in the furnace, must not be 'understood' to have been wrongful. The use of such fictions obscures from our view the real issue at hand, that is, the nature and scope of the duties that come into existence when one lights a fire, operates on a patient *etc.* Instead, the preferred approach is to acknowledge that the active conduct in these cases was lawful, and then proceed to determine to what extent the inactive conduct can be said to have been unlawful.[26] A similar approach appears to have commended itself to Ulpian. *Coll.* 12.7.7:

(. . .) but if one man lit the furnace and another watched it negligently, who should be liable? For the one who failed to watch it did nothing, while the one who lit it in the proper way was not at fault. Just like in the case in which a doctor operated, but either he himself or someone else neglected the aftercare, the *lex Aquilia* does not apply. What then are we to say? I think that an *actio ad exemplum Aquiliae* lies against both the man who fell asleep at the furnace or the man who negligently watched it and against the doctor who neglected the aftercare, either if the man dies or if he is disabled.[27]

The level of abstraction here achieved is remarkable. Ulpian observes that 'the one who failed to watch [the fire] did nothing', while the one who lit it 'was not at fault'.[28] He then proceeds to draw a parallel between his case and that of Gaius's doctor. In neither case, he says, the direct action is available. This strongly suggests that, to Ulpian, the *Lex Aquilia* did not directly apply to cases of nonfeasance. If liability was nevertheless to arise, as Ulpian argued it should, praetorian intervention was required, the result being an *actio ad exemplum Aquiliae* (or *utilis*[29]).[30]

[24] J. Voet, *Commentarius ad Pandectas*, Vol I (6th edn 1731), p. 537 (*ad* legem Aquiliam, 3): '*(. . .) delinquerunt namque hi omnes suscipiendo officium, ac susceptum non adimplendo. Liberum erat ipsis artem operamve suam alteri non addicere: ad addictam implere necesse erat: in quo dum cessant (derelinquendo curationem, ignem non extinguendo, vel non muniendo ne evagetur dum obdormirent (..)) suscipiendo aeque ac non adimplendo peccasse intelliguntur*'. Translation: P. Gane, *The Selective Voet*, Vol 2 (1955), p. 548–549.

[25] See also J.C. Smith, *Smith and Hogan; Criminal Law* (10th edn 2002), p. 61.

[26] *Contra*: E. Grueber, *The Roman Law of Damage to Property* (1886), p. 214, footnote 1.

[27] *(. . .) ceterum si alius ignem subiecerit fornaci, alius neglegenter custodierit, an tenetur? Namque qui non custodit, nihil fecit, qui recte ignem subiecit, non peccavit: quemadmodum si hominem medicus recte secuerit, sed neglegenter vel ipse vel alius curaverit, Aquilia cessat. Quid ergo est? Et hic puto ad exemplum Aquiliae dandam actionem tam in eum, qui ad fornacem obdormivit vel neglegenter custodit, quam in medicum qui neglegenter curavit, sive homo periit sive debilitatus est.* Translation: F.H. Lawson, *Negligence in the Civil Law* (1950), pp. 103–105. Cf. *D.* 9.2.27.9.

[28] Lawson remarks that the phrase '*Namque qui . . . peccavit*' is probably a gloss: F.H. Lawson, *Negligence in the Civil Law* (1950), p. 103. However, the fact that the phrase features both in the *Collatio* and in the Digest would suggest otherwise.

[29] See *D.* 9.2.27.9 (Ulpian).

[30] Compare also *D.* 9.2.30.3, in which Paul argues that someone who fails to control a fire is deemed to have caused damage, with *Coll.* 12.7.4–5 where Ulpian states that a majority is of the opinion that the direct action is not available in such cases.

4.2 The Law in France

Until the seventeenth century, the French law of delict had been a mixture of Roman law, canon law and local laws and customs.[31] There was no general rule of liability, neither was there a clear distinction between the compensatory and the punitive function of awarding damages. In 1689 Domat published his '*Les loix civiles dans leur ordre naturel*', a most influential work that would eventually provide the fundamentals of the modern French law of delictual liability. Central to Domat's understanding of delictual liability was the notion of *faute*. Domat distinguished three types of *fautes*: those that consist of a crime or offence, those that are a breach of agreements, and those that are neither, 'like when one thoughtlessly throws something out of a window and spoils someone's clothes, when animals that are not properly looked after cause damage, when one causes a fire through carelessness, or when a building under the threat of falling down is not repaired and collapses on another building and causes damage'.[32] Delictual liability is concerned with the latter type of fault. When under a duty to act, Domat continued, a defendant could be held liable for a failure to prevent harm:

> Those who, being able to prevent harm from occurring, when a certain duty committed them to prevent this harm, failed to do so, may be held liable depending on the circumstances. Thus, a master who sees and allows the infliction of harm by his servant, is held liable.[33]

Domat's ideas were adopted, expanded and improved by Pothier, the most influential French scholar of the eighteenth century. By the end of that century, the French legislator decided to draft a liability rule that was meant to be universally and eternally applicable.[34] Domat's and Pothier's theories were clearly the source of inspiration of the articles 1382 and 1383 of the French Civil Code (*C. civ.*) of 1804:

> **1382** Any conduct whatever of man which causes damage to another obliges him by whose fault ('*faute*') it occurred to make reparation.[35]

[31] J-L Gazzaniga, *Introduction historique au droit des obligations* (1992), p. 243.

[32] J. Domat, *Les loix civiles dans leur ordre naturel* (rev. edn 1745), p. 179 (*Livre II, Titre VIII*): '(. . .) *comme si par legereté on jette quelque chose par une fenêtre qui gâte un habit: Si des animaux mal gardez font quelque dommage: Si on cause un incendie par une imprudence: Si un bâtiment qui menace ruine n'étant pas réparé tombe sur un autre, & y fait du dommage.*'

[33] *Ibid.*, p. 185 (*Livre II, Titre VIII, Section VIII*): '*Ceux qui pouvant empêcher un dommage, que quelque devoir les engageoit de prévenir, y auront manqué, pourront en être tenus selon les circonstances. Ainsi un maître qui voit & souffre le dommage que fait son domestique, pouvant l'empêcher, en est responsable.*' Cf. *D.* 9.2.44.1 and 9.2.45.*pr*.

[34] C.H. Sieburgh, 'Faute als grond voor aansprakelijkheid', [1998] *Groninger Opmerkingen en Mededelingen*, pp. 68–90 at p. 71. Cf. also G. Viney, *Traité de Droit Civil; Introduction à la responsabilité* (2nd edn 1995), nr. 14.

[35] '***1382*** *Tout fait quelconque de l'homme, qui cause à autrui un dommage, oblige celui par la faute duquel il est arrivé, à le réparer.*' The translation is largely based on J.H. Crabb, *The French Civil Code* (rev. edn 1995), p. 252. It was necessary to amend this translation in one respect: Crabb's translation of '*fait*' was 'act'. A '*fait*' however, can refer to an act as well as to inaction. See J. Mihura in his annotation under the judgment of the *Cour de Cassation* in the Branly case, [1951] II *JCP* 6193, with further references.

1383 Each one is liable for the damage which he causes not only by his own conduct but also by his negligence or imprudence.[36]

When defining the notion of *faute*, the French legal system usually distinguishes between fault by commission ('*faute de commission*') and fault by omission ('*faute d'abstention*').[37] With regard to the latter, a further distinction is made between omissions that are part of a larger activity ('*abstentions dans l'action*') – such as a car driver's failure to apply the brakes – and pure omissions ('*abstentions pures et simples*').[38] Again, it is here submitted that this further distinction is more confusing than it is useful.[39] The same has been argued by Tunc and the brothers Mazeaud in their influential *Traité Théorique et Pratique de la Responsabilité Civile*.[40] However, a majority of academics continues to adopt the distinction.

In cases of *abstentions dans l'action*, the courts do not seem to have had any problems with imposing liability.[41] The so-called '*Branly case*' provides what is probably the most well-known example of an *abstention dans l'action*; Professor Turpain, the author of an article with the title '*Historique de la T.S.F*' ('History of Wireless Telegraphy') had omitted to mention the name and the works of the plaintiff, Edouard Branly. The French *Cour de Cassation* decided:

That the court should have investigated whether Turpain, when writing a history of wireless telegraphy in which the name and the works of Branly were wilfully omitted, had behaved like a prudent writer or historian, aware and conscious of the duty to be objective that rested upon him.[42]

It is worth noting that the *Cour de Cassation* was apparently of the opinion that imposition of liability was not too much of an invasion of Professor Turpain's freedom of speech and expression.[43] Thus, *abstentions dans l'action* are measured against

[36] '***1383*** *Chacun est responsable du dommage qu'il a causé non seulement par son fait, mais encore par sa négligence ou par son imprudence.*' Translation: see previous footnote.

[37] E.g. H. Mazeaud, L. Mazeaud and A. Tunc, *Traité Théorique et Pratique de la Responsabilité Civile* (6th edn 1965), nrs 524 and 525; G. Viney and P. Jourdain, *Traité de Droit Civil*, Vol IV (2nd edn 1998), nrs 451–452 and F. Terré, P. Simler and Y. Lequette, *Droit civil; Les Obligations* (8th edn 2002), nr 719.

[38] G. Viney and P. Jourdain, *Traité de Droit Civil*, Vol IV (2nd edn 1998), nr 456; F. Terré, P. Simler and Y. Lequette, *Droit Civil; Les Obligations* (8th edn 2002), nrs 720–721 and J. Limpens, R.M. Kruithof and A. Meinertzhagen-Limpens, 'Liability for One's Own Act', in A. Tunc (ed.), *International Encyclopedia of Comparative Law*, Vol XI Torts (1983), ch. 2, p. 36 with further references in footnote 332.

[39] See above Chapter 2.

[40] H. Mazeaud, L. Mazeaud and A. Tunc, *Traité Théorique et Pratique de la Responsabilité Civile* (6th edn 1965), nr 525.

[41] F. Terré, P. Simler and Y. Lequette, *Droit Civil; Les Obligations* (8th edn 2002), nr 720; J. Limpens, R.M. Kruithof and A. Meinertzhagen-Limpens, 'Liability for One's Own Act', in A. Tunc (ed.), *International Encyclopedia of Comparative Law*, Vol XI Torts (1983), ch. 2, p. 36.

[42] *Civ.* 27 February 1951, *D.* 1951, 329: '*que la cour devait rechercher si, en écrivant une histoire de la T.S.F. dans laquelle les travaux et le nom d'Edouard Branly étaient volontairement omis, Turpain s'était comporté comme un écrivain ou un historien prudent, avisé et conscient des devoirs d'objectivité qui lui incombaient*'.

[43] G. Viney and P. Jourdain, *Traité de Droit Civil*, Vol IV (2nd edn 1998), nr 456 and F. Terré, P. Simler and Y. Lequette, *Droit Civil; Les Obligations* (8th edn 2002), nr 720.

the same standard as actions are:[44] *i.e.* the French equivalent of the 'reasonable man standard'.[45] On the same principle those who, however blamelessly, create a risk, have an obligation to take reasonable care to prevent this risk from materializing.[46] Hence the liability of a railway company for failing to provide the appropriate warning signals at a level crossing.[47]

In the area of *abstentions pures et simples*, too, the *Branly case* would play a pivotal role. Initially, the courts showed a reluctance to impose liability for 'pure' omissions. In a 1924 judgment, the *Cour de Cassation* held that:

(. . .) if everyone is liable for his negligence, an omission can only bring about liability if the person who is held liable had an obligation to do that which was omitted.[48]

At the time, this judgment was interpreted as meaning that liability for nonfeasance would only be imposed if it violated an affirmative duty that had been created by statute or at least by custom.[49] Obviously, this requirement restricted the scope of liability for *abstentions pures et simples*.[50] The main reason for the reluctance of the courts is said to have been that one should be allowed at least the freedom not to act. Additionally, it was doubted whether a causal connection could exist between nonfeasance and harm.[51] In the 1940s, the recognition of affirmative duties by the courts was accelerated by a development in the area of criminal law. Unlike the German legal system,[52] the French system regards the commission of any criminal offence which causes harm to others as a '*faute*' for the purpose of articles 1382 and 1383 *C. civ.* No further inquiry into the intended scope of the criminal provision is necessary. This concept is referred to as the 'unity of criminal and civil faults'.[53] Thus, when the legislator introduced a duty to act under criminal law, this was bound to have an immediate effect on the interpretation of '*faute*' in the law of negligence.[54] The first two paragraphs

[44] G. Viney and P. Jourdain, *Traité de Droit Civil*, Vol IV (2nd edn 1998), nr 456.

[45] E.g. the '*personne avisée placée dans les mêmes circonstances "externes" que l'auteur du dommage*', H. Mazeaud, L. Mazeaud and A. Tunc, *Traité Théorique et Pratique de la Responsabilité Civile* (6th edn 1965), nr 540; or the '*bon père de famille du même âge (voire de la même profession), placé dans une situation comparable*', P. le Tourneau and L. Cadiet, *Droit de la Responsabilité* (1998), nr 3065.

[46] G. Viney and P. Jourdain, *Traité de Droit Civil*, Vol IV (2nd edn 1998), nr 456 and F. Terré, P. Simler and Y. Lequette, *Droit Civil; Les Obligations* (8th edn 2002), nr 720.

[47] *Civ.* 8 April 1932, *DH* 1932, 297.

[48] *Civ.* 24 December 1924, *DH* 1925, 120 at 121: *(. . .) si chacun est responsable de sa négligence, l'omission ne peut entraîner une responsabilité qu'autant qu'il y avait, pour celui auquel on l'impute, obligation d'accomplir le fait omis.*

[49] H. Mazeaud, L. Mazeaud and A. Tunc, *Traité Théorique et Pratique de la Responsabilité Civile* (6th edn 1965), nr 544.

[50] J. Limpens, R.M. Kruithof and A. Meinertzhagen-Limpens, 'Liability for One's Own Act', in A. Tunc (ed.), *International Encyclopedia of Comparative Law*, Vol XI Torts (1983), ch. 2, pp. 36–43 at p. 37.

[51] P. Catala and J.A. Weir, 'Delict and Torts: a Study in Parallel', (1962–1963) 37 Tulane LR 573–620 at 615.

[52] Cf. the references in footnote 101, below, and the corresponding part of the main text.

[53] J. Bell, S. Boyron and S. Whittaker, *Principles of French Law* (1998), p. 361, with further references.

[54] A. Tunc, 'The Volunteer and the Good Samaritan' in J.M. Ratcliffe, (ed.), *The Good Samaritan and the Law* (1966), pp. 43–62 at p. 49.

of article 63 of the French Criminal Code (*C. pén.*), after it was amended in 1945,[55] read:

Article 63 Any person who, by his immediate action and without danger to himself or others, could have prevented either a felonious act or a misdemeanor against the person, wilfully fails to do so, shall be punished by jailing for no less than one month nor more than three years and by fine from 12,000 to 500,000 francs, or either punishment, unless more severe punishments are provided by this Code or special law.

Any person who wilfully fails to render or to obtain assistance to an endangered person when such was possible without danger to himself or others, shall be subject to like punishments.[56]

The courts translated the criminal duties imposed by article 63 *C. pén.* into private law duties. In 1947, the *Tribunal Correctionnel d'Aix* decided to award 25,000 francs in damages to the plaintiff, who had nearly drowned when he fell through ice into a deep canal. The defendant, who was the plaintiff's father-in-law, had walked away from the scene after refusing to assist a third person who tried to rescue the plaintiff by handing him an iron bar to which he might cling.[57]

In a later case, a doctor who was held liable by the *Cour d'Appel* of Paris for failing to assist a patient in need, argued that article 63 *C. pén.* was merely intended to protect the public interest, and should not give rise to private law claims. The *Cour de Cassation* dismissed the submission:

(. . .) if the provisions of article 63, 2nd paragraph of the Criminal Code concern the general interest of society and repress the disturbance caused by a delictual abstention to law and order, they also aim to protect private interests;[58]

One noteworthy consequence of the civil liability arising from article 63 *C. pén.*, is that members of the medical profession are only allowed to strike in non-emergency cases.[59]

It should be mentioned that a new Criminal Code has come into force in 1994. The former article 63 *C. pén.* is now incorporated in a larger section, which increases the penalties imposed by article 63 *C. pén.* and introduces a further affirmative duty

[55] *Ordinance* of 25 June 1945, [1945] *JO* 3862.

[56] '***Article 63*** *Sans préjudice de l'application, le cas échéant, des peines plus fortes prévues par le présent code et les lois spéciales, sera puni d'un emprisonment d'un mois à trois ans et d'une amende de 12.000 à 500.000 francs, ou de l'une de ces deux peines seulement, quiconque, pouvant empêcher par son action immédiate, sans risque pour lui ou pour les tiers, soit un fait qualifié crime, soit un délit contre l'intégrité corporelle de la personne, s'abstient volontairement de le faire.*

Sera puni des mêmes peines quiconque s'abstient volontairement de porter à une personne en péril l'assistance que, sans risque pour lui ni pour les tiers, il pouvait lui prêter, soit par son action personnelle soit en provoquant un secours.' Translation based on G.O.W. Mueller, *The French Penal Code* (1960), p. 38. Mueller's translation was of the text of art. 63 *C. pén.* after it was amended on 13 April 1954, [1954] *JO* 3580.

[57] *Tribunal Correctionnel d'Aix* 27 March 1947, *D* 1947, 304.

[58] *Crim.* 16 March 1972, *D* 1972, 394 at 395: '*(. . .) si les dispositions de l'art. 63, al. 2, c.pén. ont pour objet l'intérêt général de la collectivité et répriment le trouble causé à l'ordre public par une abstention délictueuse, elles ont aussi pour but la protection des intérêts privés;*'.

[59] K.J. Kemp, *Delictual Liability for Omissions* (1978) (Unpublished thesis, University of Port Elizabeth, South Africa), p. 564.

to assist in the case of a natural disaster, even when there is no immediate danger to any person.[60]

The decisive breakthrough towards a complete recognition of liability for negligent nonfeasance came with the aforementioned *Branly case*. Technically, the *Branly case* was only concerned with an *abstention dans l'action* and not with *abstentions pures et simples*. The *Cour de Cassation* however, probably strongly influenced by the works of the brothers Mazeaud,[61] did not draw such distinction:

(. . .) fault within the articles 1382 and 1383 C. civ. can consist of an abstention as well as a positive act; (. . .) an abstention gives rise to liability of the person responsible – even if there was no malice and intention to harm – when the act that was omitted should have been done either by virtue of a legal, statutory or contractual obligation, or by virtue of the demand for objective information within a profession, particularly when a historian is concerned.[62]

If interpreted to the letter, this judgment would not necessarily represent a big change in the area of liability for nonfeasance.[63] In the majority of the subsequent case law, however, the courts proceeded on the presumption that the *Branly case* constituted a breach with the distinction between feasance and nonfeasance.[64] At present, legal theory appears to have adopted a similar position. Whenever they think it appropriate the courts should be able to impose liability, whether the behaviour complained of is active or passive.[65]

In practice however, the courts appear to adopt a more cautious approach where omissions are concerned.[66] In particular, the personal characteristics of the defendant are taken into account. Thus, the courts are reluctant to hold children accountable for their omissions.[67] Also, the courts are not likely to impose liability where the defendant did not understand that his intervention was necessary or where he was physically or mentally unable to render the required assistance.[68] If,

[60] *Nouveau Code Pénal, Livre II, Titre Premier, Chapitre III, Section III* (artt. 223-5-223-7). Cf. the accompanying notes in the *Circulaire* of 14 May 1993.

[61] H. Mazeaud and L. Mazeaud, '*Obligations en général et responsabilité civile*', (1943) 41 *Rev.trim.dr.civ.* 109–121 at 111 and *eidem, Traité Théorique et Pratique de la Responsabilité Civile*, Vol 1 (4th edn 1947), nr 525.

[62] Civ. 27 February 1951, *D* 1951, 329: '*(. . .) la faute prévue par les art. 1382 et 1383 peut consister aussi bien dans une abstention que dans un acte positif; que l'abstention, même non dictée par la malice et l'intention de nuire, engage la responsabilité de son auteur lorsque le fait omis devait être accompli soit en vertu d'une obligation légale, réglementaire ou conventionnelle, soit aussi, dans l'ordre professionnel, s'il s'agit notamment d'un historien, en vertu des exigences d'une information objective;*'.

[63] H. Mazeaud, L. Mazeaud and A. Tunc, *Traité Théorique et Pratique de la Responsabilité Civile* (6th edn 1965), nr 544.

[64] *Ibid.*, nr 544 with further references to the relevant case law in footnotes 8, 9, 10 and 11.

[65] H. Mazeaud, L. Mazeaud and A. Tunc, *Traité Théorique et Pratique de la Responsabilité Civile* (6th edn 1965), nr 544; G. Viney and P. Jourdain, *Traité de Droit Civil*, Vol IV (2nd edn 1998), nr 453 and J. Limpens, R.M. Kruithof and A. Meinertzhagen-Limpens, 'Liability for One's Own Act', in A. Tunc (ed.), *International Encyclopedia of Comparative Law*, Vol XI Torts (1983), ch. 2, pp. 36–43 at 37.

[66] F. Terré, P. Simler and Y. Lequette, *Droit Civil; Les Obligations* (8th edn 2002), nr 721.

[67] N. Dejean de la Bâtie, *Aubry et Rau, Droit Civil Français*, Vol VI-2 (8th edn 1989), nr 38 with further references.

[68] N. Dejean de la Bâtie, *Aubry et Rau, Droit Civil Français*, Vol VI-2 (8th edn 1989), nr 38 and H. Desbois in his *Note* under *Civ.*, 27 February 1951, *D* 1951, 329 at 331.

on the other hand, the omission was malicious and harm was intended, case law and legal theory agree that liability should arise.[69]

4.3 The Law in Germany

Since the introduction of the German Civil Code (*BGB*) in the year 1900, the Roman texts have lost force of law in Germany. The liability rules for the German equivalent of 'negligence' can now be found in § 823 *BGB*:

§ 823 [Duty to compensate for damage]

(1) A person who, wilfully or negligently, unlawfully injures the life, body, health, freedom, property or other right of another is bound to compensate him for any damage arising therefrom.

(2) The same obligation is placed upon a person who infringes a statute intended for the protection of others. If, according to the provisions of the statute, an infringement of this is possible even without fault, the duty to make compensation arises only in the event of fault.[70]

Thus, the German legislator does not appear to have differentiated between liability for feasance and for nonfeasance.[71] However, when interpreting the requirement of 'unlawfulness' in section (1) of § 823, the courts have taken a different approach towards actions on the one hand and inaction on the other.

If one of the protected interests of section (1) has been infringed through a positive act, this act is presumed to have been unlawful. The only way for the defendant to rebut this presumption is by invoking a special justification for his act (e.g. self-defence).[72] However, if one of the protected interests of section (1) has

[69] *Civ.* 13 December 1972, *D* 1973, 493; H. Mazeaud, L. Mazeaud and A. Tunc, *Traité Théorique et Pratique de la Responsabilité Civile* (6th edn 1965), nr 534; G. Viney and P. Jourdain, *Traité de Droit Civil*, Vol IV (2nd edn 1998), nr 455 and F. Terré, P. Simler and Y. Lequette, *Droit civil; Les Obligations* (8th edn 2002), nr 721.

[70] ***823 [Schadensersatzpflicht]***

(1) Wer vorsätzlich oder fahrlässig das Leben, den Körper, die Gesundheit, die Freiheit, das Eigentum oder ein sonstiges Recht eines anderen widerrechtlich verletzt, ist dem anderen zum Ersatze des daraus entstehenden Schadens verpflichtet.

(2) Die gleiche Verpflichtung trifft denjenigen, welcher gegen ein den Schutz eines anderen bezweckendes Gesetz verstößt. Ist nach dem Inhalte des Gesetzes ein Verstoß gegen dieses auch ohne Verschulden möglich, so tritt die Ersatzpflicht nur im Falle des Verschuldens ein.' Translation: S.L. Goren, *The German Civil Code* (rev. edn 1994), p. 153.

[71] *RG* 30 October 1902, *RGZ* 52, 373 at 376; R. Hübner, *Grundzüge des Deutschen Privatrechts* (5th edn 1930), p. 609; R. Zimmermann, *The Law of Obligations, Roman Foundations of the Civilian Tradition* (1996), p. 1045 and C. von Bar, *The Common European Law of Torts*, Vol 1 (1998), p. 125.

[72] H. Kötz, *Deliktsrecht* (4th edn 1988), nr 94; K. Larenz/C-H. Canaris, *Lehrbuch des Schuldrechts*, Vol 2 (13th edn 1994), p. 364; B.S. Markesinis and H. Unberath, *The German Law of Torts* (4th edn 2002), pp. 79–80; J. Limpens, R.M. Kruithof and A. Meinertzhagen-Limpens, 'Liability for One's Own Act', in A. Tunc (ed.), *International Encyclopedia of Comparative Law*, Vol XI Torts (1983), ch. 2, p. 15; and F.H. Lawson, *Negligence in the Civil Law* (1950), p. 30.

been infringed by inaction, this inaction is not automatically presumed to have been unlawful. Inaction is only regarded as unlawful if it violated a 'duty to act' (*Pflicht zum Handeln*).[73]

During the second half of this century the different approach taken by the courts towards cases of feasance and of nonfeasance has been criticized by many influential authors.[74] According to these authors one should not presume positive acts to be unlawful, merely on the ground of their harmful result. As with inaction, positive acts should only be regarded as unlawful if they violate a pre-existing duty.[75] Thus, according to this view, there should no longer be a difference in approach towards cases of nonfeasance and cases of feasance: both action and inaction should only be regarded as unlawful if a duty is violated. In theory this development could have serious implications for cases of nonfeasance.[76] In practice however, the courts have been – and are likely to continue to be – much more reluctant to recognize the existence of affirmative duties than of negative duties.[77]

German law roughly distinguishes between three types of affirmative duties. Firstly, the defendant may voluntarily have entered into a relationship of proximity with the claimant. Thus, contractual parties have a duty to act in good faith, regardless of the exact wording of the contract. In the absence of a contract, too, an undertaking may give rise to an affirmative duty. A neighbour who promises to look after a child or dog, can be held liable for not doing so, even though his promise may not have been contractually binding.[78]

Because their occupations put them in a special position of responsibility, specific protective duties are imposed on nannies, doctors, the police, sports teachers *etc.* Similar duties to ensure the safety of others are imposed on those who have a family relationship or a relationship of love and affection with the person in need of protection. Thus, although the Levite may not be required to render assistance to everyone, he does have a duty to aid his close relatives, his spouse, or his close friends.[79]

Where the first two types of affirmative duties arise out of the special responsibility the defendant has for the safety of the endangered person, a third type arises

[73] E. Deutsch, *Haftungsrecht*, Vol 1 (1976), p. 127; *Idem, Unerlaubte Handlungen, Schadensersatz und Schmerzensgeld* (3rd edn 1995), nrs 38 and 86; Staudinger/Hager (1999), § 823, *RdNr* H5 and B.S. Markesinis and H. Unberath, *The German Law of Torts* (4th edn 2002), pp. 85–86.

[74] L. Enneccerus and H.C. Nipperdey, *Allgemeiner Teil des Bürgerlichen Rechts*, Vol 2 (15th edn 1960), par. 209; W. Münzberg, *Verhalten und Erfolg als Grundlagen der Rechtswidrigkeit und Haftung* (1966), pp. 109–112; H. Kötz, *Deliktsrecht* (4th edn 1988), nrs 98–103 and K. Larenz/C-H. Canaris, *Lehrbuch des Schuldrechts*, Vol 2 (13th edn 1994), pp. 364–370 (with further references on p. 365, footnote 37).

[75] . . . or if they were intentional; H. Kötz, *Deliktsrecht* (4th edn 1988), nr 98. Cf. *ibid.*, nr 103 and K. Larenz/C-H. Canaris, *Lehrbuch des Schuldrechts*, Vol 2 (13th edn 1994), p. 365.

[76] B.S. Markesinis and H. Unberath, *The German Law of Torts* (4th edn 2002), p. 83.

[77] R. Zimmermann, *The Law of Obligations, Roman Foundations of the Civilian Tradition* (1996), p. 1045.

[78] E. Deutsch, *Haftungsrecht*, Vol 1 (1976), p. 128 and J. Esser/E. Schmidt, *Schuldrecht*, Vol I (6th edn 1984), pp. 354–355.

[79] E. Deutsch, *Haftungsrecht*, Vol 1 (1976), p. 128 and J. Esser/E. Schmidt, *Schuldrecht*, Vol I (6th edn 1984), p. 355.

when the defendant is in some way connected with the danger itself. Examples are the duty of owners of dangerous premises, substances or animals to prevent others from being harmed. Under this heading one usually also includes the duty arising from a 'previous act' ('*aus vorangegangenem Tun*'); those who, no matter how inculpably, create a danger, have a duty to prevent the danger from harming others. Thus, as under Roman law, someone who lights a fire will be liable under German law if he fails to control the fire.[80]

Most of the above affirmative duties have been expressly recognized by the courts through creation of the so-called '*Verkehrspflichten*' and '*Verkehrssicherungspflichten*'.[81] These terms are not easily translated. For present purposes it will suffice to say that *Verkehrs(sicherungs)pflichten* are legal duties that require someone who, within the scope of his responsibility establishes a source of potential danger or allows it to remain, to protect the interests and rights of others against such danger.[82] Very soon after the introduction of the *BGB*, the German courts started recognizing the existence of *Verkehrs(sicherungs)pflichten*.[83] The following case was considered by the *Reichsgericht* in 1903:[84] On a cold winter evening the plaintiff had lost his balance when walking on slippery stone steps in his home town. He brought a claim for damages against the local authorities, arguing that they ought to have gritted the steps. The *Reichsgericht* found for the plaintiff, establishing that the local authorities had a general duty to take care[85] that the steps were safe for the public to walk on. This duty, argued the *Reichsgericht*, arose from the local authorities' 'power of disposition'[86] over the steps. Although the local authorities in this case were the legal owners of the steps, it was explicitly stated that this duty of care was not limited to legal owners:

> The main focus does not lie on the right of ownership as such; those who possess other rights that entail power of disposition may have a similar duty to take care. The question is, whether the person concerned, by dint of his actual and legal relationship with the property, ought to take any kind of care towards third parties when disposing of this property, respectively when handling or using it in legal relations.[87]

[80] E. Deutsch, *Haftungsrecht*, Vol 1 (1976), pp. 128–129 and J. Esser/E. Schmidt, *Schuldrecht*, Vol I (6th edn 1984), pp. 354–356.

[81] On the terminological distinction between *Verkehrspflichten* and *Verkehrssicherungspflichten*, see H. Kötz, *Deliktsrecht* (4th edn 1988), nr 233.

[82] Staudinger/Hager (1999), § 823, *RdNr* E1-2; B.S. Markesinis and H. Unberath, *The German Law of Torts* (4th edn 2002), p. 86; C. von Bar, *The Common European Law of Torts*, Vol 1 (1998), nr 104 and *idem, Verkehrspflichten: richterliche Gefahrensteuerungsgebote im deutschen Deliktsrecht* (1980), p. 113 with further references to the relevant case law in footnote 77.

[83] *RG* 30 October 1902, *RGZ* 52, 373.

[84] *RG* 23 February 1903, *RGZ* 54, 53.

[85] *Ibid.* at 56; '*Pflicht zur Anwendung von Sorgfalt*'.

[86] *Ibid.* at 56; '*Verfügungsmacht*'.

[87] *Ibid.* at 56: '*Der Schwerpunkt liegt hierbei nicht in dem Eigentumsrecht als solchem; eine gleiche Pflicht zur Anwendung von Sorgfalt besteht möglicherweise auch für den aus einem anderen Recht als dem Eigentum Verfügungsberechtigten. Die Frage ist, ob der Betreffende vermöge seiner tatsächlichen und rechtlichen Beziehung zu der Sache bei der Verfügung über diese Sache, bezw. bei der Handhabung oder dem Gebrauch derselben im Rechtsverkehr irgend welche Sorgfalt gegenüber Dritten anzuwenden habe.*'

The amount of *Verkehrs(sicherungs)pflichten* that is recognized by the courts has increased immensely over the years. In the majority of cases they entail an affirmative duty to act, and arise either out of the special relationship the defendant has with a particular thing or piece of property or out of the defendant's special position of responsibility.[88] Examples are the duty of local authorities to ensure the safety of the roads,[89] the duty of hosts to ensure the safety of their guests on their premises,[90] the duty of care that road users owe to other road users[91] and the duty of those whose trade or profession may affect others, to use particular care and skill in exercising their trade or profession.[92] What standard of care the *Verkehrs(sicherungs)pflichten* impose, depends on the particular circumstances of each individual case. The most important factors that are taken into account are the likelihood of a particular risk to materialize, the serious nature of its consequences if the risk does materialize and the difficulty of preventing the risk from materializing.[93]

Another possible source of affirmative duties are the statutory provisions. If a statutory duty is violated, as a result of which someone is harmed, the victim can bring a claim under section (2) of § 823 *BGB*. This claim will only be successful if the statute was intended to protect others (if the statute is a so-called '*Schutzgesetz*'). Hence, if someone forgets to light his car lights at night, as is required by § 17 of the German traffic regulations,[94] he will be liable to those who suffer harm as a consequence of his omission.[95] Of particular interest in this context is § 323c of the German Criminal Code (*StGB*), a provision originating from the days of the Nazi regime:[96]

§ 323c [Failure to render assistance to those in need] Whoever fails to render assistance in case of accident, common danger or emergency, although such assistance was needed and could have been expected from him under the circumstances, especially since he could have rendered it without placing himself in significant danger and without violating any important duties, shall be punished by up to one year's imprisonment or by fine.[97]

[88] E. Deutsch, *Haftungsrecht*, Vol 1 (1976), p. 128.

[89] H. Kötz, *Deliktsrecht* (4th edn 1988), nrs 241–242; *BGH* 30 April 1953, *BGHZ* 9, 373; *BGH* 15 June 1954, *BGHZ* 14, 83 and *BGH* 30 December 1954, *BGHZ* 16, 95.

[90] *BGH* 25 February 1958, *VersR* 1958, 308 and *BGH* 19 May 1967, *VersR* 1967, 801.

[91] C. von Bar, *Verkehrspflichten: richterliche Gefahrensteuerungsgebote im deutschen Deliktsrecht* (1980), pp. 56–57 and Staudinger/Hager (1999), § 823, *RdNr* E73 ff.

[92] *BGH* 16 December 1953, *VersR* 1954, 100. See for a more detailed investigation into the case law C. von Bar, *Verkehrspflichten: richterliche Gefahrensteuerungsgebote im deutschen Deliktsrecht* (1980), pp. 43–82; *idem*, *The Common European Law of Torts*, Vol I (1998), nrs 104–105; Staudinger/Hager (1999), § 823, *RdNr* E73 ff. and B.S. Markesinis and H. Unberath, *The German Law of Torts* (4th edn 2002), pp. 85–102.

[93] C. von Bar, *Verkehrspflichten: richterliche Gefahrensteuerungsgebote im deutschen Deliktsrecht* (1980), p. 114 and H. Kötz, *Deliktsrecht* (4th edn 1988), nr 234.

[94] '*Straßenverkehrsordnung*'.

[95] E. Deutsch, *Haftungsrecht*, Vol 1 (1976), pp. 125–126.

[96] *Reichsgesetzblatt* 1935 (1), 839.

[97] '***323c [Unterlassene Hilfeleistung]***

Wer bei Unglücksfällen oder gemeiner Gefahr oder Not nicht Hilfe leistet, obwohl dies erforderlich und ihm den Umständen nach zuzumuten, insbesondere ohne erhebliche eigene Gefahr und ohne Verletzung

After the collapse of the Nazi regime, the question arose whether § 323c *StGB*[98] was still in force. The *Großer Senat für Strafsachen* answered this question in the affirmative, stating that the duty to render assistance in emergencies is a 'moral obligation that has existed from time immemorial' and adding that 'aid to neighbours in need was, in particular, always an imperative command of Christian doctrine'.[99]

Thus, German law continues to impose a criminal law duty to rescue on those who can do so without the risk of harming themselves. At first sight, this statutory provision would seem to be 'intended for the protection of others', in the sense of § 823 (2) *BGB*. Indeed, it is likely that the German legislator in 1935 was of the opinion that the criminal law duty of § 323c *StGB* would give rise to a private law duty under § 823 (2) *BGB*.[100] However, legal opinion has changed and it is now the predominant view that § 323 *StGB* was not intended to protect individual persons but only society as a whole.[101] This legalistic argument does seem peculiar, especially considering the following words by Haager:

> (. . .) It is sufficient, that a statutory provision mainly pursues another goal, but simultaneously seeks to protect certain individual interests. (. . .) Only statutory provisions that are exclusively intended to protect the order of society, the entire state as such, its external intactness and its internal constitution and administration, fall completely outside of the context of such '*Schutzgesetz*', like the criminal provisions on high treason and treason, on resistance against state authority, on breach of the constitution etc.[102]

It is hard to imagine that § 323c *StGB* was exclusively intended to protect the 'entire state as such' and not (at least) also certain individual interests. It is

anderer wichtiger Pflichten möglich ist, wird mit Freiheitsstrafe bis zu einem Jahr oder mit Geldstrafe bestraft. Translation: J.J. Darby, *The Penal Code of the Federal Republic of Germany* (1987), p. 231.

98 Then § 330c *StGB*.

99 *BGH* 10 March 1954, *BGHSt* 6, 147 at 151: '*Es kann nicht bestritten werden, daß gegenseitige Hilfe in Notfällen einem von jeher bestehenden sittlichen Gebot entspricht. Die Hilfe für den notleidenden Nächsten war insbesondere immer ein Hauptgebot der christlichen Lehre.*' Translation: J.P. Dawson, '*Negotiorum Gestio*: the Altruistic Intermeddler', (1961) 74 Harvard LR 817–865 and 1073–1129 at 1104.

100 Weimar, '*Schadensersatzpflicht bei Schädigungen durch Unterlassen*', *DR* 1937, 77; E. Krupp, '*Kameradschaftspflichten und Rechtspflichten*', *DR* 1938, 465 at 467 and H. Stoll, *Vertrag und Unrecht*, Vol 2 (3rd edn 1943), p. 197. Cf. W. Weimar, '*Besteht eine Schadensersatzpflicht eines Krankenhauses bei Abweisung Schwerverletzter? JR* 1975, 145 at 146.

101 H. Welzel, '*Zur Dogmatik der echten Unterlassungsdelikte, insbesondere des § 330c StGB*', *NJW* 1953, 327 at 328; W. Dütz, '*Zur privatrechtlichen Bedeutung unterlassener Hilfeleistung (§ 330c StGB)*', *NJW* 1970, 1822–1826, at 1825; Staudinger/Hager (1999), § 823, *RdNr* H9 and *OLG Frankfurt* 27 October 1988, *NJW-RR* 1989 (2), 794. A similar approach is taken towards § 138 *StGB*. *Contra*: K. Larenz/C-H. Canaris, *Lehrbuch des Schuldrechts*, Vol II/2 (13th edn 1994), p. 441, where it is argued that both § 138 and § 323c *StGB* are *Schutzgesetze*.

102 K. Haager, *BGB-RGRK*, Vol II, Part 2 (11th edn 1960), § 823, *Anm*. 103, p. 1290: '*Es genügt, daß eine Vorschrift in der Hauptsache andere Zwecke verfolgt, nebenher aber zum Schutz bestimmter einzelner Interessen bestimmt ist. (. . .) Nur Gesetze, die ausschließlich die Ordnung der Gesamtheit, das Staatganze als solches, seine äußere Unversehrtheit, seine innere Verfassung und Verwaltung, zu schützen bestimmt sind, wie die Strafgesetze über Hoch- und Landesverrat, über Widerstand gegen die Staatsgewalt, über Verfassungsbruch und andere, fallen vollständig außerhalb des Rahmens eines solchen Schutzgesetzes, auch wenn sie gewissen Personen nützen.*'

likely that there are other, more profound reasons that lie behind the denial of a private law duty to rescue under § 823 (2) *BGB*. In a judgment in 1988, the *Oberlandesgericht* of Frankfurt used an argument which strongly resembles the 'Why pick on me?' argument:

The criminal provision [of § 323c *StGB*] is not a '*Schutzgesetz*' in the sense of § 823 (2) *BGB*, because there is no reason to hold the person who omits to render assistance liable in the same way as the person who inflicted the harm.[103]

Even in the absence of a *Verkehrspflicht* or a *Schutzgesetz*, liability for nonfeasance may arise if the defendant's refusal to act was intentional and *contra bonos mores*.[104] § 826 *BGB* reads:

§ 826 [Intentional damage *contra bonos mores*] A person who, in a manner *contra bonos mores*, intentionally causes damage to another, is bound to compensate him for the damage.[105]

'Intention' is taken to exist, if the defendant was aware of the harmful nature of his behaviour. It is not necessary that the motive of his behaviour was to cause harm.[106] However, not every intentional refusal to act is regarded to be *contra bonos mores*. Schäfer, for example, submits that an intentional refusal to render assistance to someone in need is not *contra bonos mores*, unless such refusal will lead to death, serious bodily harm, or a dangerous road accident and unless rendering assistance is easy and can be done without disregarding one's own important interests.[107]

There are relatively few cases involving nonfeasance in which successful claims have been brought under § 826 *BGB*. Contractual parties have been held liable for intentionally failing to disclose relevant information in the course of the negotiations.[108] Also, claims have been allowed against persons who noticed that their signature had been forged on an official document, but failed to give a warning to that effect.[109]

In summary, in the absence of express statutory provisions, liability for nonfeasance may be imposed under one of three main headings: § 823 *BGB* in

[103] *OLG Frankfurt*, 27 October 1988, *NJW-RR* 1989/II, 794 at 795: *Die Strafbestimmung ist kein Schutzgesetz i.S. des § 823 II BGB, denn es geht nicht an denjenigen, der Hilfeleistung unterläßt, in gleicher Weise haften zu lassen wie den Schädiger* (footnotes omitted).

[104] *RG* 1 June 1937, *RGZ* 155, 257 at 285 and *BGH* 5 November 1962, *NJW* 1963, 148 at 149–150.

[105] '***826 [Sittenwidrige vorsätzliche Schädigung]***

Wer in einer gegen die gute Sitten verstoßenden Weise einem anderen vorsätzlich Schaden zufügt, ist dem anderen zum Ersatze des Schadens verpflichtet.

[106] Staudinger/Oechsler (2003), § 826, *RdNr* 75–76 and B.S. Markesinis and H. Unberath, *The German Law of Torts* (4th edn 2002), pp. 85–102, 889.

[107] Staudinger/Schäfer (1985), § 826, *RdNr* 51. Cf. W. Dütz, '*Zur privatrechtlichen Bedeutung unterlassener Hilfeleistung (§ 330c StGB)*', *NJW* 1970, 1822–1826 at 1825–1826.

[108] *OLG Köln*, 2 November 1971, *NJW* 1972, 497; *BGH* 17 May 1982, *NJW* 1982, 2815 and Staudinger/Oechsler (2003), § 826, *RdNr* 158–161, with further references.

[109] Staudinger/Schäfer (1985), § 826, *RdNr* 55–57, with further references.

connection with the *Verkehrspflichten*, § 823 (2) *BGB* and its *Schutzgesetze*, and § 826 *BGB*. It must however be noted that the courts have thus far only imposed such affirmative duties when the defendant was in some way connected with the endangered person or with the danger itself. If a case like the one of the good Samaritan were to be considered now, it seems unlikely that the German courts would have held the priest or the Levite liable for the harm that was caused by their inaction.

4.4 The *Actio Negotiorum Gestorum (Directa)* in Roman, German, and French Law

A. Historical Introduction

'*Negotiorum gestio*' means, loosely translated, 'the management of affairs'.[110] As a legal concept, it finds its roots in Roman law[111] and is concerned with the legal relationship that arises from the unsolicited management of the affairs of another.[112] In modern legal writings, it is almost invariably associated with claims granted to the intervener. However, *negotiorum gestio* is a bilateral[113] relationship and as such creates obligations both on the part of the intervener (*gestor*) and on the part of the person he seeks to assist.[114] Indeed, the Romans regarded the action of the person assisted *against* the intervener as the main claim.[115] This action is now commonly referred to as the 'direct action', the '*actio negotiorum gestorum directa*'. By contrast, the action of the intervener is referred to as the *actio (negotiorum gestorum) contraria*. The *actio contraria* will be subjected to a more detailed investigation in Part II of this book. With the *actio directa*, however, the intervener could in certain circumstances be held liable for a failure to act. Therefore, this direct action needs to be considered in this chapter.

Anyone who without request intervened in the affairs of another could be held liable with the direct action. The principal could demand to be compensated for losses caused by the intervener's failure to exercise due care,[116] and the intervener would have to account for his management and surrender any benefits that he had received from the enterprise.[117] Although the standard of care was subject of

[110] D.H. van Zyl, *Negotiorum Gestio in South African Law* (1985), p. 3. Cf. M. Kaser, *Das Römische Privatrecht*, Vol II (2nd edn 1975), p. 417.

[111] F. Schulz, *Classical Roman Law* (1951), p. 624.

[112] Cf. S.J. Stoljar, 'Negotiorum Gestio' in E. von Caemmerer and P. Schlechtriem (eds), *International Encyclopedia of Comparative Law*, Vol X Restitution – Unjust Enrichment and Negotiorum Gestio (1984), ch. 17, p. 3.

[113] Albeit imperfectly bilateral: R. Zimmermann, *The Law of Obligations, Roman Foundations of the Civilian Tradition* (1996), p. 433.

[114] *D.* 3.5.2 (Gaius).

[115] It appears that Cicero knew only the direct action, which might indicate that the *actio contraria* developed later; Cicero, Topica XVII.66. See also R. Zimmermann, *The Law of Obligations, Roman Foundations of the Civilian Tradition* (1996), p. 443.

[116] *D.* 3.5.10 (Pomponius).

[117] *D.* 3.5.2 (Gaius) and *D.* 3.5.22 (Paul).

debate,[118] there is at least one text that would seem to suggest that, in cases of emergency, the intervener was liable only for his intentional wrongdoing.[119] Finally – and this is where liability for nonfeasance comes in – it is widely thought that once the intervener had embarked on the *gestio*, he was bound to continue and complete it.[120] This view draws support from *D.* 3.5.20.2 (Paul):

If I began to manage Titius's affairs during his lifetime, I ought not to leave off at his death. However, there is no necessity for me to enter into new transactions, though it is necessary to complete and look after old ones. (. . .)[121]

Thus, although Roman law may not have imposed a duty to assist one's fellow human beings, those who decided to intervene would have to carry through their intervention. 'However', Paul states, 'there is no necessity (. . .) to enter into new transactions'. This could be taken as stating a general rule that the intervener only had to complete those transactions or elements of the affairs in which he had specifically involved himself. If this was the law, someone who after a heavy storm started to fix the roof on the house of his absent neighbour would have to complete the repair, but would be free to decide not to repair the broken window shutters. Yet, the text is concerned with a case in which the person assisted passed away during the *gestio*. This in turn could be taken to suggest that as long as the latter was alive, the intervener might be obliged to involve himself in other elements of the affairs, too. In other words, once one had started to assist another, one may have come under a duty to assist the other in all his affairs that urgently needed to be looked after. This interpretation would appear to be supported by another text that is attributed to Paul, *D.* 3.5.15:

Again, when someone transacts business of mine, it is not a number of transactions but a single obligation, unless initially he took on only one transaction with the intention of getting out on its completion. For in this case, if he makes a fresh decision to tackle another as well, it is a different obligation.[122]

Here, Paul appears to say that someone who intervenes in another's affairs must be deemed to have accepted full responsibility over all the affairs of the person

[118] R. Zimmermann, *The Law of Obligations, Roman Foundations of the Civilian Tradition* (1996), pp. 445–447 with further references.

[119] *D.* 3.5.3.9 (Ulpian); see also H. Dernburg, *Pandekten*, Vol 2 (7th edn 1903), p. 338.

[120] *E.g.* P. Mac Chombaich De Colquhoun, *A Summary of the Roman Civil Law*, Vol III (1854), p. 110 (§ 1770); J.P. Dawson, '*Negotiorum Gestio*: the Altruistic Intermeddler', (1961) 74 Harvard LR 817–865 and 1073–1129 at 819–820 and S.J. Stoljar, 'Negotiorum Gestio' in E. von Caemmerer and P. Schlechtriem (eds), *International Encyclopedia of Comparative Law*, Vol X Restitution – Unjust Enrichment and Negotiorum Gestio (1984), ch. 17, p. 156.

[121] *Si vivo Titio negotia eius administrare coepi, intermittere mortuo eo non debeo: nova tamen inchoare necesse mihi non est, vetera explicare ac conservare necessarium est.* (. . .) Unless it is otherwise stated, translations of the Digest texts are taken from Th. Mommsen, P. Krueger and A. Watson (eds), *The Digest of Justinian*, Vol I (1985).

[122] *Sed et cum aliquis negotia mea gerat, non multa negotia sunt, sed unus contractus, nise si ab initio ad unum negotium accessit, ut finito eo discederet: hoc enim casu si nova voluntate aliud quoque adgredi coeperit, alius contractus est.*

assisted, 'unless initially he took on only one transaction with the intention of getting out on its completion'. However, *D.* 3.5.5.14 (Ulpian) reveals that this view may not have been shared by all of their contemporaries:

As regards the duty of an intervener, if he has done certain things but not others, while because of him someone else has not taken on the latter things, and if a careful person (and this is what we demand of him) would have done these also, should it be said that he is liable to an action for *negotiorum gestio* for what he has not done as well? In my opinion, this is the more reasonable view. (. . .)[123]

Ulpian's example involves an intervention that has detrimental consequences; because the intervener has intervened in some affairs, other potential interveners have refrained from intervening. Ulpian indicates that in such circumstances the intervener should in his view be held under a duty to look after all of the principal's interests. However, because he indicates that this is 'the more reasonable view', it must be suspected that other jurists of the time may have disagreed with Ulpian. *A fortiori*, the imposition of a duty to look after all the affairs of the person assisted must have been controversial in cases in which the intervention did not discourage third parties from intervening.

In the absence of texts that deal more thoroughly with the intervener's liability for a failure to act, any conclusion must be subject to reservation. It would appear that the intervener was – at least – bound to complete the specific affair he had embarked on.[124] Over and above that, he may well have been bound to look after those affairs that, as a result of his intervention, had been left unattended by other potential interveners. Finally, there is at least one text that suggests that – in the absence of evidence to the contrary – an intervention in the affairs of the person assisted was deemed to imply an acceptance of responsibility over all his affairs that needed looking after.[125]

Again, these cases must not be mistaken for cases involving liability for active conduct. Although active conduct is involved (the initial intervention), this

[123] *Videamus in persona eius, qui negotia administrat, si quaedam gessit quaedam non, contemplatione tamen eius alius ad heac non accessit, et si vir diligens (quod ab eo exigimus) etiam ea gesturus fuit: an dici debeat negotiorum gestorum eum teneri et propter ea quae non gessit? quod puto verius.* (. . .) Translation slightly altered.

[124] If this is correct, liability for nonfeasance would have been more readily imposed on the intervener in *negotiorum gestio* than on the *mandatarius* in the contract of *mandatum*. *D.* 17.1.22.11 (Paul) would seem to suggest that the *mandatarius* had the right to renounce his undertaking by giving notice to the *mandator*, provided that the non-performance would not put the *mandator* in a worse position than he was before the undertaking. However, in *D.* 17.1.27.2 Gaius appears to say that the *mandatarius* was only allowed to renounce if he was unable to perform. See A. Watson, *Contract of Mandate in Roman Law* (1961), pp. 71–73. Two things need to be noted here. Firstly, it is difficult to see how an intervener in *negotiorum* could 'give notice' of the renunciation of his undertaking, as the 'principal' would typically have been absent. Secondly, French law, too, requires the *gestor*, but not the *mandatarius*, to complete the management. See below, footnote 131 and the corresponding part of the main text.

[125] Cf. J. Voet, *Commentarius ad Pandectas*, Vol I (6th edn 1731), *ad D.* 3.5, § 6 and, for more detailed investigation, R.J. Pothier, *Pandectae de Justinianeae in Novum Ordinem Digestae*, Vol III, translated into French by M. de Bréard-Neuville (1819), pp. 165–175.

would usually not have been wrongful. The element of wrongfulness must be sought in the failure to carry through a primarily rightful intervention.[126]

B. The *actio directa* in French law

The *gérant d'affaires d'autrui* is, like the Roman *negotiorum gestor*, bound to account for his management and hand over benefits that he received from the *gestio*.[127] Also, he is required to meet the standard of care of a '*bon père de famille*';[128] a standard which is a contemporary adaptation of the Roman standard of the '*bonus paterfamilias*'. Moreover, article 1372 of the French Civil Code explicitly states that the *gérant* is bound to continue and complete his intervention:

> When one voluntarily manages the affairs of another, whether the owner knows of the management or whether he does not know, he who manages contracts the tacit agreement to continue the management he has commenced and to complete it until the owner is in a position to be able to do it himself; he must also take responsibility for all the incidentals of these affairs.
>
> He is subject to all the obligations which would have resulted had the owner given him an express agency.[129]

And, apparently inspired by Paul's comments in *D.* 3.5.20.2,[130] article 1373 states that the intervener is also bound to continue and complete his intervention if the principal has meanwhile passed away. In this respect the duties of the unsolicited intervener are more burdensome than those of the mandatary.[131] In principle the mandatary is entitled to renounce the mandate, provided that his withdrawal does not leave the mandator worse off.[132]

A 1985 judgment by the *Cour de Cassation* provides a rare example of the judicial application of this rule.[133] A customer at a supermarket had left her handbag, containing valuables, in her supermarket trolley. Two other customers found the bag and brought it to the customer service desk. There a supermarket employee opened the bag, identified its owner and repeatedly called her name over the

126 See chapter 2, above.

127 Art. 1993 *C. civ.* (which applies not only to mandate, but also to *gestion d'affaires*, cf. art. 1372 *C. civ.*)

128 Art. 1374 *C. civ.*

129 '**1372** *Lorsque volontairement on gère l'affaire d'autrui, soit que le propriétaire connaisse la gestion, soit qu'il l'ignore, celui qui gère contracte l'engagement tacite de continuer la gestion qu'il a commencée, et de l'achever jusqu'à ce que le propriétaire soit en état d'y pourvoir lui-même; il doit se charger également de toutes les dépendances de cette même affaire.*

Il se soumet à toutes les obligations qui résulteraient d'un mandat exprès que lui aurait donné le propriétaire.'

Translation: J.H. Crabb, *The French Civil Code* (rev. edn 1995), p. 251.

130 See also J. Domat, *Les loix civiles dans leur ordre naturel* (rev. edn 1745), p. 169 (*Livre II, Titre IV, Section I, VII*).

131 See for a not entirely convincing defence of this distinction H., L. and J. Mazeaud and F. Chabas, *Leçons de Droit Civil*, Part II, Vol I, *Obligations, Théorie Générale* (8th edn 1991), nr 687 and B. Starck, H. Roland and L. Boyer, *Droit Civil, Les Obligations, Contrat* (6th edn 1998), p. 758 (nr 2159).

132 Art. 2007 *C. civ.*

133 *Civ.*, 3 January 1985, *Gaz Pal* 1985 (*Panorama*) 90.

intercom. A little while later, the two customers who had found the bag returned to the customer service desk and asked for the bag, stating that they would return it to its rightful owner. The employee handed them the bag and failed to ask them to identify themselves. The owner of the bag returned to the supermarket and – never having received her handbag – sued the supermarket. The *Cour de Cassation* confirmed the judgment of the lower courts, holding that by accepting the handbag the employee had started to manage the affairs of the claimant and was bound to complete the management with due care. Not having met the standard of the *bon père de famille*, the supermarket was held liable under the direct action to compensate for the value of the handbag and its contents.[134] It is true, of course, that in this particular case the defendant was held liable for active wrongdoing, *i.e.* carelessly handing the bag to the finders. However, it should not be doubted that the same principle would have applied if the defendant had been guilty only of a passive failure to continue the management of another's affairs, *e.g.* if he had failed to take any steps to identify or contact the bag's owner.[135]

C. The *actio directa* in German law

The provisions on *negotiorum gestio* in the German *BGB* follow Roman law very closely.[136] Like his Roman and French counterparts, the German *Geschäftsführer ohne Auftrag* will have to account for his management[137] and hand over benefits that he received from the intervention.[138] As soon as it is practicable he will have to inform the principal of his intervention and, unless there is danger in delay, wait for the principal to authorize continuation of the intervention.[139] Also, the *BGB* contains a specific provision that limits the liability of the intervener who attempts to avert imminent danger that threatens the principal, to loss caused by his intentional wrongdoing or gross negligence.[140] However, unlike their French counterparts, the drafters of the BGB consciously refrained from including a provision that would impose a duty on the intervener to continue and complete the intervention once it was undertaken. In a 1906 judgment, the *Reichsgericht* summarized the motives behind the legislator's decision succinctly:

The *Berufungsgericht* (Court of Appeal) correctly holds that, in general, a duty of the intervener to complete the intervention once undertaken, does not exist under the present laws. A provision to that effect – like those included in several state codes, i.e. § 257 I 13 of the

[134] The decision has been criticized on the grounds that it was not obvious whether the supermarket intended to manage the claimant's affairs. Indeed, it has been argued that this case involves a contract of deposit between the finders and the supermarket, and that the supermarket was thus bound to return the handbag to them. See A. Piedelievre in his case note on *Civ.*, 3 January 1985, Gaz Pal 1985 (*Panorama*) 90. Cf. also J. Mestre, *Rev.trim.dr.civ.* 1985, 575.

[135] Cf. *Cour d'Appel de Toulouse*, 10 January 1930, *DH* 1930, 237.

[136] R. Zimmermann, *The Law of Obligations, Roman Foundations of the Civilian Tradition* (1996), p. 435.

[137] § 666 *BGB* (which applies not only to mandate, but also to *negotiorum gestio*, cf. § 681 *BGB*).

[138] § 667 *BGB*. [139] § 681 *BGB*. [140] § 680 *BGB*.

Prussian *ALR*, § 1346 of the Saxon *BGB* and art. 1372 of the *Code civil* – has not been incorporated in the German *BGB*. The 'Explanatory Notes' ('*Motive*', Vol. 2, p. 858) say: under the rule of § 749 (677), the intervener should attend the affairs of another in accordance with the standard of care of a *bonus paterfamilias*, and he must take the discernible wishes of the principal into account. This rule must also provide an answer to the question whether the intervener, once he has undertaken the intervention, is allowed to withdraw. If the withdrawal is likely to result in a loss, which the principal would not have suffered if the intervener had never intervened, than the latter is bound to continue the intervention in order to avoid liability to pay compensation.[141]

When taken at face value, this judgment leaves sufficient room to argue that the intervener is usually under a duty to complete his intervention, because a *bonus paterfamilias* would normally do so. However, most of the German commentaries on § 677 *BGB* regard the absence of a duty to complete one's intervention as the general rule. Only in exceptional circumstances will the standard of the *bonus paterfamilias* – or more generally the requirement of 'good faith' of § 242 *BGB* – require the intervener to complete his intervention.[142] As was indicated by the *Reichsgericht* in the above passage, such exceptional circumstances may be present in cases in which the withdrawal would put the principal in a worse position than he was before the intervention took place. In other words: liability for failure to complete the intervention may arise where the overall result of the intervention is detrimental.[143]

It has been suggested that the intervener is also not allowed to withdraw at an untimely moment.[144] This view appears to have been taken from Larenz's *Lehrbuch des Schuldrechts*, where it is argued that section 2 of § 671 *BGB*, a provision concerning the contract of mandate,[145] should be applied by analogy to cases of *Geschäftsführung ohne Auftrag*.[146] § 671, s. 2 *BGB* reads:

The mandatary must give notice (of termination) only in such manner, that the mandator can make other arrangements for taking care of the matter, unless there is a serious reason

[141] *RG* 10 May 1906, *RGZ* 63, 280 at 283: '*Dem Berufungsgericht ist nun darin Recht zu geben, daß nach dem geltenden Gesetze eine Verpflichtung des nicht beauftragten Geschäftsführers, das begonnene Geschäft zu Ende zu führen, grundsätzlich nicht besteht. Das deutsche Bürgerliche Gesetzbuch hat eine hierauf abzielende Vorschrift, wie sie von mehreren Landesgesetzen – namentlich in § 257 preuß. A.L.R. I. 13, § 1346 sächs. B.G.B., Art. 1372 Code civil – getroffen war, nicht aufgenommen. Die Motive (Bd. 2 S. 858) bemerken: nach der Regel des § 749 (677) habe der Geschäftsführer für den andern das Geschäft so zu führen, wie es der Sorgfalt eines ordentlichen Hausvaters entspreche, und habe hierbei auf die erkennbaren Intentionen des Geschäftsherrn zu achten. Hiernach beurteilte sich auch die Frage, ob der Geschäftsführer von der einmal unternommenen Geschäftsführung zurücktreten dürfe. Drohe auf den zurücktreten für den Geschäftsherrn ein Schade, welcher nicht entstanden sein würde, wenn der Geschäftsführer sich nicht eingemischt hätte, so sei der letztere zur Vermeidung der Haftung wegen Schadensersatzes die Geschäftsbesorgung fortzusetzen verpflichtet. Im übrigen sei eine besondere Verpflichtung zu Fortsetzung der Geschäftsbesorgung nicht anzuerkennen.*'

[142] *E.g.* J. Denecke, *BGB-RGRK*, *Band* II., Vol I (11th edn 1959), § 677, *Anm.* 4; *MünchKomm* – Seiler (1997), § 677, *RdNr* 46; Staudinger/Wittmann (1995), § 677, *RdNr* 5; H. Thomas in *Palandt Bürgerliches Gesetzbuch* (57th edn 1998), § 677, *Anm.* 5e.

[143] *E.g. RG* 5 December 1929, *RGZ* 126, 287 at 292.

[144] *E.g.* M. Vollkommer, *Jauernig/Vollkommer* (8th edn 1997), § 677, *Anm.* 3b.

[145] '*Auftrag*'.

[146] K. Larenz, *Lehrbuch des Schuldrechts*, Vol II/1 (13th edn 1986), p. 448 (§ 57 Ib).

for the untimely notice. If he gives an untimely notice without such reason, he shall compensate the mandator for the loss arising therefrom.[147]

If Larenz was correct in holding that this provision is to be applied by analogy to cases involving *Geschäftsführung ohne Auftrag*, this would have serious consequences for the liability of the German intervener. For in many cases of *Geschäftsführung ohne Auftrag* the principal is absent, hence unable to 'make other arrangements' for the management of his affairs. In the absence of the principal, the intervener's withdrawal would therefore invariably be 'untimely'. Thus, analogous application of § 671, s. 2 *BGB* would mean that in many cases of unsolicited intervention the intervener would only be able to withdraw with impunity if he had serious reasons to do so. However, in light of the fact that Larenz's view seems to contradict German doctrine and does not appear to be supported by any authority, we must regard his view with scepticism.

In summary, it appears that the German intervener is entitled to withdraw from the unsolicited intervention, provided that the overall result of his intervention is not detrimental to the principal. As we will see in Part I, Chapter 5.4 (2), the German law position in this respect bears some resemblance to at least one view of the position in Common law; in the Canadian case called *The 'Ogopogo'*, Schroeder JA argued that 'even if a person embarks upon a rescue and does not carry it through, he is not under a liability to the person to whose aid he had come so long as discontinuance of his efforts did not leave the other in a worse condition than when he took charge'.[148]

[147] '*Der Beauftragte darf nur in der Art kündigen, daß der Auftraggeber für die Besorgung des Geschäfts anderweit Fürsorge treffen kann, es sei denn, daß ein wichtiger Grund für die unzeitige Kündigung vorliegt. Kündigt er ohne solchen Grund zur Unzeit, so hat er dem Auftraggeber den daraus entstehenden Schaden zu ersetzen.*'

[148] *The 'Ogopogo'* [1970] 1 Lloyd's Rep 257 at 263.

5

Liability for Nonfeasance in English Private Law

5.1 Historical Background

In a letter dated 1 August 1888 Thomas Hardy wrote to his good friend Edmund Gosse that he was 'at present up to the elbows in a cold blooded murder which I hope to get finished in a day or two'.[1] Hardy was referring to a short story he was writing, entitled 'A Tale of Two Ambitions'. In this story the two main characters, Joshua and Cornelius Halborough (both studying to become clergymen), witness their father – an obnoxious drunk – fall into a weir. The two brothers, who fear that their father will ruin their younger sister Rosa's chances of marrying a wealthy gentleman, refuse to come to the rescue. After a short struggle he drowns.

The inaction of the brothers Halborough, no matter how cold-blooded and repulsive, would not in the time of Hardy have amounted to 'murder'.[2] Indeed, it is doubtful whether there would have been any legal repercussions for their immoral conduct. Central to the later medieval law of torts were the action of trespass and the action upon the case.[3] An action of trespass would almost certainly not have been available in cases of nonfeasance. For by analogy with the Roman requirement that damage be done *corpore suo*,[4] the defendant's behaviour was only considered a 'trespass' if it had directly harmed the plaintiff.[5] This requirement of 'directness' was illustrated by Fortescue J in *Reynolds v Clarke*:

> If a man throws a log into the highway, and in that act it hits me; I may maintain trespass, because it is an immediate wrong; but if as it lies there I tumble over it, and receive an injury, I must bring an action on the case; because it is only prejudicial in consequence, for which originally I could have no action at all.[6]

[1] R.L. Purdy an M. Millgate (eds), *The Collected Letters of Thomas Hardy*, Vol I (1978), 179.
[2] J.F. Stephen, *A Digest of the Criminal Law, Crimes and Punishment* (4th edn 1887), art. 212.
[3] D.J. Ibbetson, *A Historical Introduction to the Law of Obligations* (1999), p. 155.
[4] Cf. above, section 4.1, footnote 17 and the corresponding part of the main text.
[5] D.J. Ibbetson, *A Historical Introduction to the Law of Obligations* (1999), p. 159.
[6] (1725) 1 Strange 634, 93 ER 747 at 636. This case is also reported in 2 Ld Raym 1399, under the name *Reynolds v Clerk* and in 8 Mod. 272 under the name *Reynolds v Clark* in Fort 212. However, the passage here quoted does not appear in these reports.

Because in cases of nonfeasance the harm is caused indirectly, the action of trespass would not have lain. Indeed, in *The Six Carpenters' Case* of 1611, it was confirmed that 'not doing is no trespass'.[7]

The action upon the case on the other hand, would typically have lain in cases of indirect or 'consequential' loss. In 1762, Sir John Comyns, Chief Baron of the Exchequer, included in his *Digest* a title for the 'Action upon the Case for Negligence'. 'Negligence', rather unlike its wide modern connotations, was understood to mean 'neglect' or 'omission'.[8] An action upon the case based on such an omission would have lain for 'negligence in a man's trust' or 'duty',[9] for negligence in a man's office,[10] for a man's 'neglect in doing that, which by law he ought to do', for his 'neglect to do that, which he has undertaken', for negligence in taking care of one's animals and for negligently keeping a fire.[11] As we will see in the remaining sections of this chapter, many similar categories still feature in the modern law.

In the course of the nineteenth century the division between the action of trespass and the action upon the case was overshadowed by the development of a new tort: the tort of negligence. 'Negligence' was no longer understood as merely referring to omissions, but came to cover cases of both acts and inaction.[12] In *Blyth v Birmingham Waterworks Company*,[13] Baron Alderson defined negligence as follows:

> Negligence is the omission to do something which a reasonable man, guided upon those considerations which ordinarily regulate the conduct of human affairs, would do, or doing something which a prudent and reasonable man would not do.[14]

On the face of it, this definition does not indicate that there was any difference in the law's approach towards feasance and nonfeasance; apparently both types of behaviour were measured against the standard of the reasonable man. However, as Pollock was careful to point out, Baron Alderson's definition must have been based on the presumption that the party whose conduct was in question, was already under a 'duty of taking care'.[15] And it was at this 'duty'-stage of the trial, that the judicial approach in cases of nonfeasance differed from that in cases of feasance. For acts and their results, Pollock explained, the actor was generally speaking held answerable. For mere omission he was not, unless he was under

[7] (1611) 8 Co Rep 146a, 77 ER 695 at 146b. Cf. however S.F.C. Milsom, 'Not Doing is No Trespass' (1954) 12 CLJ 105–117.

[8] D.J. Ibbetson, *A Historical Introduction to the Law of Obligations* (1999), p. 165, footnote 53 and J.H. Baker, *An Introduction to English Legal History* (4th edn 2002), p. 413.

[9] *E.g.* when by the negligence of a servant, cattle perish.

[10] *E.g.* when a sheriff allows a prisoner to escape.

[11] J. Comyns, *A Digest of the Laws of England*, Vol I (1762), pp. 223–228. It was decreed in s. 86 of the Fires Prevention (Metropolis) Act 1776, that no action could be brought against any person on whose premises a fire accidentally began. While this provision is still in force, its effect is limited owing to the restrictive interpretation by the Privy Council in *Goldman v Hargrave* [1966] 2 All ER 989 at 996–997, *per* Lord Wilberforce (see for a discussion of this case below, Part I, section 5.6 (2)).

[12] Cf. for the opposite view J. Austin, *Lectures on Jurisprudence*, Vol II (1863), p. 101 (Lecture XX).

[13] (1856) 11 Ex. 781.

[14] *Ibid.* at 784.

[15] F. Pollock, *The Law Of Torts* (1887), p. 355.

some specific duty.[16] An example of the judicial reluctance to impose affirmative duties can be found in *Gantret v Egerton*. The defendants owned land, which was intersected, by a canal and cuttings, and bridges 'leading to certain docks of the defendants'.[17] Leon Gantret, who was lawfully passing over and using this land and these bridges, fell into one of the cuttings and drowned. His wife claimed that the defendants had wrongfully and improperly kept and maintained their land, canal, cuttings and bridges, and had allowed them to continue to be in a condition that rendered them unsafe for persons lawfully passing along. Herschell, for the plaintiff, argued that the defendants would have to prove that they did not owe a duty of care towards the plaintiff. At this point, according to the Bar Reports, Willes J interrupted Herschell:

> There is no duty to do anything, but there is a duty to abstain from doing anything that would injure.[18]

In the Law Reports, where this case appears under the name *Gautret v Egerton*, he is said to have added the following illustration:

> No action will lie against a spiteful man who, seeing another running into a position of danger, merely omits the warning.[19]

Because the plaintiff's declaration did not reveal the breach of a specific affirmative duty, it was held that the plaintiff had no cause of action.

5.2 The Law in England at Present

More than a hundred and thirty years have passed since Willes J gave his decision in *Gantret/Gautret v Egerton*. In that time it has been generally assumed that English law persisted in its reluctance to impose liability for nonfeasance. In the words of Professor Markesinis: 'it is a well-known fact that the common law, first for historical reasons and later on philosophical grounds, has taken a hostile view towards imposing tortious liability for pure omissions'.[20] Yet, until 1996 it was surprisingly difficult to find binding authority for this no-liability rule.[21] *Gantret/Gautret v Egerton* itself continued to be good law,[22] but was probably too

[16] *Ibid.*, p. 352. See also *Bulman v Furness Rly Company* (1875) 32 LT 430 at 432, where a distinction is made between 'active' and 'passive' negligence and F.T. Piggott, *Principles of the Law of Torts* (1885), p. 208, who distinguishes 'positive' and 'negative' duties.

[17] *Gantret v Egerton* (1867) 16 LT 17 at 17.

[18] *Ibid.* (1867) 16 LT 17 at 18. This interruption does not appear in this form in the Law Reports, [1867] LR 2 CP 371.

[19] *Gautret v Egerton* [1867] LR 2 CP 371 at 375. This quote does not appear in the Bar Reports, (1867) 16 LT 17.

[20] B.S. Markesinis, 'Negligence, Nuisance and Affirmative Duties of Action' (1989) 105 LQR 104 at 104.

[21] This observation was also made by M.A. Millner in his *Negligence in Modern Law* (1967), p. 30.

[22] See *McGeown v Northern Ireland Housing Executive* [1994] 3 All ER 53 and *Gulliksen v Pembrokeshire CC* [2002] EWCA Civ 968.

narrow a basis for a principle as broad as the no-liability rule. In *Pride of Derby Ltd v British Celanese Ltd*, Lord Denning stated that 'the distinction between misfeasance and nonfeasance is valid only in the case of highways repairable by the public at large' and that 'it does not apply to any other area of the law'.[23] Indeed, there was not much concrete evidence for the existence of a general rule of no liability for nonfeasance. True, there had been occasional references to the rule in *obiter dicta*.[24] Yet cases in which it was part of the *ratio decidendi* were scarce. One of the few exceptions, which for that reason featured in almost every textbook as authority on the matter, was said to be *Smith v Littlewoods*, in which Lord Goff stated:

> Why does the law not recognise a general duty of care to prevent others from suffering loss or damage caused by the deliberate wrongdoing of third parties? The fundamental reason is that the common law does not impose liability for what are called pure omissions.[25]

Although the no-liability rule was here clearly an important argument in Lord Goff's speech, it must be doubted whether *Smith v Littlewoods* provided binding authority. Firstly, Lord Goff was the only one of their Lordships to refer to the doctrine of no liability for nonfeasance.[26] Secondly, Lord Goff himself went on to express his doubts about the no-liability rule, saying that it 'may (. . .) require one day to be reconsidered'.[27]

Encouraged by Lord Goff's latter statement, Markesinis expressed in a 1989 article the hope and expectation that the no-liability rule would soon belong to the past.[28] Many other influential scholars too, have argued in favour of abandoning the rigid distinction between cases of feasance and of nonfeasance.[29] However, in its 1996 decision in *Stovin v Wise*[30] the House of Lords made clear that such

[23] [1953] Ch 149 at 188. See also *Duff v Highland and Islands Fire Board* (Outer House, Scotland) [1995] SLT 1362 at 1363, *per* Lord Macfadyen.

[24] *E.g.* Lord Keith's famous example of a man 'who sees another about to walk over a cliff with his head in the air, and forbears to shout a warning' in *Yuen Kun Yeu v AG of Hong Kong* [1987] 2 All ER 705 at 710. (Note that this example is remarkably similar to Willes J's example of the 'spiteful man' who 'omits the warning') and Lord Diplock's speech in *Home Office v Dorset Yacht Co. Ltd* [1970] AC 1004, at 1060. In *Smith v Littlewoods* Lord Goff referred to this speech as authority for the no-liability rule. Yet the fact alone that liability was imposed in *Dorset Yacht* indicates that it must be seriously doubted whether the no-liability rule was part of the *ratio decidendi*.

[25] *Smith v Littlewoods* [1987] AC 241 at 271.

[26] Although Lord Keith expressed his agreement with Lord Goff's speech; *Smith v Littlewoods* [1987] AC 241 at 249. The other Lawlords came to the same conclusion as Lord Goff, but based this conclusion on the fact that, in short, the damage was not reasonably foreseeable. For a more detailed investigation, see B.S. Markesinis, 'Negligence, Nuisance and Affirmative Duties of Action' (1989) 105 LQR 104 and below, Part I, Section 5.6 (2).

[27] *Smith v Littlewoods* [1987] AC 241 at 271.

[28] B.S. Markesinis, 'Negligence, Nuisance and Affirmative Duties of Action' (1989) 105 LQR 104 at 122–123.

[29] *E.g.* A.M. Honoré, 'Law, Morals and Rescue' in J.M. Ratcliffe (ed.), *The Good Samaritan and the Law* (1966), pp. 225 ff., reprinted and expanded in Honoré, *Making Law Bind, Essays Legal and Philosophical* (1987), pp. 256 ff.; P. Cane, *Atiyah's Accidents, Compensation and the Law* (6th edn 1999), pp. 60 ff.; J.G. Fleming, *The Law of Torts* (9th edn 1998), pp. 162 ff. and E.J. Weinrib, 'The Case for a Duty to Rescue', (1980) 90 Yale LJ 247–293.

[30] *Stovin v Wise* [1996] 3 All ER 801.

development would not take place in the near future. In a powerful speech, Lord Hoffmann not only confirmed the principle of no liability for nonfeasance but went on to defend it. The most relevant part of this speech was quoted above, in Section 3.1. Lord Goff and Lord Jauncey agreed with Lord Hoffmann. The minority of their Lordships, consisting of Lord Nicholls and Lord Slynn, also adhered to the general no-liability rule. After stating that the distinction between liability for acts and liability for omissions is 'fundamentally sound',[31] Lord Nicholls said:

> The recognised legal position is that the bystander does not owe the drowning child or the heedless pedestrian a duty to take steps to save him. Something more is required than being a bystander. There must be some additional reason why it is fair and reasonable that one person should be regarded as his brother's keeper and have legal obligations in that regard. When this additional reason exists, there is said to be sufficient proximity. That is the customary label.[32]

On the facts of the case, Lord Nicholls and Lord Slynn were of the opinion that there were specific circumstances that gave rise to a duty of care.

Thus, *Stovin v Wise* provided new and ample authority for the no-liability rule.[33] Only if we are under a specific duty to act, will we be held liable for our failure to act. The crucial question becomes therefore: 'when do such specific duties arise?' Part of the answer was given by Lord Hoffmann in *Stovin v Wise*:

> There may be a duty to act if one has undertaken to do so or induced a person to rely upon doing so. Or the ownership or occupation of land may give rise to a duty to take positive steps for the benefit of those who come upon the land and sometimes for the benefit of neighbours.[34]

In the following sections some specific circumstances that may give rise to affirmative duties will be assessed and investigated. It should at the outset be noted that the categories of circumstances that are distinguished in these sections sometimes overlap. As we will see, in many cases it is the combination of circumstances that has given rise to the imposition of an affirmative duty.

5.3 The Defendant has Created the Risk

When the defendant has created a risk, however blamelessly, and then fails to control it, the courts tend to qualify the case as one of feasance, rather than nonfeasance. In Chapter 2 we criticized this tendency and discussed an example of a car driver who failed to brake in time to avoid hitting a pedestrian. For the reasons given there, we decided to treat his failure to brake as an instance of 'nonfeasance',

[31] *Ibid.* at 806. [32] *Ibid.* at 807.

[33] Cf. however *Bellefield Computer Services Ltd v E. Turner & Sons Ltd* [2000] Build LR 97 at 101, *per* Schiemann LJ: 'Clearly the principles underlying the decision in [*Stovin v Wise*] have no direct application (. . .) where no public law element is present'.

[34] *Stovin v Wise* [1996] 3 All ER 801 at 819.

rather than, as Fleming argues, 'the element that makes his *active* conduct – driving – negligent'.[35] Accordingly, we regarded the stoker who fell asleep at the furnace as an example of someone who would incur liability for nonfeasance in Roman law.[36]

Most English courts however, would regard both the car driver's failure to brake and the stoker's failure to control the fire as active. Thus, by qualifying the defendant's behaviour as active rather than passive, the courts allow themselves to impose liability without having to address the issue of liability for nonfeasance. This technique is not unlike that of the French courts, when they distinguish '*abstentions dans l'action*' from the 'real' nonfeasance, the '*abstentions pures et simples*'.[37]

One notable exception is the 1961 case of *Johnson v Rea*.[38] There, the defendant firm of stevedores was handling sacks of soda ash. In the process, small quantities of soda ash seeped onto the floor, which became very slippery as a result. The defendant mentioned this fact to the plaintiff. Despite this warning, the plaintiff, who was carrying a heavy keg, slipped and injured his hand. In the view of the Court of Appeal, the defendants were not to blame for the fact that some soda ash had seeped onto the floor.[39] Nevertheless, the defendants were held liable for their failure to clean the floor. The principle being, as Ormerod LJ put it, that 'if any person creates a danger, it is his duty to do something more than to warn people coming on to the premises or coming within the ambit of the danger that it exists. He must take reasonable steps, if such steps can be taken, to obviate the danger to people likely to encounter it'.[40] There is a host of cases in which the same principle has been applied, albeit often implicitly.[41] Hence, there can be little doubt that in English law, as in French and Roman law, creating a risk gives rise to an affirmative duty to take reasonable steps to prevent the risk from culminating in injury.[42]

On the same principle a man who has made a representation that was initially true, but has become false due to a change in circumstances, is under a duty to disclose this change in circumstances:[43] he has created a risk and is under a duty to

[35] J.G. Fleming, *The Law of Torts* (9th edn 1998), p. 163.

[36] See above, Section 4.1.

[37] See above, Section 4.2.

[38] [1961] 1 WLR 1400. See also *Kane v New Forest DC* [2001] 3 All ER 914 and *R. v Miller* [1983] 2 AC 161 at 178–179, *per* Lord Diplock.

[39] *Ibid.* at 1407, *per* Harman LJ.

[40] *Ibid.* at 1405.

[41] *Kelly v Metropolitan Rly Co.* [1895] 1 QB 944; *Morrison v Sheffield Corporation* [1917] 2 KB 866; *Musgrove v Pandelis* [1919] 2 KB 43; *Sheppard v Glossop Corporation* [1921] 3 KB 132 at 145, *per* Scrutton LJ; *Fisher v Ruislip-Northwood Urban District Council and Middlesex County Council* [1945] KB 584; *Hughes v Lord Advocate* [1963] 1 All ER 705; *Hill v Chief Constable of West Yorkshire* [1989] AC 53 at 61 *per* Lord Keith and *Wright v Lodge* [1993] 4 All ER 299.

[42] C.K. Allen, 'Legal Duties' [1931] 40 Yale LJ 331–380, reprinted in C.K. Allen, *Legal Duties and Other Essays in Jurisprudence* (1931), pp. 156–220 at 206 with further references in footnote 2; M.R. Brazier in M.R. Brazier and others (eds), *Clerk & Lindsell on Torts* (18th edn 2000), para. 7–45 and W.V.H. Rogers, *Winfield and Jolowicz on Torts* (16th edn 2002), pp. 136–137 and J.G. Fleming, *The Law of Torts* (9th edn 1998), pp. 163–164.

[43] *Cherry Ltd v Allied Insurance Brokers Ltd* [1978] 1 Lloyd's Rep 274 and D.K. Allen, *Misrepresentation* (1988), pp. 85–86. A similar duty lies on a man who unwittingly makes a false representation and later realizes that he has made a mistake; *Briess v Woolley* [1954] AC 333 at 359 *per* Lord Tucker and G. Spencer Bower and A.K. Turner, *The Law of Actionable Misrepresentation* (3rd edn 1974), pp. 120–121.

prevent this risk from culminating in harm. Application of this principle does not, in general, give rise to a duty to safeguard one's belongings against abuse by third parties. Thus, if I leave my car unattended with the keys still in the ignition and a thief drives off with it and kills a cyclist, I am not liable, even though it may rightly be argued that I increased the risk of such an accident happening.[44] Only if there are additional circumstances, such as a special relationship with the plaintiff or with the third party, will I be liable for the deliberate wrongdoing of that third party.[45]

A slightly different, but obviously related issue is whether someone whose blameless behaviour has not just created a risk, but already caused harm to occur, owes the harmed person a duty to minimize the consequences of this harm. The answer is not all that obvious. When in 1903 a railroad engine, without negligence of its crew, cut off an arm and a leg of a trespasser, the Supreme Court of Kansas refused to impose liability on the railway company for its failure to render aid.[46] Twenty-seven years later, the Supreme Court of Alabama came to a similar conclusion in the case of *Turbeville v Mobile Light & R. Co.*[47] The defendant company operated a street railroad. Without negligence on the part of the defendant or its servants, one of the defendant's streetcars ran into the plaintiff. The plaintiff got caught under or against the streetcar and 'the safety guard' attached to this car fell on the plaintiff. The defendant's servants could easily have reversed the car or lifted the safety guard off the plaintiff, but failed to do so. The plaintiff was suffocated by the weight of the safety guard. Brown J. considered:

> (. . .) we know of no principle of municipal law that imposed on the defendants or its servants a legal duty to relieve him by backing the car off his body or lifting it up so as to relieve his peril. It certainly could not be said that such duty rested on a mere bystander who witnessed his misfortune and who was in no way legally responsible for his predicament. If this be so, what reason can be found in the law to say that the defendant or its servants were under a duty to act, when they were guilty of no wrong or negligence in producing or bringing about the unfortunate situation.[48]

During the second half of this century American law appears to have given way to the strong criticism[49] these and similar decisions gave rise to. It is now generally recognized that a duty to act arises where the defendant's prior conduct, though innocent, has caused an injury.[50]

44 *Topp v London County Bus Co* [1993] 3 All ER 448. Cf. *Perl Ltd v Camden London Borough Council* [1984] QB 342.

45 *Stansbie v Troman* [1948] 2 KB 48 and below, Part I, Sections 5.5 and 5.6.

46 *Union Pacific Rly Co. v Cappier* 66 Kan. 649, 72 Pac. 281 (Sup. Ct of Kansas, 1903).

47 221 Ala. 91, 127 So. 519 (Sup Ct of Alabama, 1930), with further references.

48 *Ibid.* at 521.

49 *E.g.* Ch.O. Gregory, 'The Good Samaritan and the Bad' in J.M. Ratcliffe, (ed.), *The Good Samaritan and the Law* (1966), pp. 23–41 at 26–27.

50 W. Page Keeton (ed.), *Prosser and Keeton on The Law of Torts* (5th edn 1984), p. 377 and F.V. Harper, F. James and O.S. Gray, *The Law of Torts* (2nd edn 1986), pp. 720–721 (para. 18.6) with further references in footnote 16.

In English law, too, it must be presumed that he who innocently causes an injury owes a duty to minimize the consequences of this injury.[51]

Thus, both in cases in which the defendant created a risk and in cases in which the defendant blamelessly caused an injury, English law allows an exception to the rule of no liability for nonfeasance. A possible justification for allowing an exception in these cases is that the 'why pick on me?' argument is easily met: the defendant is not merely one of a large number of bystanders. Moreover, there is a more obvious causal connection between the defendant's behaviour and the damage than in most cases involving nonfeasance.

5.4 The Defendant has Undertaken to Act and/or has Induced the Plaintiff to Rely on Him

As I am walking over a bridge a woman falls into the water. I hear her scream for help and decide to come to the rescue. I throw her a rope, which she grabs and holds on to.[52] In English law I was under no duty to come to the woman's rescue; I was free to ignore her.[53] Now that I have thrown the rope and thus embarked on the rescue, the question arises whether my legal position has changed. Am I still allowed to change my mind about the rescue – and let go of the rope – or have I come under a duty to carry it through? And if I have come under a duty to carry through my rescue attempt, when exactly did this duty arise? Was it when I undertook the rescue or was it when the woman in the water swam towards the rope and grabbed it, thus acting in reliance upon my undertaking?

A. Can a mere undertaking give rise to a duty to act?

When one analyses the case law it is not always clear what, in the courts' understanding, amounts to an 'undertaking'. Not only do the courts use different terms – usually either 'undertaking' or 'assumption of responsibility'[54] – but the ways the courts interpret the concept varies considerably. One can roughly distinguish two types of interpretation. Sometimes the courts mean that the defendant has expressly or implicitly made a promise. At other times, the judges have interpreted the term to mean no more than that the defendant has voluntarily acted.[55] A good example of the first type of undertaking, 'the implied promise', is by

[51] A.M. Honoré, 'Are Omissions Less Culpable?' in P. Cane and J. Stapleton (eds), *Essays for Patrick Atiyah* (1991), pp. 31 ff. at pp. 43–45.

[52] Example loosely based on J.B. Ames, 'Law and Morals' 22 Harvard LR 97–113 (1908), reprinted in J.M. Ratcliffe, (ed.), *The Good Samaritan and the Law* (1966), pp. 1–21 at p. 19.

[53] B.S. Markesinis and S.F. Deakin, *Tort Law* (4th edn 1999), pp. 138–141 with further references.

[54] See for various other terms K. Barker, 'Unreliable Assumptions in the Modern Law of Negligence' (1993) 109 LQR 461–484 at 463.

[55] *Ibid.* at 462. Barker distinguishes a third type of undertaking which is based on 'choice'.

Lord Devlin in *Hedley Byrne & Co. Ltd v Heller & Partners Ltd*:[56]

(. . .) the categories of special relationships which may give rise to a duty to take care in word as well as in deed are not limited to contractual relationships or to relationships of fiduciary duty, but include also relationships which in the words of Lord Shaw in *Nocton v Lord Ashburton* are 'equivalent to contract', that is, where there is an assumption of responsibility in circumstances in which, but for the absence of consideration, there would be a contract. Where there is an express undertaking, an express warranty as distinct from a mere representation, there can be little difficulty. The difficulty arises in discerning cases in which the undertaking is to be implied.[57]

Although *Hedley Byrne* was not strictly speaking a case of nonfeasance, we may safely assume that its principle can equally apply in cases involving nonfeasance. This is confirmed by Lord Goff in *Henderson v Merrett Syndicates Ltd*:[58]

I wish to add in parenthesis that (. . .) an assumption of responsibility by, for example, a professional man may give rise to liability in respect of negligent omissions as much as negligent acts of commission, as for example when a solicitor assumes responsibility for business on behalf of his client and omits to take a certain step, such as the service of a document, which falls within the responsibility so assumed by him.[59]

A case that can be said to have involved an implied promise is *Barnett v Chelsea and Kensington Hospital*.[60] There, a hospital came under a duty to treat three men suffering from poisoning because, amongst other reasons, they had been allowed to enter the hospital and their complaints were passed on to the medical casualty officer.[61]

It is more difficult to establish on what basis liability was imposed in *White v Jones*.[62] The defendants – solicitors – had failed to change a will in accordance with the testator's instructions. As a result the testator's daughters – plaintiffs – received a considerably smaller sum than their father had intended them to have. In one view, the defendants' implied promise gave rise to a duty towards the plaintiffs. However, it is difficult to see how the defendants' contractual promise to the testator incorporated an implied promise to the plaintiffs. As Lord Goff observed:

(. . .) there is great difficulty in holding, on ordinary principles, that the solicitor has assumed any responsibility towards an intended beneficiary under a will which he has undertaken to prepare on behalf of his client (. . .).[63]

Nevertheless Lord Goff found in favour of allowing the plaintiffs' claim. Of 'cardinal importance' to this decision was a peculiarity which Lord Goff regarded as a 'lacuna in the law': if the plaintiffs were not allowed a claim in negligence, there would have been no effective remedy for the defendants' negligence. The only

56 [1964] AC 465. 57 *Ibid.* at 528–529 (footnotes omitted). 58 [1995] 2 AC 145.
59 *Ibid.* at 181. Cf. *Midland Bank Trust Co. Ltd v Hett, Stubs & Kemp* [1979] Ch 384 *per* Oliver J.
60 [1969] 1 QB 428. 61 *Ibid.* at 435–436, *per* Nield J. 62 (HoL) [1995] 2 AC 207.
63 *Ibid.* at 262.

person who had a valid claim on contract – the (executor of the) estate – had suffered no loss:[64]

(. . .) it seems to me that it is open to your Lordships' House (. . .) to fashion a remedy to fill a lacuna in the law to solve the problem of transferred loss in the case before them. (. . .) In my opinion, therefore, your Lordships' House should in cases such as these extend to the intended beneficiary a remedy under the *Hedley Byrne* principle by holding that the assumption of responsibility by the solicitor towards his client should be held in law to extend to the intended beneficiary (. . .).[65]

Thus, Lord Goff was careful to make clear that his decision in *White v Jones* was instigated by the exceptional circumstances of the case. Considerably different in this respect was Lord Browne-Wilkinson's speech in the same case. His Lordship considered that in previous cases special relationships had been found to exist where the defendant had voluntarily assumed to act in the matter by involving himself in the plaintiff's affairs or by choosing to speak.[66] By analogy, he argued, the solicitor came into a special relationship with those intended to benefit under the will when he accepted the instructions to draw the will.[67] Rather than exceptional, Lord Browne-Wilkinson appears to have regarded this decision as the straightforward application of an overriding principle; a principle that, it should be noted, bears some resemblance to the principle underlying the Roman *actio negotiorum gestorum (directa)*:

If the responsibility for the task is assumed by the defendant he thereby creates a special relationship between himself and the plaintiff in relation to which the law (not the defendant) attaches a duty to carry out carefully the task so assumed.[68]

Whereas Lord Goff used the phrase 'assumption of responsibility' in its meaning of 'implied promise', Lord Browne-Wilkinson spoke of 'assuming the task' which appears to mean 'choosing to act'.[69] Or, as Lord Nolan put it, 'embarking upon a potentially harmful activity'.[70] On one view, an undertaking in this sense does not generally give rise to liability in tort. This view appears to have been supported by Stuart-Smith LJ in *Capital and Counties v Hampshire CC*,[71] where he said:

It is not clear why a rescuer who is not under an obligation to attempt a rescue should assume a duty to be careful in effecting the rescue merely by undertaking the attempt.[72]

[64] (HoL) [1995] 2 AC, at 259–260. Cf. *Ross v Caunters* [1980] Ch 297 at 303, *per* Megarry V-C and the decision of the Court of Appeal in *White v Jones* (CA) [1993] 3 WLR 730, at 749, *per* Farquharson LJ and at 751, *per* Steyn LJ.

[65] *White v Jones* (HoL) [1995] 2 AC 207 at 268. Cf. *Leigh and Sillivan Ltd v Aliakmon Shipping Co. Ltd* [1986] 2 All ER 145.

[66] *Ibid.* at 274.

[67] *Ibid.* at 276.

[68] *Ibid.* at 273.

[69] Their Lordships would have imposed a duty to act even in the absence of any reliance by the plaintiffs on the defendants' undertaking. Cf. *White v Jones* (HoL) [1995] 2 AC 207 at 272 *per* Lord Browne-Wilkinson.

[70] *Ibid.* at 293.

[71] [1997] 2 All ER 865.

[72] *Ibid.* at 885. Cf. also *Sheppard v Glossop Corporation* [1921] 3 KB 132 at 145, *per* Scrutton LJ.

On another view, however, an attempt to rescue can give rise to an affirmative duty of care. Some support for this view can be drawn from the speech by Lord Morris in *Hedley Byrne & Co. Ltd v Heller & Partners Ltd*:

A medical man may unexpectedly come across an unconscious man, who is a complete stranger to him, and who is in urgent need of skilled attention: if the medical man, following the fine traditions of his profession, proceeds to treat the unconscious man he must exercise reasonable skill and care in doing so.[73]

The same view was adopted by the Court of Appeal in *Barrett v Ministry of Defence*.[74] In Barrett, a naval airman died after he became so drunk that he passed out into a coma and suffocated on his own vomit. The Queen's Regulations for the Royal Navy 1967 stated that all officers owed a duty to discourage drunkenness and in the event of alcohol abuse 'to take appropriate action to prevent any likely breaches of discipline, possible injury or fatality, including medical assistance if . . . available'.[75] The deceased's widow sued the Ministry of Defence. Beldam LJ held that the provisions in the Queen's Regulations did not give rise to a duty towards individual sailors because:

The purpose of Queen's Regulations and standing orders is to preserve good order and discipline in the service and to ensure that personnel remain fit for duty and while on duty obey commands and off duty do not misbehave bringing the service into disrepute.[76]

However, after the deceased had collapsed, one of the officers had arranged for him to be put on a stretcher and to be taken to his cabin. On the ground that by doing so the officer had voluntarily undertaken responsibility, Beldam LJ held the Ministry of Defence liable:

Until he collapsed I would hold that the deceased was in law alone responsible for his condition. Thereafter, when the appellant assumed responsibility for him, it accepts that the measures taken fell short of the standard reasonably to be expected.[77]

Despite the fact that the undertaking was not accompanied by reliance, liability was imposed. According to Stuart-Smith LJ, *Barrett v Ministry of Defence* is an exceptional case. Because the deceased was under command of the officer, he argued, there was already a sufficiently close relationship of proximity to give rise to a duty of care.[78] This view may seem convincing, but fails to explain why in *Barrett v Ministry of Defence* no duty of care arose until the officer undertook the rescue. Before this undertaking, Beldam LJ's words are clear in this respect, 'the deceased was in law alone responsible for his condition'.[79]

[73] *Hedley Byrne & Co. Ltd v Heller & Partners Ltd* [1964] AC 465 at 495. See also M.A. Jones, *Medical Negligence* (2nd edn 1996), pp. 34–35 and I. Kennedy and A. Grubb, *Principles of Medical Law* (1998), p. 294 with further references.

[74] [1995] 3 All ER 87.

[75] *Ibid.* at 87.

[76] *Ibid.* at 94. Note the resemblance between this speech and the prevailing opinion in Germany on the question whether or not § 323c *StGB* is a *Schutzgesetz*; above, Section 4.3.

[77] *Ibid.* at 96.

[78] *Capital and Counties v Hampshire CC* [1997] 2 All ER 865 at 886.

[79] *Barrett v Ministry of Defence* [1995] 3 All ER 87 at 96 (quoted immediately above).

In the recent ambulance case of *Kent v Griffiths*,[80] the Court of Appeal appears to have confirmed that an undertaking, in the sense here discussed, can give rise to a duty of care. In *Kent*, an ambulance service had accepted a 999 call but turned up excessively late. The ambulance service was held liable. The 'acceptance of the call', Lord Woolf held, gave rise to a duty of care.[81] Admittedly, this phrase is somewhat ambiguous. Was the call 'accepted' when the phone was picked up, or when the request for an ambulance was agreed to? However, his Lordship indicated that it was sufficient that the ambulance service had decided to intervene. Thus, an undertaking in the sense of an 'implied promise' does not seem to have been required: 'having decided to provide an ambulance an explanation is required to justify a failure to attend within reasonable time'.[82]

B Does an undertaking give rise to a duty to act when coupled with reliance?

If an undertaking alone does not suffice to give rise to a duty of care, then perhaps the fact that the claimant relied on the defendant's undertaking might change matters. When dealing with reliance, one usually distinguishes detrimental and non-detrimental reliance.[83]

Let us first consider a case of so-called detrimental reliance, by assuming that the woman to whom I threw the rope has an alternative option that might save her life. She could swim to a sandbank in the middle of the river, although this sandbank will flood during high tide. Relying on my willingness to carry through my rescue attempt, she chooses for (what she thinks is) the safer option and holds on to the rope I threw her. I let go of the rope and the woman, whose firm grasp of the rope has taken its toll on her physical resources, immediately drowns. It should not be doubted that my undertaking coupled with the woman's detrimental reliance gives rise to a duty of care.[84] More doubtful, however, is the scope of this duty of care.[85]

On one view my duty is merely to make sure that my undertaking, whether initially made in good faith or not, does not end up putting the woman in a worse position than she was before I threw her the rope. I could perform such a duty by dragging her by the rope to the middle of the bridge, thus enabling her to make it to the sandbank after all. She is then in the same position as she was before I threw her the rope, and even if she drowns as the high tide comes in I am not liable. To use Bagshaw's terminology: liability arises in respect of 'the detrimental reliance

[80] (CA) [2001] QB 36. For a more detailed discussion of this case, see K. Williams, 'Medical Samaritans: Is There A Duty To Treat?' (2001) 21 OJLS 393–413 at 401–403.

[81] *Ibid.* at 54.

[82] *Ibid.* at 53, *per* Lord Woolf. See also K. Williams, 'Medical Samaritans: Is There A Duty To Treat?' (2001) 21 OJLS 393–413 at 410.

[83] K. Barker, 'Unreliable Assumptions in the Modern Law of Negligence' (1993) 109 LQR 461–484 at 475.

[84] P. Cane, *Atiyah's Accidents, Compensation and the Law* (6th edn 1999), p. 64.

[85] J.G. Fleming, *The Law of Torts* (9th edn 1998), pp. 164–168.

itself', not 'the expectation which prompted the detrimental reliance'.[86] If this is the law, the doctrine of 'detrimental reliance' is in essence nothing but an analogous application of the rule set out in Section 5.3 (above); by throwing a rope I increased the risk that the woman would not make it to safety on her own strength. All I would need to do to avoid liability is to neutralize the detriment that followed from the woman's reliance, thus preventing the additional risk I created from culminating in harm.[87] This view appears to be supported by Schroeder JA in a Canadian case called *The 'Ogopogo'* where he refers to the principle that 'even if a person embarks upon a rescue and does not carry it through, he is not under any liability to the person to whose aid he had come so long as discontinuance of his efforts did not leave the other in a worse condition than when he took charge'.[88]

On another view, however, an undertaking coupled with detrimental reliance gives rise to a wider duty to perform the task that was undertaken. If this is the law, I am not allowed to put the woman back in the same position as she was before I threw her the rope; I will have to take reasonable care in carrying through my rescue attempt. If I do not, I may be held liable for the woman's whole loss, including the benefits she expected to receive from my undertaking. This is the view that appears to have been adopted by the Court of Appeal in *London Borough of Bromley v Ellis*,[89] although the case is not entirely clear in this respect. An insurance agent had undertaken to arrange the transfer of an insurance policy to a Mr Ellis free of charge. In the belief that he was thus insured, Mr Ellis refrained from taking out new insurance. He became involved in a car accident and after he found out that he had not been insured after all, he brought a claim for indemnity against the insurance agent. The Court of Appeal held that even though there was no contractual relationship between Mr Ellis and the insurance agent, the latter's undertaking gave rise to a duty to arrange the transfer with reasonable care.[90] If this duty were merely to take care that his undertaking did not end up putting Mr Ellis in a worse position than he was before the undertaking was made, one would have expected the average charge of an insurance agent to be a reducing factor in the assessment of damages. After all, if the insurance agent had not undertaken the task of arranging the transfer free of charge, Mr Ellis would in all likelihood have had to pay another agent to perform this task. However, nothing in the case report indicates that a reduction was made. Bagshaw argues that a similar view – albeit with regard to detriment rather than detrimental reliance – is adopted in *Capital and Counties v Hampshire CC*:

> (. . .) the Court of Appeal held that where the fire brigade had caused additional harm, or increased the risk of harm, it should be treated as having caused the damage represented by

[86] R. Bagshaw, 'The Duties of Care of Emergency Service Providers' [1999] LMCLQ 71–92 at 75.

[87] It should be noted that this view does not imply that liability is merely imposed for the act of 'undertaking' rather than the inaction of failing to prevent harm from occurring. The undertaking itself did not amount to negligence. Cf. above, Chapter 2.

[88] *The 'Ogopogo'* [1970] 1 Lloyd's Rep 257 at 263.

[89] [1971] 1 Lloyd's Rep 97.

[90] *Ibid.* at 99 *per* Lord Denning MR. See also *Wilkinson v Coverdale* (1793) 1 Esp 75, 170 ER 284.

the difference between the plaintiff's actual position after the fire, and the position the plaintiff would have been in if the fire brigade had fought the fire in a reasonably competent manner. This seems incorrect, because it means that the damage the fire brigade is said to have negligently caused (for instance by switching off the sprinkler) is more than the damage which it was its duty to take care not to cause.[91]

It must however be noted that Stuart-Smith LJ's judgment is not quite as clear in this respect as Bagshaw implies it is. True, Stuart-Smith LJ does initially appear to say that the fire brigade should be liable for the whole damage, taking into account the expectation that resulted from the fire brigade's undertaking.[92] Yet he later qualifies this by saying that the fire brigade is not liable for the damage insofar as it can prove that it would have occurred 'in any event, even if they had never come upon the scene'.[93]

Amongst those who argue that an undertaking, without reliance, does not suffice to give rise to a duty of care, the predominant view would appear to be that in general an undertaking that is coupled with detrimental reliance merely gives rise to a duty to make sure that this undertaking does not end up leaving the victim worse off.[94]

The second type of reliance, non-detrimental reliance, must be regarded as of little legal importance.[95] With a small adjustment our example of the drowning woman can again serve as an illustration; if we assume that the woman would never have been able to swim to safety,[96] her holding on to the rope I threw her is not a detrimental act of reliance. In truth, it is debatable whether her holding on to the rope should altogether be regarded as an act of reliance. After all, we can hardly speak of 'reliance' when the person concerned was not offered a real choice; she could either drown immediately or grab hold of the rope for as long as I let her. The more appropriate term would therefore be 'dependence' which, as we learn from the parable of the good Samaritan, is not regarded as a ground to impose liability. No matter how much the victim depended on the Levite, the latter would not have had a duty to aid him in English law.

[91] R. Bagshaw, 'The duties of care of emergency service providers' [1999] LMCLQ 71–92 at 74–75 (footnotes omitted) and *idem*, 'Proximity's Siren Song: Negligence Liability of Fire Brigades in England', (1998) 6 Tort L Rev 109–113 at 111–112.

[92] *Capital and Counties v Hampshire CC* [1997] 2 All ER 865 at 882: 'It is not to be supposed that having arrived on the fire ground the fire brigade would simply have sat on their hands'.

[93] *Ibid.* at 882. It remains unclear why the fire brigade should bear the burden of proof in this respect. See also J. Hartshorne, 'The liability in negligence of the fire service – the Court of Appeal decides', (1997) 13 PN 53–58 at 58 and *Kent v Griffiths* (CA) [2001] QB 36 at 48, *per* Lord Woolf: 'if the fire brigade by their own actions increased the risk of danger they would be liable for negligence *in respect of the damage which was caused by the increased risk*'. (Emphasis added).

[94] . . . and, perhaps, not to cause any 'substitute harm', as Bagshaw calls it; R. Bagshaw, 'The duties of care of emergency service providers' [1999] LMCLQ 71–92 at 76. Cf. M. Spence, *Protecting Reliance: The Emergent Doctrine of Equitable Estoppel* (1999), pp. 6–7.

[95] K. Barker, 'Unreliable Assumptions in the Modern Law of Negligence' (1993) 109 LQR 461–484 at 475.

[96] . . . and that no other option than the rope would have given her a chance to survive.

C. 'General reliance'

In recent case law attention has been drawn to a third type of reliance, the concept of so-called 'general reliance'.[97] The clearest exposition of this type of reliance is by Mason J in the High Court of Australia, where he stated that:

(. . .) there will be cases in which the plaintiff's reasonable reliance will arise out of a general dependence on an authority's performance of its function with due care, without the need for contributing conduct on the part of a defendant or action to his detriment on the part of a plaintiff. Reliance or dependence in this sense is in general the product of the grant (and exercise) of powers designed to prevent or minimize a risk of personal injury or disability, recognized by the legislature as being of such magnitude or complexity that individuals cannot, or may not, take adequate steps for their own protection. This situation generates on one side (the individual) a general expectation that the power will be exercised and on the other side (the authority) a realization that there is a general reliance or dependence on its exercise of power (. . .).[98]

'General reliance' appears to provide an argument in favour of the imposition of a duty of care on a class of defendants, rather than on any specific defendant. It is a factor in the decision whether it would be fair, just and reasonable to impose a duty of care. The concept of general reliance refers to the reliance of society as a whole, rather than the reliance of an individual plaintiff. Even if the plaintiff himself did not expect the defendant to act, he can invoke the doctrine of general reliance.[99] Although it is not immediately apparent whether general reliance is reliance of the detrimental or the non-detrimental kind, it is likely to possess some detrimental characteristics. For in most (if not all) situations in which society as a whole has relied on the defendant to fulfill a task undertaken, society (or elements within it) would have performed this task if only it (they) had known that the defendant was not going to do so.

To illustrate the types of cases in which this policy argument could play an important role, Mason J mentioned the control of air traffic, the safety inspection of aircraft and the fighting of a fire in a building by a fire authority.[100] Although the doctrine of general reliance would typically apply in cases in which the defendant is a public authority, there is no obvious reason why the doctrine could not also apply in cases that do not involve public authorities. Indeed, Lord Browne-Wilkinson's speech in *White v Jones* contains a fine example of such application:

Although in any particular case it may not be possible to demonstrate that the intended beneficiary relied upon the solicitor, society as a whole does rely on solicitors to carry out their will making functions carefully.[101]

[97] *E.g. Stovin v Wise* [1996] 3 All ER 801 at 828–830 *per* Lord Hoffmann and *Capital and Counties v Hampshire CC* [1997] 2 All ER 865 at 876–878 *per* Stuart-Smith LJ.

[98] *Sutherland Shire Council v Heyman* (1985) 157 CLR 424 at 464.

[99] *Stovin v Wise* [1996] 3 All ER 801 at 829, *per* Lord Hoffmann and R. Bagshaw, 'The duties of care of emergency service providers' [1999] LMCLQ 71–92 at 80.

[100] *Sutherland Shire Council v Heyman* (1985) 157 CLR 424 at 464.

[101] *White v Jones* [1995] 2 AC 207 at 276.

It is as yet uncertain if, and if so to what extent, the doctrine of general reliance will be of practical importance in cases before the English courts. In *Stovin v Wise* Lord Hoffmann stressed that if the doctrine was to be accepted, its application would require 'some very careful analysis of the role which the expected exercise of the statutory power plays in community behaviour'.[102] Addressing one of the examples given by Mason J, Lord Hoffmann indicated that in cases involving the fire brigade this careful analysis might lead the courts to decide that liability ought not to be imposed:[103]

> For example, in one sense it is true that the fire brigade is there to protect people in situations in which they could not be expected to be able to protect themselves. On the other hand, they can and do protect themselves by insurance against the risk of fire.[104]

Soon after Lord Hoffmann gave his speech in *Stovin v Wise*, a case involving fire brigades, *Capital and Counties v Hampshire CC*,[105] came before the Court of Appeal. The Court of Appeal was not convinced by arguments based on general reliance or more generally on the fire brigade's undertaking. It was decided that a fire brigade did not owe a duty to extinguish a fire, regardless of whether or not it had accepted an emergency call. Moreover, even if it did attend the fire its only duty was not to make the situation worse.[106] Similar views have since been expressed in a case involving the police[107] and one involving the coastguard.[108]

However, this line of authority is difficult to reconcile with the position adopted by the Court of Appeal in the more recent case of *Kent v Griffiths*.[109] While the decisive factor in that decision was the ambulance service's specific undertaking, an argument based on general reliance does appear to have lurked in the background. Lord Woolf stated that 'the ambulance call having been made, apparently attendance is automatic'. His Lordship added that in his view 'the reaction of the judge to the facts of this case accords with the likely reaction of any

[102] *Stovin v Wise* [1996] 3 All ER 801 at 829. Cf. however *Invercargill City Council v Hamlin* (PC) [1996] 1 All ER 756 at 761–764, *per* Lord Lloyd with further references.

[103] In *Philcox v Civil Aviation Authority, The Times* 8 June 1995, it had already been decided that the Aviation Authority, the other example used by Mason J, owed no duty to the owner of an aircraft to take care in the inspection of his aircraft and the certification of its airworthiness.

[104] *Stovin v Wise* [1996] 3 All ER 801 at 829.

[105] [1997] 2 All ER 865.

[106] *Ibid.* at 883–886 and 889, *per* Stuart-Smith LJ.

[107] *Costello v Chief Constable* [1999] 1 All ER 550 at 563, *per* May LJ and *Cowan v Chief Constable for Avon & Somerset Constabulary* [2001] EWCA Civ 1699. Cf. *Alexandrou v Oxford* [1993] 4 All ER 328 at 338, *per* Glidewell LJ and at 343–344, *per* Slade LJ.

[108] *Oll v Secretary of State for Transport* [1997] 3 All ER 897 at 905, *per* May J.

[109] (CA) [2001] QB 36, discussed above at pp. 100–101. Lord Woolf, at 45, stated that he accepted 'unhesitatingly the good sense of [the *Capital and Counties*] line of authority'. However, when closely read, Lord Woolf's speech gives the contrary impression, not least because *Kent* involved detrimental reliance, and could thus have been decided by simply applying the principle enunciated in *Capital and Counties*. See also *Kent v London Ambulance Service* (CA, strike-out) [1999] Lloyd's Rep Med 58 at 62 (reported under the name *Kent v Griffiths* in (1999) 47 BMLR 125), in which Kennedy LJ openly questioned the Court of Appeal's reluctance to recognize a relationship of proximity in *Alexandrou v Oxford*. 'Could there not be a special relationship with all 999 callers whose calls were accepted?', he wondered.

well-informed member of the public'.[110] A consideration based on general reliance was more clearly articulated by Kennedy LJ when *Kent v Griffiths* first came to the Court of Appeal, on appeal against a strikeout.[111] One of the important reasons for allowing the appeal appears to have been that the public generally – and detrimentally – relies on an ambulance to turn up once a call has been accepted:

(. . .) if the ambulance service undertakes to attend the person who has been promised that assistance, and those acting on his or her behalf, *normally* abandon the search for other possible means of transporting the patient to hospital in a situation in which other means of transport may readily be available.[112]

All in all, it has become rather difficult to predict whether the courts will impose a duty of care on public authorities, and with that whether the doctrine of general reliance will gain more judicial support in the future.[113] As Brooke LJ said in *Musgrave v The Chief Constable of Hampshire*:

This is an extremely difficult area of the law. There are a number of cases which go either way and in the last resort it is a matter for the judge after establishing the facts to decide, if the necessary proximity exists between the parties, [and] whether it is just, fair and reasonable to impose the duty complained of.[114]

In summary, the presence of an undertaking – especially if accompanied by detrimental reliance – may give rise to an affirmative duty and thus to an exception to the rule of no liability for nonfeasance. There are several justifications for allowing such an exception in these cases. Firstly, the 'why pick on me?' argument is easily met: by his undertaking the defendant has rendered himself easily identifiable. Secondly, there is a more obvious causal connection between the defendant's conduct and the damage than in most cases of nonfeasance, especially in those cases involving detrimental reliance. Thirdly, although the imposition of liability may still be regarded as an interference with an individual's freedom, the defendant has had the choice to avoid this interference by refusing to undertake responsibility.[115] To use the words of Oliver Wendell Holmes:

Although a man has a perfect right to stand by and see his neighbor's property destroyed, or, for the matter of that, to watch his neighbor perish for want of his help, yet if he once intermeddles he has no longer the same freedom. He cannot withdraw at will.[116]

On the other hand, the 'culpability argument' seems to oppose at least as strongly against imposing liability as it does in all other cases of nonfeasance. For if

110 *Ibid.* at 54.

111 *Kent v London Ambulance Service* (CA, strike-out) [1999] Lloyd's Rep Med 58 at 63 (reported under the name *Kent v Griffiths* in (1999) 47 BMLR 125). (Emphasis added.)

112 *Ibid.* at 63.

113 The High Court of Australia rejected the doctrine of general reliance in *Pyrenees Shire Council v Day* (1998) 72 ALJR 152.

114 *Musgrave v the Chief Constable of Hampshire*, Court of Appeal 10 February 1999 (unreported).

115 J.C. Smith and P. Burns, 'Donoghue v. Stevenson – The Not So Golden Anniversary' (1983) 46 MLR 147 at 156–157.

116 O.W. Holmes, *The Common Law* (1881), p. 278.

I undertake but fail to rescue am I not less culpable than if I do not even try in the first place?

5.5 The Defendant is in a Special Position of Responsibility towards the Plaintiff

As we have seen in Section 4.3, above, German law is less reluctant to impose liability for nonfeasance in cases where the defendant had a special relationship with the plaintiff. Thus, we observed, 'although the Levite may not be required to render assistance to everyone, he does have a duty to aid his close relatives, his spouse or his close friends'.[117] Whether the same is true for English law is not entirely clear. Cases involving relatives suing each other are rare.[118] Most English scholars accept that parenthood may give rise to a duty to protect or help one's children.[119] A similar view appears to have been adopted by the Court of Appeal in *Surtees v Royal Borough of Kingston upon Thames* in which Stocker LJ considered the duty owed by a foster parent to her foster child:

> I have no doubt that stated in general terms the duty imposed on Mrs. Hughes was to take such care as in all the circumstances was reasonable to ensure that the plaintiff was not exposed to unnecessary risk of injury, the standard of care being that of a careful parent in the prevailing circumstances.[120]

Stocker LJ went on to say that when establishing the scope of this parental duty, the courts should take account of the domestic circumstances of the individual parent.[121] The Vice-Chancellor emphasized the point:

> We should be slow to characterise as negligent the care which ordinary loving and careful mothers are able to give to individual children, given the rough and tumble of home life.[122]

Given the scarcity of authority on the matter, we can but speculate about the scope of the parental duty. It probably does not incorporate a duty to insure one's children against the risk of injury.[123]

117 Above, Section 4.3, footnote 79 and the corresponding part of the main text.

118 W.V.H. Rogers, *Winfield and Jolowicz on Tort* (16th edn 2002), p. 138.

119 P. Cane, *Atiyah's Accidents, Compensation and the Law* (6th edn 1999), p. 65; B.S. Markesinis and S.F. Deakin, *Tort Law* (4th edn 1999), pp. 138–139; W.V.H. Rogers, *Winfield and Jolowicz on Tort* (16th edn 2002), p. 138 and M.A. Jones, *Textbook on Torts* (8th edn 2002), p. 59. Cf. also J.G. Fleming, *The Law of Torts* (9th edn 1998), p. 169 and *Marc Rich & Co. v Bishop Rock Marine Co. Ltd* [1994] 1 WLR 1071 at 1077 *per* Saville LJ, as well as the Congenital Disabilities (Civil Liability) Act 1976, s. 2.

120 *Surtees v Royal Borough of Kingston upon Thames* [1992] PIQR P101 at P111.

121 *Ibid.* at P111–P112. 122 *Ibid.* at P124.

123 *Van Oppen v Bedford Charity Trustees* [1989] 1 All ER 273 at 291, *per* Boreham J, as confirmed by the Court of Appeal in *Van Oppen v Bedford Charity Trustees* (CA) [1989] 3 All ER 389 at 412, *per* Balcombe LJ.

Short of attempting to give a complete list of all the other special relationships that may give rise to a duty to protect, a few examples will suffice for present purposes. A school may be liable for releasing its pupils before closing time[124] or more generally for failing to take reasonable care of the safety of the person and property of each pupil.[125] An employer must not only secure the safety in the workplace but also look after an employee who is injured or falls ill at work.[126] Similarly, prison authorities have a duty to provide medical care to their prisoners.[127] Finally, the close relationship between police officers gives rise to 'a duty to comply with a specific or acknowledged police duty where failure to do so will expose a fellow officer to unnecessary risk of injury'. Thus, the Chief Constable of Northumbria was held vicariously liable when one of his police inspectors failed to render assistance to a female police constable who was attacked by a prisoner.[128]

There are several possible reasons why the courts allow exceptions to the no-liability rule in cases involving a defendant who was in a special position of responsibility towards the plaintiff. Firstly, owing to his special position the defendant is easily identified, hence easily 'picked on'. Secondly, in most of the above cases the defendant has entered into a special position of responsibility by his own choice; parents usually choose to have children, teachers choose to become teachers, *etc.* It could be argued that by making this choice one voluntarily accepts a limitation of one's liberty.[129] Thirdly, most of the above protective duties, though not the parental duty, arise in the course of the defendant's profession. Through the defendant's salary, it may be argued, he is indirectly rewarded for the performance of his protective duty.

5.6 The Defendant is in a Special Position of Control over the Source of the Damage

One can roughly distinguish two types of situations in which the fact that the defendant can be said to be in a position of control over a potential source of damage gives rise to an affirmative duty to act. The defendant may have control over the potentially harmful conduct of others or over land.

124 *Barnes v Hampshire CC* [1969] 1 WLR 1563.

125 *Van Oppen v Bedford Charity Trustees* [1989] 3 All ER 389 at 414–415, *per* Croom-Johnson LJ. Cf. *Woodbridge School v Simon Paul Chittock* [2002] EWCA Civ 915.

126 *Kasapis v Laimos Bros.* [1959] 2 Lloyd's LR 378 at 381, *per* Salmon J.

127 *Knight v Home Office* [1990] 3 All ER 237 at 243, *per* Pill J.

128 *Costello v Chief Constable of the Northumbria Police* [1999] 1 All ER 550.

129 J.C. Smith and P. Burns, 'Donoghue v. Stevenson – The Not So Golden Anniversary' (1983) 46 MLR 147 at 157.

A. Control over the conduct of others

As a general rule, one is not responsible for injury or loss caused by the conduct of others.[130] There are however exceptions to this rule, as we learn from a judgment of Dixon J. in the High Court of Australia:

> The general rule is that one man is under no duty of controlling another man to prevent his doing damage to a third. There are, however, special relations which are the source of a duty of this nature. It appears now to be recognized that it is incumbent upon a parent who maintains control over a young child to take reasonable care so to exercise that control as to avoid conduct on his part exposing the person or property of others to unreasonable danger. Parental control, where it exists, must be exercised with due care to prevent the child inflicting intentional damage on others or causing damage by conduct involving unreasonable risk of injury to others.[131]

Not just the parent–child relationship,[132] but also most of the other relationships mentioned in the previous section give rise to a duty to control. Thus, in addition to the duty to protect its pupils against harm, a school is under a duty to prevent its pupils from causing harm to others.[133] Prison authorities may be liable for the damage caused by escaping prisoners.[134] Similarly, a mental hospital may be liable for injury caused by one of its patients while he was on authorized leave.[135]

The possible justifications for allowing an exception to the no-liability rule in cases in which the defendant is in a position of control over the conduct of others are the same as those mentioned in the previous section: the defendant is easily 'picked on', the defendant has usually entered into a position of responsibility by his own choice and in most cases he is rewarded for the performance of his affirmative duty.

A fortiori a duty may be imposed in cases where the defendant is both in a position of responsibility towards the plaintiff and in a position of control over the wrongdoer.[136] Thus, an employer is under a duty to prevent his employees from causing injury to their fellow workmen.[137] Likewise, prison authorities may be

[130] *Weld-Blundell v Stephens* [1920] AC 956 at 986, *per* Lord Sumner. The same is true in respect of self-inflicted harm. See *Tomlinson v Congleton Borough Council* [2003] UKHL 47 at nr 46, *per* Lord Hoffmann: 'A duty to protect against obvious risks or self-inflicted harm exists only in cases in which there is no genuine and informed choice, as in the case of employees, or some lack of capacity, such as the inability of children to recognise danger or the despair of prisoners which may lead them to inflict injury on themselves.' (References omitted.)

[131] *Smith v Leurs* (1945) 70 CLR 256 at 262 (footnotes omitted). This passage was quoted with apparent approval by both Lord Pearson and Lord Diplock in *Home Office v Dorset Yacht Co. Ltd* [1970] AC 1004 at 1055 and 1063 respectively.

[132] *Newton v Edgerley* [1959] 1 WLR 1031.

[133] *Carmarthenshire CC v Lewis* [1955] AC 549.

[134] *Home Office v Dorset Yacht Co. Ltd* [1970] AC 1004. It should however be noted that liability in this case might have had a different basis. In *Hill v Chief Constable of West Yorkshire* [1989] AC 53 at 61 Lord Keith suggested that the prison officers had created a 'potential situation of danger' by bringing the Borstal boys in the locality where the damage was done.

[135] *Holgate v Lancashire Mental Hospitals Board* [1937] 4 All ER 19.

[136] *Home Office v Dorset Yacht Co. Ltd* [1970] AC 1004 at 1062, *per* Lord Diplock and W.V.H. Rogers, *Winfield and Jolowicz on Tort* (16th edn 2002), p. 140.

[137] *Hudson v Ridge Manufacturing Co. Ltd* [1957] 2 QB 348.

liable for failing to prevent prisoners from injuring each other[138] or even from injuring themselves.[139] Hospitals owe a similar duty to a patient who is a known suicide risk.[140]

B. Control over Land

It is often said that ownership of land is a source of obligations as well as of rights.[141] Indeed, there are several areas of the law that impose affirmative duties on landowners.

Firstly, a claim may arise in negligence against an occupier who fails to neutralize a potential danger that occurs on his land. In *Goldman v Hargrave*[142] a tall red gum tree on the defendant's land was hit by lightening and caught fire. Instead of extinguishing the fire by putting water on it, the defendant decided to let the tree burn itself out. Five days later a fresh gust of wind revived the fire, which spread to the plaintiff's land and caused extensive damage. The Judicial Committee of the Privy Council decided in favour of imposing liability. In his speech Lord Wilberforce stated that an occupier's duty was 'one of a more positive character than merely to abstain from creating, or adding to, a source of danger or annoyance'.[143] The occupier was under a 'measured duty of care' to 'remove or reduce hazards to neighbours'.[144] Lord Wilberforce, however, did not rest there and added an important observation with regard to the standard of care required from such occupiers:

> (. . .) the standard ought to be to require of the occupier what is reasonable to expect of him in his individual circumstances. Thus, less must be expected of the infirm than of the able bodied (. . .)[145]

Thus, using the words of Atiyah, Lord Wilberforce 'subjectivized' the standard of care for cases in which the occupier did not create the original danger.[146]

The case of *Smith v Littlewoods Ltd*[147] also involved a fire which spread to neighbouring land, but differed from *Goldman v Hargrave* in that the fire was caused by vandals setting fire to a deserted cinema rather than by a natural event. With respect to the question whether the defendants should have secured their cinema against vandals, the two main speeches, Lord Mackay's and Lord Goff's, displayed some considerable differences in approach. Lord Mackay made no mention of the no-liability rule for nonfeasance and dismissed doctrinal objections

[138] *Ellis v Home Office* [1953] 2 All ER 149 and *Stenning v Home Office* [2002] EWCA Civ 793.

[139] *Kirkham v Chief Constable of Manchester* [1990] 2 QB 283 and *Reeves v Commissioner of Police of the Metropolis* [1999] 3 All ER 897. Cf. *Vellino v Chief Constable of the Greater Manchester Police* [2002] 3 All ER 78.

[140] *Selfe v Ilford and District Hospital Management Committee, The Times* 26 November 1970.

[141] *E.g.* W.V.H. Rogers, *Winfield and Jolowicz on Tort* (16th edn 2002), p. 141; P. Cane, *Atiyah's Accidents, Compensation and the Law* (6th edn 1999), p. 68.

[142] [1966] 2 All ER 989.

[143] *Ibid.* at 992.

[144] *Ibid.* at 995.

[145] *Ibid.* at 996.

[146] P. Cane, *Atiyah's Accidents, Compensation and the Law* (6th edn 1999), p. 69.

[147] [1987] AC 241.

against liability for the act of another with considerable ease.[148] Instead, he focused his attention on the requirement of foreseeability. Because human conduct is particularly unpredictable, he argued, the requirement of foreseeability will not readily be fulfilled:

> In summary I conclude, in agreement with both counsel, that what the reasonable man is bound to foresee in a case involving injury or damage by independent human agency, just as in cases where such agency plays no part, is the probable consequences of his own act or omission, but that, in such a case, a clear basis will be required on which to assert that the injury or damage is more than a mere possibility.[149]

Lord Mackay came to the conclusion that the Inner House of the Court of Session had failed to establish that the vandals' act of arson was not a probable consequence of leaving the cinema unattended and unlocked.

Lord Goff expressly rejected Lord Mackay's use of the 'mechanism of foreseeability'.[150] His Lordship commenced his speech by stressing the principle that in general one is not liable for the act of another; a principle which he said was founded on the rule of no liability for omission.[151] However, in exceptional circumstances a duty could be imposed to guard against the wrongdoing of others. Lord Goff mentioned some specific relationships that could give rise to such a duty before touching on a more general circumstance:

> (. . .) an occupier who negligently causes or permits a source of danger to be created on his land, and can reasonably foresee that third parties may trespass on his land and, interfering with the source of danger, may spark it off, thereby causing damage to the person or property of those in the vicinity, should be held liable to such a person for damage so caused to him.[152]

Since the cinema could not properly be described as a source of danger in the nature of a fire hazard, no liability ought to arise.[153]

Lord Goff added that once an occupier knew that a third party had created a fire on his premises, he ought to take reasonable steps to prevent such fire from damaging neighbouring property.[154] Again, however, the evidence of the case showed no such knowledge on the part of the defendant.

The law of nuisance, too, may create liability for a failure to act in situations involving relations between adjoining landowners. In general a person who unlawfully interferes with another's use or enjoyment of land is liable in nuisance.[155] However, the occupier of the premises from which the nuisance originates may be liable even if the nuisance was not created by himself or by someone for whom he is responsible. It was implied in the Court of Appeal's decision in *St Anne's Well Brewery Co. v Roberts* that an occupier is liable for damages caused to neighbouring

148 [1987] AC at 259–260. 149 *Ibid.* at 261. 150 *Ibid.* at 279.
151 *Ibid.* at 271. 152 *Ibid.* at 273. 153 *Ibid.* at 275–276.
154 *Ibid.* 274, *per* Lord Goff. Cf. *ibid.* at 268, *per* Lord Mackay.
155 W.V.H. Rogers, *Winfield and Jolowicz on Tort* (16th edn 2002), p. 508 with further references.

land by the collapse of a wall, if he knew or ought to have known that his predecessor's excavations had rendered the wall unstable.[156] Similarly, in *Sedleigh-Denfield v O'Callaghan*[157] an occupier of land was held liable for a nuisance that had been created by a trespasser on his land. The trespasser had placed a pipe in a ditch on the defendant's land in order to carry off rainwater. During a heavy rainstorm the pipe became choked with leaves, so that the water overflowed onto the plaintiff's land and caused damage. The House of Lords found for the plaintiff because even though the defendant had not created the nuisance, he was aware or ought to have been aware of its existence. Both Viscount Maugham and Lord Wright adopted a statement of law in Salmond's *The Law of Torts*:[158]

> When a nuisance has been created by the act of a trespasser, or otherwise without the act, authority, or permission of the occupier, the occupier is not responsible for that nuisance unless, with knowledge or means of knowledge of its existence, he suffers it to continue without taking reasonably prompt and efficient means for its abatement.[159]

In *Leakey v National Trust* Megaw LJ quoted the very same passage and applied its principles to a case in which the nuisance originated in a natural occurrence.[160] Echoing a statement by Lord Wilberforce in *Goldman v Hargrave*, the Court of Appeal recognized 'a general duty on occupiers in relation to hazards occurring on their land, whether natural or man-made'.[161] Moreover, Lord Wilberforce's 'subjectivized' standard of care was incorporated into the law of nuisance.[162] Hence in nuisance as in negligence, the financial and physical resources available to the particular occupier are taken into account when defining the standard of care.

Thirdly, there are statutory provisions that create affirmative duties. The Occupiers' Liability Act 1957 imposes a general duty on occupiers of land to take care to see that visitors and their belongings are reasonably safe.[163] The Occupiers' Liability Act 1984 creates an additional duty towards persons other than visitors in respect of risk of their suffering injury on the premises.[164] Although both Acts contain a reference to 'the circumstances of the case',[165] there is no specific mention of the physical and financial resources of the occupier. Hence it remains unclear whether the standard of care is objective or 'subjectivized'.[166] 'The foundation of occupier's liability is occupational control, *i.e.*, control associated with

156 *St Anne's Well Brewery Co. v Roberts* (1929) 140 LT 1 at 7, *per* Scrutton LJ.

157 [1940] AC 880.

158 *Ibid.* at 893–894, *per* Viscount Maugham and at 910, *per* Lord Wright.

159 J. Salmond, *The Law of Torts* (5th edn 1920), p. 260.

160 *Leakey v National Trust* [1980] QB 485 at 516. See also *Delaware Mansions Ltd v Westminster CC* [2001] 4 All ER 737 at 747–749, *per* Lord Cooke.

161 *Ibid.* at 516; cf. *Goldman v Hargrave* [1966] 2 All ER 989 at 995.

162 *Ibid.* at 524–527.

163 Occupiers' Liability Act 1957, ss. 2(2) and 1(3)(b).

164 Occupiers' Liability Act 1984, ss. 1(1) and 1(3).

165 Occupiers' Liability Act 1957, s. 2(2) and Occupiers' Liability Act 1984, s. 1(3)(c).

166 The pre-1984 case of *British Railways Board v Herrington* adopted a subjectivized standard towards trespassers; [1972] AC 877 at 899, *per* Lord Reid, at 920, *per* Lord Wilberforce and at 941–942, *per* Lord Diplock.

and arising from presence in and use of or activity in the premises'.[167] Thus, the dangers against which the occupier is required to guard are not necessarily dangers arising from a defect in the land itself, but can equally arise from the use of the land. In *Cunningham & Others v Reading Football Club Ltd*[168] the defendant club was held liable under the 1957 Act for failing to prevent hooligans from injuring police officers by throwing missiles. These missiles included, besides the 'usual' sharpened coins, pieces of concrete that had been broken off the 'east terrace'. According to Drake J. a 'reasonably prudent and careful occupier' would not have left the concrete in the bad state it was in, especially in a situation in which it was probable that the concrete would be broken up and used as missiles.[169] The Highways Act 1980 imposes a comparable duty on the highway authority to maintain the highway.[170]

The justification for creating an exception to the rule of no liability in cases of occupiers of land is twofold. Firstly, the occupier is in the best position to recognize and remove the risk, hence easily 'picked on'. Secondly, it has been argued that the ownership of land should entail responsibilities as well as rights.[171]

[167] *Wheat v E. Lacon & Co. Ltd* [1966] AC 552 at 589, *per* Lord Pearson and Occupiers' Liability Act 1984, s. 1(2)(a).

[168] [1992] PIQR P141.

[169] *Ibid.* at P152.

[170] Highways Act 1980, s. 41(1).

[171] P. Cane, *Atiyah's Accidents, Compensation and the Law* (6th edn 1999), p. 68. Cf. J.C. Smith and P. Burns, 'Donoghue v. Stevenson – The Not So Golden Anniversary' (1983) 46 MLR 147 at 158.

6

Towards a More Consistent Approach

In this first Part, the legal systems of France, Germany, and England have been investigated in an attempt to assess their general approach towards cases of nonfeasance. If we allow ourselves to reflect upon the results of this investigation, we will find that there are many similarities.

In the beginning of this century both French and German courts, like their English counterparts, were reluctant to impose liability for nonfeasance in the absence of a specific duty to act. The courts in all three countries recognized specific duties to act, though only on a case-by-case basis. The Second World War appears to have provided the metaphorical junction at which the French system went its own way. In both France and Germany, the legislators introduced a duty to rescue in criminal law. The German courts refused to translate this duty into a private law duty to rescue and appear to have continued to create affirmative duties on an incremental basis. Conversely, the French courts were quick to recognize a duty to rescue in private law. Eventually, this led to a breach with the rigid feasance–nonfeasance distinction in the *Branly* case in 1951.

Although German and English law appear to have continued to coincide, in that the distinction between feasance and nonfeasance was upheld and duties to act were created incrementally, we observed some important differences. Probably the most noteworthy difference is that, with an open category of *Verkehrspflichten*, German courts are less restrictive in recognizing new affirmative duties than their English counterparts. Another difference, although of more importance in theory than in practice, is the German liability for intentionally inflicted harm (§ 826 *BGB*), which also applies to cases of nonfeasance.

Returning to the parable of the good Samaritan, we can conclude that the priest and the Levite would have had little to fear from English law. Considering that they did not actively contribute to the wounded man's suffering, they would have escaped liability:

> (. . .) both priest and Levite ensured performance of any common law duty of care to the stricken traveller when, by crossing to the other side of the road, they avoided any risk of throwing up dust in his wounds (. . .).[1]

[1] *Jaensch v Coffey* (High Court of Australia), (1984) 54 ALR 417 at 439–440, *per* Dean J.

A natural consequence, Lord Hoffmann might say, of 'the individualist values of the common law'.[2] By contrast, in Germany the priest and the Levite would have been liable in criminal law and arguably under § 826 *BGB* if it could have been established that they 'passed by on the other side' with the intent to harm. In French law they would also have incurred criminal liability, while the victim would have had a claim for damages in negligence.

The question we need to ask ourselves is whether English law should start moving towards a breach with the rigid feasance–nonfeasance distinction. It is here submitted that it should. It has been argued that the law should reinforce the rules of our shared morality wherever it is not oppressive, impracticable, or pointless.[3] Of course, we need not accept that the moral obligation to aid other people should necessarily be translated into a legal duty. However, we cannot ignore the sense of unease caused by the fact that by upholding the feasance–nonfeasance distinction the law not only fails to encourage altruistic behaviour, but in effect discourages it. As it stands, the law gives potential interveners the choice between apathy, which is rewarded with legal immunity, and intervention, which comes with the threat of legal repercussions. The well-informed and calculating bystander will tend towards apathy.[4]

A second argument is one of consistency. Our present legal regime aims to compensate loss at the expense of the person whose negligent behaviour caused it. Or, as Lord Hutton put it in *Darker v Chief Constable of West Midlands*, 'the predominant requirement of public policy is that those who suffer a wrong should have a right to a remedy'.[5] If we accept our present regime, the exclusion of one particular type of negligent behaviour – nonfeasance – from this regime needs to be justified. And, as we observed in Chapter 3, it is doubtful whether it can. Of the many justifications that have been put forward, only two could withstand scrutiny.

One was the '*quid pro quo*' argument; the law does not give interveners anything in return for their intervention, so, Lord Hoffmann stated, 'there must be some special reason why he should have to put his hand in his pocket'.[6] As we shall see in Part II, it is not altogether certain whether the law does not award interveners any '*quid pro quo*'. However, to the extent that it does not, why should it necessarily follow that no duty to intervene should be imposed? It may be, as indeed it will here be argued, that *both* areas of the law require reconsideration.

At the very heart of the distinction, however, is the 'freedom' argument, and more particularly Lord Nicholls's version of it. Lord Nicholls, it may be remembered,

[2] *Tomlinson v Congleton Borough Council* [2003] UKHL 47 at nr 47.

[3] A.M. Honoré, 'Law, Morals and Rescue' in J.M. Ratcliffe (ed.), *The Good Samaritan and the Law* (1966), pp. 225 ff., reprinted and expanded in A.M. Honoré, *Making Law Bind, Essays Legal and Philosophical* (1987), pp. 256 ff. at p. 269.

[4] See also D. Birnbacher, *Tun und Unterlassen* (1995), p. 264.

[5] *Darker v Chief Constable of West Midlands* [2000] 3 WLR 747 at 771. See also *ibid.*, at p. 750, *per* Lord Hope: 'It is the principle that a wrong ought not to be without a remedy'.

[6] *Stovin v Wise* [1996] 3 All ER 801 at 819.

argued that the main problem with imposing a general duty to intervene is that it does not leave the defendant the option of avoiding being subjected to this duty. 'He who wishes to act must act carefully or not at all. (. . .) With liability for omissions, however, a person is not offered a choice. The law compels him to act when left to himself he might do nothing.'[7] Yet, as we observed in Section 3.2 (a), this is a distinction of degree, not of principle. Rather than impossible, it is on average *less easy* to avoid being subjected to affirmative duties than it is of negative duties. And because the distinction is one of degree, the preferred response is to adjust the measure of care that is required, not deny a duty altogether. Indeed, Lord Nicholls himself discussed this possibility. Having referred to Lord Wilberforce's speech in *Goldman v Hargrave*, his Lordship stated:

> The solution adopted is to have regard to the circumstances of the individual. He must act as would a reasonable person in his position. The standard of reasonableness is to be measured by what may reasonably be expected of the defendant in his individual circumstances. Where action calls for expenditure, the court if necessary will have regard to the financial resources of the defendant.[8]

Earlier in this book, we have already encountered similar 'subjectivized' versions of the standard of care. In *Surtees v Royal Borough of Kingston upon Thames*[9] it was held that a mother owes her children a duty to protect them, but that the standard of care depends on the domestic circumstances of the individual parent.[10] Similarly, we observed that the French courts pay more attention to the personal characteristics of the defendant when defining the standard of care in cases of nonfeasance. Thus, we found that the French courts are not likely to hold someone liable who does not understand that his intervention is necessary, nor someone who is physically or mentally unable to render aid.

The reason for this distinction is evident. In most cases involving misfeasance, we can be reasonably expected to anticipate being subjected to a negative duty of care. Thus, if we go hunting we know we will have to observe the hunting laws and exercise due care. If we find these duties too burdensome, *e.g.* if we cannot afford a gun licence or if we do not have enough patience to take the appropriate safety precautions, we have the option not to go hunting. Accordingly, in cases of feasance, the financial resources and physical and mental abilities of the defendant are often ignored.[11] However, in many cases of nonfeasance – as in some cases of feasance – this possibility to anticipate being subjected to a duty of care is virtually absent. For example, if I walk over a bridge and a woman falls into the water, the fact that I cannot swim or that I am deaf and did not hear her screams for help cannot reasonably be held against me. In those cases there is good reason to pay more attention than usual to the individual circumstances of the defendant.

7 *Ibid.* at 809.

8 *Stovin v Wise* [1996] 3 All ER 801 at 809. See *Goldman v Hargrave* [1966] 2 All ER 989 at 995–996, *per* Lord Wilberforce.

9 [1992] PIQR P101.

10 *Ibid.* at P111 and P111–P112, *per* Stocker LJ and at P124, *per* the Vice-Chancellor.

11 P. Cane, *The Anatomy of Tort Law* (1997), p. 43.

However, it should be noted that the absence of the possibility to anticipate being subjected to a duty is not confined to cases of nonfeasance. Nor, indeed, is there such an absence in all cases of nonfeasance. In some cases of professional undertaking, for example, the defendant knew the duty of care required of people within his profession, and could have anticipated it. Thus, there is no reason to apply a more 'subjectivized' standard of care in cases like *White v Jones*. Indeed, it is debatable whether *Goldman v Hargrave* was a case in which the possibility of anticipation was absent. Salmond appears to have been of the opinion that landowners could anticipate being subjected to a duty of care:

> (. . .) an occupier is liable even for a continuing nuisance which already existed on the premises when he first entered into possession of them; for it is his duty either to refrain from taking possession of such premises or else to abate the nuisance so soon as he becomes the occupier.[12]

If a landowner does not have the financial resources to neutralize hazards that may occur on his land, should we not expect him to consider selling part of his land or indeed all of it?[13] The application of a more 'subjectivized' standard of care is appropriate only in cases in which the defendant could not reasonably be expected to anticipate being subjected to the duty concerned.

Let us now return to the example with which we started. The priest and the Levite could not reasonably be expected to have anticipated their encounter with a wounded man in need of their help. This does not prevent us from imposing a duty on them to render assistance. However, in establishing whether their behaviour was reasonable, special attention ought to be paid to their individual circumstances. If, for example, they both had a bad back and no 'beast' on which to put the man, they could be forgiven for their refusal to carry the man. After all, the law requires reasonable behaviour, not heroism. Yet this does not mean that the law should not oblige them to 'make the best of a difficult situation' and attempt to obtain assistance from a third party.[14] If anyone were to object that it would be too difficult the draw the line between a reasonable and an unreasonable refusal to intervene, they should be reminded that this difficulty 'has continually to be faced in the law'.[15]

[12] J. Salmond, *The Law of Torts* (5th edn 1920), p. 259.

[13] Cf. P. Cane, *Atiyah's Accidents, Compensation and the Law* (6th edn 1999), p. 69 and F.H. Lawson and B.S. Markesinis, *Tortious Liability for Unintentional Harm in the Common Law and the Civil Law*, Vol I (1982), p. 77.

[14] K.J. Kemp, *Delictual Liability for Omissions* (1978) (Unpublished thesis, University of Port Elizabeth, South Africa), p. 386.

[15] J.B. Ames, *Lectures on Legal History* (1913), p. 451 ('Law and Morals').

PART II

GRANTING A CLAIM TO THE INTERVENER

7

The Different Measures of Recovery and their Terminology

When discussing the rights of the good Samaritan, the question that appears to surface most often is whether he should be entitled to 'reimbursement of his expenses'. Yet, reimbursement of expenses is by no means the only measure of recovery that might be made available to him. Instead of focusing on his expenditure, the law might allow him to recover the loss he suffered ('compensation'). Alternatively, he might be entitled to claim payment for services rendered ('remuneration') or be given a further 'reward'. Finally, he might be granted a claim for the value of the benefits he conferred ('restitution'). Before we can start investigating to what measure of recovery, if any, the good Samaritan is or should be entitled, we must first agree on the meaning of each of these terms. For while 'reimbursement', 'compensation', 'remuneration', 'reward', and 'restitution' are part of every lawyer's vocabulary, these terms can have many different meanings, depending on the context in which they are employed. The aim of this short chapter is merely to avoid confusion by defining the terms that will here be used at the outset. It is not suggested thereby that these definitions are in any way superior to those adopted in other writings on the subject.

'Reimbursement', from the French '*remboursement*' means little more than 'repayment'. Thus, the term can be used to describe the repayment of a loan: the borrower 'reimburses' the lender.[1] However, more recently the term has been confined to three party relationships: a borrower '*repays*' his lender, but if a surety has already paid his loan he '*reimburses*' the latter. Reimbursement is then no longer synonymous with 'repayment', but is narrower. It is used only in cases in which, as it was put by Harris, 'the defendant is obliged to repay the claimant in respect of money paid by the plaintiff to a third person'.[2] It is this narrower notion of reimbursement that will be adopted here. It is perhaps worth noting that a different definition is adopted by Lord Goff and Professor Jones. These writers employ the term to describe situations in which the defendant is obliged to 'reimburse' the plaintiff, *other than on the basis of a contract*, and *to the extent that the defendant has*

[1] Cf. *Bank of New South Wales v Campbell* (1886) 11 App Cas 192.

[2] D.R. Harris in J. Morris (ed.), *Chitty on Contracts*, Vol I (22nd edn 1961), p. 664. See also the 28th edition of this work, at p. 1474.

benefited from his payment.[3] Our definition is both broader and narrower. 'Broader', because it includes repayment of expenses on the basis of a contract, *e.g.* in the context of contractual indemnity to sureties,[4] and 'narrower', because it will not be applied to situations where the plaintiff can only recover his expenses in so far as they represent a benefit on the part of the defendant. In the latter type of case, the term 'restitution' shall be used (see below).

From this right to reimbursement must be distinguished the right to be 'compensated'. It has been said that the distinction between reimbursement of expenses and compensation of loss is sometimes 'obscure'.[5] This is hardly surprising, considering that expenses are in truth a type of (economic) loss, albeit voluntarily suffered. It could therefore be argued that reimbursement of expenses constitutes a sub-category under the larger heading of 'compensation'. However, in order to avoid confusion, the terms will for present purposes be regarded as mutually exclusive. Thus, unless it is otherwise indicated, 'compensation' will here be used to denote the 'making up' for losses other than expenses voluntarily incurred.

When it comes to 'remuneration' for services rendered, there is again room for semantic overlap. For the verb 'to remunerate', from the Latin *remunerare*, has a twofold meaning. In its first meaning, it denotes nothing more specific than 'to repay'. In this sense, it covers both of the two terms discussed earlier. Not only can one be remunerated for one's expenses,[6] but one can even be remunerated for one's losses. For example, in *The Lamentable Tragedy of Locrine*, King Brutus's son Albanact can be heard to say:

> And you good fellowes for your houses burnt,
> We will remunerate you store of gold, (. . .)[7]

However, 'remuneration' is much more commonly used in its second meaning: 'payment for services rendered'. It is in this sense that the term will be used here. As Blackburn J once put it:

> (. . .) 'remuneration' (. . .) means a *quid pro quo*. If a man gives his services, whatever consideration he gets for giving his services seems to me a remuneration for them.[8]

Payment does not need to be adequate in order to be called remuneration. Child labourers in the Third World may be shamefully underpaid, yet for present purposes their services will be regarded as 'remunerated'. This distinguishes

[3] Lord Goff of Chieveley and G. Jones, *The Law of Restitution* (6th edn 2002), pp. 439–440.

[4] See also J.H. Munkman, *The Law of Quasi-Contracts* (1950), pp. 19–20.

[5] K. Takayanagi, 'Liability without Fault in the Modern Civil and Common Law-II' (1921) 16 Ill LR 268–303 at 270.

[6] *E.g.* R. Cobden, *Speeches on Peace, Financial Reform, Colonial Reform, and Other Subjects* (1849), p. 34: '(. . .) our exclusive trade with the colonies remunerates us for the expense of colonial establishments'.

[7] *The Lamentable Tragedy of Locrine* (1595), ascribed to William Shakespeare, Act 2, Scene 4 (in some editions this is Scene 3).

[8] *R. v Postmaster General* (1876) 1 QBD 658 at 663.

'remuneration' from the next measure of recovery to be discussed here: 'reward'. In everyday usage, reward and remuneration are often used interchangeably.[9] Indeed, in the law of salvage the 'salvage reward' incorporates elements of reimbursement, compensation as well as remuneration.[10] However, the term will here be used in the more narrow sense of 'payment over and above the other measures of recovery, by way of encouragement of interveners'.[11]

Finally, a word or two should here be said on the meaning of the word 'restitution'. 'A word or two' because this is neither the time nor the place to rehearse the many learned writings on the meaning of the term. Suffice it to say that in this book we shall speak of 'restitution' when the defendant is forced to give up a benefit – or its value in money – to the claimant.[12]

[9] *E.g. The Goring* (CA) [1987] 1 QB 687 at 690.

[10] International Convention on Salvage 1989, art. 13.1(f), on which F.D. Rose, *Kennedy and Rose; The Law of Salvage* (6th edn 2002), pp. 664–671.

[11] Cf. F.D. Rose, 'Restitution for the Rescuer' (1989) 9 OJLS 167–204 at 200; A. Burrows, *The Law of Restitution* (2nd edn 2002), p. 321; Lord Goff of Chieveley and G. Jones, *The Law of Restitution* (6th edn 2002), p. 458 and G. Virgo, *The Principles of the Law of Restitution* (1999), p. 308.

[12] Cf. P.B.H. Birks, *An Introduction to the Law of Restitution* (1985), pp. 9–16 and L.D. Smith, 'The Province of the Law of Restitution' (1992) 71 Can BR 672–699. The definition here adopted incorporates both 'disgorgement' and 'restitution' as defined by Smith.

8

Theoretical Arguments against Granting a Remedy to the Intervener

It is a principle of Stoic philosophy that we have a *moral* duty to show gratitude to those who assist us, by returning the favour. Thus, Aristotle wrote in his *Ethica Nicomachea* that, as a general rule, we have a duty to repay services that have been done to us.[1] Indeed, Cicero argued that no duty is more indispensable than that of returning a kindness.[2] It is probably safe to say that we still regard it as our moral duty to be grateful to – and act in a manner that reflects this gratitude towards – those who come to our assistance in our time of need. However, when asked whether this moral duty should have a legal equivalent and, if so, what the scope of this duty should be, the opinions vary strongly. In his *De Beneficiis*, Seneca argued that the beauty of 'giving' lies in the fact that one leaves it wholly to the courtesy of the receivers. Hence, by rendering ingratitude actionable in the court of law, we would 'corrupt two of the most worthy things in human life, namely man's gratitude and generosity'.[3] 'Moreover', he argued, 'for the application of such a law all the courts in the world would hardly be sufficient.'[4] The common law, too, has traditionally denied the existence of a legal duty to reimburse, compensate, remunerate or even reward the altruistic intervener for his assistance. In the case of *Glenn v Savage*, the Supreme Court of Oregon stated the reasons why there should be no such duty. The judgment echoes both of Seneca's arguments, and adds a third one:

> The great and leading rule of law is to deem an act done for the benefit of another, without his request, as a voluntary act of courtesy, for which no action can be sustained. The world abounds with acts of this kind, done upon no request; but would more abound with ruinous litigation, and the overthrow of personal rights and civil freedom, if the law was otherwise. (. . .) The law will never permit a friendly act, or such as was intended to be an act of kindness or benevolence, to be afterwards converted into a pecuniary demand. It would be doing violence to some of the kindest and best effusions of the heart to suffer them afterwards to be perverted by sordid avarice.[5]

[1] Aristotle, *Nicomachean Ethics*, Book IX, Ch. 2.

[2] M.T. Cicero, *De Officiis*, *lib.* I, *cap.* XV.

[3] L.A. Seneca, *De Beneficiis*, III, VII, 3: '*Ita duas res, quibus in vita humana nihil pulchrius est, corrumpimus, gratum hominem et beneficium*'.

[4] *Ibid.*: '*Adice nunc, quod huic uni legi omnia fora vix sufficient.*'

[5] *Glenn v Savage* 13 Pac 442 (Sup. Ct of Or. 1887) at 448, *per* Strahan J.

In this passage one can distinguish the following three main arguments against the imposition of a duty to reward or remunerate the good Samaritan or even to merely reimburse his expenses: granting a claim would lead to 'ruinous litigation', it would lead to 'the overthrow of personal rights and civil freedom' and it would do 'violence to some of the kindest and best effusions of the heart'. In this chapter each of these arguments will be discussed. In addition, we shall investigate whether a change in the law might lead to abuse by meddlesome interveners looking to make a profit.

8.1 Granting a Claim would lead to Ruinous Litigation

Of the three arguments put forward by the Supreme Court of Oregon, this one is probably most easily countered. First and foremost, it lacks a factual basis. Evidence from the continent would suggest that the courts are perfectly capable of dealing with an increased volume of litigation on issues of voluntary intervention. Yet, it is by no means certain that the introduction of a general principle would lead to such an increase. Indeed, it is equally possible that the volume of litigation on the subject would decrease instead of increase. While English law generally denies the intervener a claim, it has – as we shall see in Chapter 11, below – created a number of exceptions to this general rule in different areas of the law. Almost invariably, these exceptions have been contentious and have required further elaboration in subsequent case law. Much of the litigation concerning the scope of these exceptions would be rendered superfluous by the introduction of a general principle. Any prediction of whether the sum of the litigation concerning exceptions to the English rule would be exceeded in volume by the litigation on the scope of a new principle, could only be speculative.

However, even if we were to accept that litigation would increase with the introduction of a general principle, this would not *per se* be a reason to decide against it. If justice requires that the voluntary intervener be allowed a claim, then perhaps the state should ensure that there are enough judges to enable the intervener to enforce his claim.

8.2 Granting a Claim would lead to the Overthrow of Personal Rights and Civil Freedom

In *Falcke v Scottish Imperial Insurance Co.* Bowen LJ famously defended the refusal of English law to grant the altruistic intervener a right to recover his expenditure:

> The general principle is, beyond all question, that work or labour done or money expended by one man to preserve or benefit the property of another do not according to English law create any lien upon the property saved or benefited, nor, even if standing

alone,[6] create any obligation to repay the expenditure. Liabilities are not to be forced on people behind their backs any more than you can confer a benefit upon a man against his will.[7]

The principle that neither liabilities nor benefits ought to be forced on people, finds its roots in the ideal of 'freedom of will', or, as the Second Restatement of Restitution puts it, 'self-determination'.[8] Ideally, everyone should be able to decide for themselves what benefits they receive and what obligations they incur. In its long history, this principle has by no means been advocated by common lawyers uniquely. Indeed, the Roman provisions regarding 'gifts' can serve to illustrate an early application of the principle. It is generally presumed that under Justinian a *donatio inter vivos* required the receiver's consent.[9] This view draws support from *D.* 39.5.19.2, in which Ulpian is reported to have written:

A gift given as an act of liberality cannot be acquired by someone who does not want it.[10]

These days, all the major codes of continental Europe regard 'gift' as a contract. This contract is not concluded unless and until both parties agree to it.[11] With regard to the German provision, § 516 *BGB*, the *Münchener Kommentar* identifies the following general principle:

(. . .) the *BGB* does not merely [take] the donator's unilateral intention to confer a benefit [into account], but requires a *contract*. Here is expressed the general principle underlying the *BGB*, that no one needs to allow anything to be forced on him.[12]

[6] Goff and Jones indicate that the comma between 'nor' and 'even' ought to be placed between 'even' and 'if': Lord Goff of Chieveley and G. Jones, *The Law of Restitution* (6th edn 2002), p. 453, footnote 59.

[7] *Falcke v Scottish Imperial Insurance Co.* (1886) 34 Ch D 234, at 248. See also *China Pacific S.A. v Food Corporation of India* [1982] AC 939 at 961, *per* Lord Diplock.

[8] Restatement (Second) of Restitution, § 2. See also J.P. Dawson, 'The Self-Serving Intermeddler', (1974) 87 Harvard LR 1409–1458, at 1409.

[9] Cicero, *Topica* 8: '*Neque donationem sine acceptione intellegi (posse?)*'; J.M. Ricard, *Traité des Donations Entre-Vifs et Testamentaires*, Vol 1 (last edn 1685), p. 186 (*Partie* I, *Chapitre*, IV, *Section* I); J.E. Goudsmit, *The Pandects*, translated by R. de Tracy Gould (1873), p. 193 (§ 68) with further references in footnote 1; J.B. Moyle, *Imperatoris Iustiniani Institutionum* (5th edn 1912), p. 232. Cf. for the *ius commune* R. Zimmermann, *The Law of Obligations, Roman Foundations of the Civilian Tradition* (1996), p. 499. *Contra*: F.C. von Savigny, *System des heutigen Römischen Rechts*, Band 4 (1841), pp. 148 ff. (§ 160) and I. II.VII.2, in which it is stated that a *donatio inter vivos* was complete and binding once the *donator* had manifested his intention to give.

[10] '*Non potest liberalitas nolenti adquiri*'.

[11] Art. 894 *C.civ.* (notwithstanding the fact that this article defines a *donation* as '*un acte*' rather than '*un contrat*'; cf. P. Esmein, *Aubry & Rau, Droit Civil*, Vol X (6 edn 1954), p. 409 (§ 646), with further references in footnote 1), § 516 *BGB*, art. 769 of the Italian Code and art. 496 of the Greek Code.

[12] H.P. Westermann (ed.), *Münchener Kommentar zum Bürgerlichen Gesetzbuch, Band* 3 (3rd edn 1995), § 516, *Rdnr* 9: '*(. . .) das BGB [stellt] nicht auf den einseitigen Bereicherungswillen des Schenkers ab, sondern erfordert einen* Vertrag. *Darin kommt zunächst der allgemeine Grundsatz des BGB zum Ausdruck, daß niemand sich etwas gegen seinen Willen aufdrängen lassen muß.* Cf. also: *Motive zu dem Entwurfe eines Bürgerlichen Gesetzbuches für das Deutsche Reich, Band* 2 (1888), p. 288. Cf. for the position in English law J. Hill, 'The Role of the Donee's Consent in the Law of Gift' (2001) 117 LQR 127–149.

Thus, both civil and common lawyers have advocated the ideal of self-determination.[13] However, it has never been suggested that 'self-determination' is or should be the only principle determining our rights and duties. In truth, both common law and civil law systems have created substantial inroads into the principle. Some of these inroads are less obvious than others. Whenever the courts create an 'objective test', for example, the ideal of self-determination is to a certain extent released. If a man agrees to buy oats in the belief that they are old oats, he will be bound 'if he so conducts himself that a reasonable man would believe that he was assenting to the terms proposed by the other party', 'whatever a man's real intention may be'.[14] More obvious inroads have been created in the area of the law of unjust enrichment. If I pay you a hundred pounds in the mistaken belief that I owed you that sum, I can claim restitution of the money. Thus, I have effectively 'forced' an obligation on you and there was little you could do to prevent it. Indeed, as Birks stated in his *Introduction to the Law of Restitution*, the entire law of unjust enrichment can be seen as an inroad into the principle of self-determination:

> Statements to the effect that liabilities are not to be forced on people behind their backs or against their will are unhelpful. (. . .) All restitutionary liabilities are technically imposed without the consent of the defendant. Only the implied contract theory of restitution could conceal this analytical fact.[15]

Hence, if we accept the validity of the principle of self-determination, we cannot but acknowledge that the law has created many exceptions to it. The question then becomes whether there are good reasons to create a similar exception for the benefit of interveners. Some potential reasons will be investigated in the next chapter.

Yet, in a 1999 article in the Michigan Law Review, Dagan appears to have gone a step further than that. In his view, to grant a claim to the intervener would not be contrary to the principle of self-determination in the first place.[16] 'Indeed', he claimed, 'liberty (. . .) can justify, in certain circumstances, acknowledging good Samaritan claims for reimbursement of expenses incurred (. . .)'.[17] Central to Dagan's theory is the presumption that the present system deters intervention:

> The reason for this disincentive is straightforward: because negotiation is impractical, a potential benefactor would fear that the beneficiary – whom she does not know and can only presume to be as rational and not particularly other-regarding as she is – would refuse ex post to reimburse her for her expenses, from which the beneficiary has already benefitted.[18]

[13] See also J. Voet, *Commentarius ad Pandectas* (ed. 1757), p. 576 (*lib.* XXXIX, *tit.* V, 11): '*non enim nolenti tribuuntur beneficia, aut liberalitates acquiruntur*'.

[14] *Smith v Hughes*, [1871] LR 6 QB 597 at 607, *per* Blackburn J.

[15] P.B.H. Birks, *An Introduction to the Law of Restitution* (1985), p. 195.

[16] H. Dagan, 'In Defense of the Good Samaritan' (1999) 97 Michigan LR 1152–1200 at 1165.

[17] *Ibid.* at 1155. [18] *Ibid.* at 1164.

As we will see in Section 9.1, below, it is probably correct to say that at least some potential interveners are deterred by the uncertainty surrounding their reimbursement. Then, logically, a majority of potential beneficiaries would want to offer reimbursement of expenses to anyone who came to their rescue or, more generally, to anyone whose intervention on their behalf was expected to be cost-beneficial. Yet, the present system ignores the will of this majority for the sole reason that they found themselves in a situation in which they were unable to express their wishes:

> Is it reasonable for the law to undermine the preferences of the majority of (rational) beneficiaries (by discouraging beneficial interferences) in the name of preventing any boundary crossing when we cannot be absolutely certain that the beneficiary would have voluntarily consented? Is it reasonable to do so even in circumstances where beneficiaries have no way of communicating their (frequent) approval or (in the rare case of idiosyncratic beneficiaries) disapproval?[19]

This is no doubt a powerful argument. However, to conclude that to grant the intervener a claim would therefore be consistent with the principle of self-determination is to stretch that principle beyond its natural boundaries. The mere fact that a legal rule honours the presumed will of a majority does not mean that any person who happens to belong to that majority has thereby been allowed to determine which rights he or she obtained and which obligations he or she incurred. In truth, the very nature of a typical emergency situation makes it impossible for either party to exercise a right of self-determination. With that in mind, it might make sense for the law to aim for a rule that represents the interest of the majority of interveners and beneficiaries. This argument will re-surface in the next chapter, under the heading of 'Interveners do not act voluntarily (compulsion)' (Chapter 9.2).

8.3 Granting a Claim would do Violence to some of the Kindest and Best Effusions of the Heart

As we will see in Chapter 10, the Continental European systems allow the good Samaritan to recover the expenses he made for the benefit of the wounded man. If we believe the Supreme Court of Oregon, these systems are doing violence to 'some of the kindest and best effusions of the heart' by allowing them afterwards to be 'perverted by sordid avarice'. Yet, how exactly would the granting of a claim do violence to the kindest of intentions? Let us presume that the good Samaritan had the kindest intentions we can possibly imagine and did not expect anything, not even gratitude, in return for his assistance. If we would nevertheless make a claim available to him, would we be doing violence to his noble intentions? Some might argue that it would become impossible for the good Samaritan to prove that

[19] H. Dagan, 'In Defense of the Good Samaritan' (1999) 97 Michigan LR 1152–1200 at 1164–5.

he acted out of altruism.[20] But why would it be? Surely, the mere fact that the Samaritan would have a right to claim does not mean that he is obliged to exercise this right. Hence if he wants to prove himself a true altruist, he can simply refrain from bringing his claim.[21]

However, even if an intervener were to decide to bring a claim, this would not necessarily negate the altruistic nature of his intervention.[22] Whether that would be the case would largely depend on the type of claim that was brought. Salvors at sea, for example, can claim a positive reward for their intervention, if successful.[23] Therefore, it is not unfair to say that if they exercise their claim they probably aim at commercial gain and that they are not moved by altruistic considerations. If, however, the courts were to allow recovery for expenditure and/or compensation only, interveners would not gain anything by their intervention and would perform a gratuitous service. Hence, it would be unfair to deny the altruistic nature of their conduct altogether.[24]

Thus, the introduction of a right to claim reimbursement or even a reward would not violate the intervener's altruistic intentions. It would merely enable the intervener to establish the true nature of his intentions. If they are entirely altruistic, he will not exercise his claim; if they are altruistic, though not to the extent that he is willing to bear the burden of the expenses, he will claim reimbursement of his expenses and/or compensation. If, on the other hand, his intentions are not altruistic at all, the law of salvage – if applicable –might allow him to claim a reward.

8.4 To Grant a Claim would lead to Abuse

In a note on quasi-contracts, John Austin briefly considered the usefulness of a general principle entitling the intervener to recover. If such a principle were not admitted at all, he thought, useful actions would be performed less often. On the other hand 'if pushed to a certain extent, it would lead to inconvenient and impertinent intermeddling, with the view of catching a reward'.[25] Similar concerns were expressed by Eyre CJ in *Nicholson v Chapman*[26] and by Lord Macnaghten in *The Gas Float Whitton No. 2*.[27]

[20] Cf. similar arguments by Posner and Landes with respect to the introduction of a duty to intervene, discussed in Part I, Section 3.4 of this book. W.M. Landes and R.A. Posner, 'Salvors, Finders, Good Samaritans, and Other Rescuers: an Economic Study of Law and Altruism', (1978) 7 J.Leg.Stud. 83–128 at 94–95 and 124.

[21] S. Levmore, 'Waiting for Rescue: An Essay on the Evolution and Incentive Structure of the Law of Affirmative Obligations', (1986) 72 Virginia LR 879–941 at 886.

[22] H. Dagan, 'In Defense of the Good Samaritan', (1999) 97 Michigan LR 1152–1200 at 1166: 'By allowing claims of Good Samaritans, do the courts in fact obliterate altruism?'

[23] See below, Section 11.9.

[24] S.J. Stoljar, *The Law of Quasi-Contract* (2nd edn 1989), p. 220 speaks in this context of 'a kindness which does not exclude [their] intention to charge for [their] services'.

[25] J. Austin, *Lectures on Jurisprudence*, Vol III (1863), p. 133.

[26] (1793) 2 H Bl 254, 126 ER 536 at 258–259, quoted below in Section 11.1.

[27] [1897] AC 337 at 349.

While the possibility of abuse might have some force as an argument against the introduction of a right to a reward, it is considerably weaker if all we intend to do is to give the intervener a claim for reimbursement and/or compensation. 'It is not reasonably to be anticipated', Edward Hope said, 'that a policy thus carefully limited would breed overnight a nation of busy-bodies anxious to perform useless and meddlesome services for others and to try their luck with the courts'.[28] After all, no calculating person would get excited at the prospect of 'breaking even'. Yet, even if we were to grant rewards to voluntary interveners, must it really be supposed that cynical members of the public would be prompted to create emergencies to earn some easy money? There is little evidence for such a supposition, as was admitted by Ralph Gibson LJ in *The Goring*:

> There is no more reason to fear that extension of the law of salvage to non-tidal waters would cause any significant increase in the number of craft going adrift in such waters than there is ground for believing that the existence of the right of salvage in tidal waters has had any such effect there.[29]

More importantly, if justice requires the introduction of a general right, the mere possibility of abuse should not be enough to reverse it. There are many existing doctrines that are open to abuse, not least of which the law of negligence. The courts are generally capable of separating the malicious from the meritorious claims.[30] Should the odd bad Samaritan that slips through the net be allowed to deny his good fellow countrymen?

[28] E.W. Hope, 'Officiousness', (1929–30) 15 Cornell LQ 25–53 and 205–242 at 36. See also S. Levmore, 'Waiting for Rescue: An Essay on the Evolution and Incentive Structure of the Law of Affirmative Obligations', (1986) 72 Virginia LR 879–941 at 886 and Lord Goff of Chieveley and G. Jones, *The Law of Restitution* (6th edn 2002), p. 456, footnote 81.

[29] *The Goring* (CA) [1987] 1 QB 687 at 709.

[30] F.D. Rose, 'Restitution for the Rescuer' (1989) 9 OJLS 167–204 at 194.

9

Theoretical Arguments in Favour of Granting a Remedy to the Intervener

9.1 Intervention ought to be Encouraged rather than Discouraged

In Continental Europe, one of the main arguments that have been used to justify the granting of a claim to the intervener has been that the law ought not to discourage interveners. Justinian, for example, acknowledged the fact that the doctrine of *negotiorum gestio* represented an inroad into the principle of self-determination. Yet, he thought this inroad justified because by not granting a claim one would discourage helpful intervention:

> (. . .) The beneficiary of the intervention incurs his obligations without even knowing the facts. This was accepted as good policy, to ensure that the affairs of the absent were not left untended if they suddenly had to set off abroad without having time to make proper arrangements. Plainly no one would intervene on their behalf without an action to recoup his outlay. (. . .)[1]

Amongst English and American scholars, too, those who argue in favour of granting a remedy to the intervener usually invoke this policy argument. Under the present English doctrine, it is assumed, potential good Samaritans are discouraged[2] because their intervention might prove to be a costly affair if the beneficiary refuses to reimburse their expenses and compensate them for their losses.[3] The solution, it is argued, is to introduce a right to be compensated for the loss incurred

[1] *I.* III.XXVII.1: (. . .) *ex qua causa ii quorum negotia gesta fuerint etiam ignorantes obligantur. Idque utilitatis causa receptum est, ne absentium, qui subita festinatione coacti nulli demandata negotiorum suorum administratione peregre profecti essent, desererentur negotia: quae sane nemo curaturus esset, si de eo quod quis impendisset nullam habiturus esset actionem.* (. . .) Translation: P.B.H. Birks and G. McLeod, *Justinian's Institutes* (1986), pp. 117–119. Cf. D. 3.5.1 (Ulpian).

[2] Of course, the present doctrine does not *actively* discourage intervention, but merely *fails to neutralize* the discouraging effect of the prospect that an intervention might prove costly. However, for the sake of clarity and brevity the term 'discourage' will here be employed to mean the same.

[3] See for example J.P. Dawson, 'Rewards for the Rescue of Human Life?' in *Essays presented to Hans Yntema*, p. 142; Lord Goff of Chieveley and G. Jones, *The Law of Restitution* (3rd edn 1986), pp. 331 and 349–50; H. Dagan, 'In Defense of the Good Samaritan' (1999) 97 Michigan LR 1152–1200 at 1156–7 and 1164.

during the intervention – to 'offset pre-legal countervailing disincentives'[4] – or even a right to a positive reward in order to actively encourage intervention.

The presumption that underlies the policy argument is that potential benefactors are influenced by economic incentives and disincentives. This presumption is widespread and not merely amongst legal writers.[5] In Wilkie Collins's *The Woman in White*, Walter Hartright finds himself at the scene of a fire, with none of the bystanders willing to help him in his attempt to rescue a man who is trapped:

> I ran down among the villagers, with the lantern in my hand. 'Five shillings apiece to every man who helps me!' They started into life at the words. That ravenous second hunger of poverty – the hunger for money – roused them into tumult and activity in a moment. 'Two of you for more lanterns if you have them! Two of you for the pickaxes and the tools! The rest after me to find the beam!' They cheered – with shrill starveling voices they cheered.[6]

The conventional view is that the potential intervener conducts a cost-benefit analysis; if the anticipated benefits (both social and material) are higher than the anticipated costs he will intervene; if they are lower he will refrain from intervening.[7] There is a large body of research to support this view. Summarizing the results of experiments conducted in the 1980's, Dovidio *et al.* stated:

> These results complement earlier findings of decreases in helping as a function of effort and time, money expended or forgone, and threat to personal freedom. Conversely, as the potential rewards associated with helping increase, intervention increases. For example, praise and monetary compensation facilitate helping. In addition, the greater the reward associated with feedback from effective helping, the more helpful bystanders are.[8]

Thus, potential interveners are thought to include monetary considerations in their cost-benefit analysis. Hence, to offer a reward will increase the likelihood of intervention, whereas the prospect of having to bear the costs of the intervention will discourage potential interveners.

However, more recent research suggests that it might not be quite as simple as that. In certain circumstances, it was found, rewards can actually have a detrimental influence. The first suggestion to that effect was made in 1970 by the sociologist Titmuss in a comparative study of the systems of blood donation in Great Britain and the United States.[9] In Great Britain, the NHS received all its blood from voluntary donors who received no reward but a cup of tea. In the United States, by

[4] H. Dagan, 'In Defense of the Good Samaritan' (1999) 97 Michigan LR 1152–1200 at 1157.

[5] See also J. Austin, *Lectures on Jurisprudence*, Vol III (1863), p. 133 (Notes on Contracts and Quasi Contracts).

[6] W. Collins, *The Woman in White* (M. Sweet, ed. 1999), pp. 517–518.

[7] J.A. Piliavin, J.F. Dovidio, S.L. Gaertner and R.D. Clark, *Emergency Intervention* (1981), pp. 94–95 and 115–116 and C.D. Batson, 'Altruism and Prosocial Behaviour' in D.T. Gilbert, S.T. Fiske and G. Lindzey (eds), *The Handbook of Social Psychology*, Vol 2 (4th edn 1998), pp. 282–316 at 285–286 with further references.

[8] J.F. Dovidio, J.A. Piliavin, S.L. Gaertner, D.A. Schroeder and R.D. Clark, 'The Arousal: Cost-Reward Model and the Process of Intervention' in M.S. Clark, *Prosocial Behavior* (1991), pp. 86–118 at 92 with further references (footnotes omitted).

[9] R.M. Titmuss, *The Gift Relationship* (original ed. with new chapters, A. Oakley and J. Ashton, eds, 1997).

contrast, blood donation was much more commercialized. Only ten per cent of all American blood came from voluntary donors. The remaining ninety per cent came from donors who were in some way rewarded, either by cash payments or otherwise.[10] Yet despite the absence of rewards, the English donated on average as much blood as their American counterparts. Titmuss did not explicitly state his views on the cause of this seemingly contradictory result. However, he did hint that it might have had something to do with the fact that the American system encouraged the notion that 'dollars can substitute for blood' which in turn would affect the motivation of potential donors.[11] Subsequent studies have come up with a more comprehensive explanation for Titmuss's findings. A simple rendering of the resulting theory runs as follows: many of the things we do, we do because of our so-called 'intrinsic motivation'; that is, because we enjoy doing these things, not because of external rewards or pressure. If someone were to decide to reward us for one of these intrinsically motivated activities, he thereby adds an extrinsic reason to our intrinsic motivation. Whereas hitherto we took part in an activity because of our intrinsic motivation, we now do so because of *extrinsic motivation* as well. The danger is, it was found, that we will now subconsciously forget our original intrinsic motivation and infer that we are acting mainly because of the external pressure. Thus, the extrinsic motivation does not just add to, but replaces the intrinsic motivation. As a result, a once enjoyable activity becomes a commodity. The disappointing conclusion is that rewarding people may actually cause them to lose interest in an activity they once enjoyed. This is what is called the 'overjustification effect' or the 'undermining effect' of extrinsic rewards.[12]

In a 1983 article, Kunda and Schwartz investigated whether the above theory applies to the activity of 'helping other people'. They conducted an experiment in which students were asked to read text material into a tape recorder to help blind students. Some of the students were promised a reward, others were not. Kunda and Schwartz came to the conclusion that offering rewards for helping other people could indeed be counter-effective:

> This study has demonstrated that internalized moral norms and values for helping are subject to the overjustification effect. (. . .) we find that paying people to help undermines their sense of moral obligation to help in related circumstances. Payment also affects the

[10] For a comprehensive summary, see R.M. Solow, 'Blood and Thunder', (1971) 80 Yale LJ 1696–1711 at 1696–1699.

[11] R.M. Titmuss, *The Gift Relationship* (original ed. with new chapters, A. Oakley and J. Ashton, eds, 1997), p. 290.

[12] See for example E.L. Deci, R.M. Ryan and R. Koestner, 'A Meta-Analytic Review of Experiments Examining the Effects of Extrinsic Rewards on Intrinsic Motivation', (1999) 125 Psychological Bulletin 627–668 and E. Aronson, T.D. Wilson and R.M. Akert, *Social Psychology* (3rd edn 1999), pp. 166–167 and 429–431. The theory is not without its critics; see for example R. Eisenberger and J. Cameron, 'Detrimental Effects of Reward: Reality or Myth?', (1996) 51 American Psychologist 1153–1166 as well as the discussion between Eisenberger *et al.* and Deci *et al.* in (1999) 125 Psychological Bulletin 677–700.

perceived reasons for having helped. It promotes attribution of the helping behavior to external rather than to internal reasons.[13]

Yet, alarming though these findings may seem at first glance, their implications should not be exaggerated. The findings do not imply, for example, that the reward mechanism that lies at the foundation of our capitalist society needs to be thrown overboard. Nor do they deny that to grant the intervener a remedy could be a sound policy to increase the occurrence of helpful interventions. Instead, the findings indicate that although a right to be rewarded would probably have a positive effect on the quantity of interventions, it might at the same time have a negative effect on the intrinsic motivation of existing volunteers. The research shows that when moving from a no-reward to a reward-based system, good Samaritans may start to attribute their helpful conduct to external reasons (the rewards) rather than to internal reasons (their sense of moral obligation). Yet, they are likely to continue to assist those in need as long as the extrinsic motivation is maintained – that is, as long as the rewards keep coming. The only *proviso* is that the reward should not be so low as to make the subject feel unappreciated.

Moreover, the 'undermining effect' does not occur with regard to those who would not intervene in a no-reward system. For, logically, rewards can only undermine intrinsic motivation if such intrinsic motivation is present. Where no intrinsic motivation exists, rewards can successfully provide incentives. Thus, with regard to the priest and the Levite, neither of whom was sufficiently intrinsically motivated to intervene, a reward system might well have its desired effect.[14]

Finally, it should be noted that not all types of extrinsic motivation undermine the intrinsic motivation. Where monetary rewards are likely to undermine intrinsic motivation, the same need not be true if the reward offered is, say, a bunch of flowers with a thank-you note. It all depends on how the extrinsic motivation is perceived by the subject.[15] And, in turn, the subject's perception depends to a large extent on how the external pressure is presented. If a reward is presented as being full payment for the required effort, it is conceivable that the subject will attribute his entire effort to the reward that is offered. In that case the extrinsic motivation completely replaces the intrinsic motivation. If, however, the reward that is offered is merely of symbolic value – the bunch of flowers with a thank-you note – the subject is likely to continue to attribute at least part of his conduct to his intrinsic motivation.

Hence, depending on what result a legislator hopes to achieve, different policies suggest themselves. If the aim is to increase the amount of helpful interventions regardless of whether the interveners' motives are extrinsic or intrinsic, offering a substantial reward would be a sound policy. The reward would encourage those who did not have an intrinsic motivation to intervene (the priest and the Levite),

[13] Z. Kunda and S.H. Schwartz, 'Undermining Intrinsic Moral Motivation: External Reward and Self-Presentation', (1983) 45 Journal of Personality and Social Psychology 763–771 at 769.

[14] E. Aronson, T.D. Wilson and R.M. Akert, *Social Psychology* (3rd edn 1999), p. 169 with further references. Cf. also T.C. Galligan, 'Aiding and Altruism: A Mythopsycholegal Analysis', (1994) 27 Univ. of Michigan Journal of Law Reform 439–520 at 507.

[15] E. Aronson, T.D. Wilson and R.M. Akert, *Social Psychology* (3rd edn 1999), p. 169.

while those who did (the good Samaritans) would be likely to continue their helpful conduct albeit for external rather than internal reasons. Such a policy appears to have been adopted in maritime law.[16] The result is a salvage industry that is well developed, though it is unlikely that many helpful interventions are still motivated by (intrinsic) moral considerations. If, on the other hand, the aim is to try and increase the amount of helpful interventions without undermining the intrinsic motivation of existing volunteers, it might be wiser to offer a reward that does not purport to represent the monetary value of the service rendered. As an incentive, the latter type of reward would probably not be as successful as the former, but it would leave room for attribution to intrinsic motivation. An example can be found in the law concerning donations to charity. The legislator rewards generosity by making donations to charity tax-deductible. This policy increases the amount that we donate to charity, but does not make us feel as though our acts are completely governed by extrinsic motivation.[17] It is here argued that the same would be true if we were to allow interveners to claim reimbursement of their expenses and/or compensation for loss suffered, as is done by the doctrine of *negotiorum gestio*; the doctrine provides comfort to potential interveners by neutralizing the costs of intervention, but at the same time prevents them from gaining monetary profit from their intervention. As a result, the decision to intervene is likely to continue to be attributed to reasons that are not of a monetary nature, for example their sense of moral duty and/or their feeling of empathy with the victim.

It should be noted that if we allow interveners reimbursement and/or compensation rather than a reward, their entitlement to such claims should not be dependent on the outcome of their interventions. For, knowing that there is always a chance that his intervention might not be successful, a calculating bystander would still feel deterred from intervening if 'no success' would mean 'no claim'.[18] If, on the other hand, the law were to offer interveners a positive reward, this problem would not necessarily occur. For, even if a successful outcome were a pre-requisite for the entitlement to a reward, the calculating intervener would not feel deterred from intervening, provided that the chance of success, multiplied by the probable reward was as high as, or higher than, the probable expenses.

9.2 Interveners do not Act Voluntarily (Compulsion)

In 1961 Dawson complained that Englishmen and North Americans stigmatized benefactors as 'officious intermeddlers' if not outright tortfeasors. 'The mildest comment', he wrote, 'will probably be that the unsolicited intervenor is a "mere volunteer"'.[19] The voluntary intervener is distinguished from the involuntary

[16] See below, Section 11.9.

[17] *Contra*: B.S. Frey and L. Goette, 'Does Pay Motivate Volunteers?' (1999), 'Conclusions'.

[18] J.P. Dawson, '*Negotiorum Gestio*: the Altruistic Intermeddler' (1961) 74 Harvard LR 817–865 and 1073–1129 at 1115.

[19] J.P. Dawson, '*Negotiorum Gestio*: the Altruistic Intermeddler' (1961) 74 Harvard LR 817–865 and 1073–1129 at 817.

(if not 'helpless') beneficiary. As a consequence, English and American scholars tend to emphasize the need to protect the freedom of the potential beneficiary, without paying attention to the position of the intervener. Indeed, even Dagan, who argued in favour of granting the intervener a claim, focused largely on the freedom of the beneficiary.[20] The freedom of the intervener, by contrast, receives relatively little attention.[21] His right of self-determination, it appears to be assumed, has remained unaffected because he himself has made the choice to intervene; he himself has determined the course of events. Therefore, in the words of the Supreme Court of Oregon: 'the great and leading rule of law is to deem an act done for the benefit of another, without his request, as a voluntary act of courtesy'.

Yet, how 'voluntarily' does the typical intervener act? In the context of the defence of '*volenti non fit iniuria*', this question has been addressed in a number of cases, one of which is *Haynes v Harwood*.[22] There, a policeman stopped two runaway horses and sustained injuries as a consequence. He brought a claim in negligence against the owners of the horses. The defendant owners, however, stated that the plaintiff had voluntarily taken the risk of injury and invoked the defence of *volenti non fit iniuria*. The Court of Appeal rejected this argument, Maugham LJ stating:

> In my opinion the police constable was not in any true sense a volunteer. (. . .) [the police] have, I think, a discretionary duty to prevent an accident arising from the presence of uncontrolled forces in the street, if they are in a position to do so. At any rate, they have a moral duty to intervene in such a case as the present where it appeared, and rightly appeared, to the plaintiff that there was a reasonable chance of preventing a most serious accident. (. . .) So regarded, the present plaintiff was not acting unreasonably in the risks he took; there was no such voluntary assumption of risk (. . .) as would bring him within the exceptions under consideration.[23]

Hence, the fact that the policeman intervened does not necessarily mean that his intervention was entirely voluntary; he may well have felt that he was obliged to intervene by a moral or maybe even a legal duty. In cases like that of the good Samaritan, the element of 'voluntariness' is often vitiated. One would hope that the choice between letting a man die and trying to save him is, at least to most people, not a choice at all. In such cases the moral duty – and in civilian jurisdictions, as we have seen in Part I, the legal duty – to assist a fellow human being does not offer the intervener a real choice. Indeed, in his *Introduction to the Law of Restitution*, Birks places this type of case in a chapter concerned with 'non-voluntary transfer'. In his view, the intervener's consent is 'vitiated' by 'moral compulsion'.[24]

[20] See Part II, Section 8.2.

[21] See for a notable exception E.W. Hope, 'Officiousness', (1929–30) 15 Cornell LQ 25–53 and 205–242 at pp. 36–38.

[22] *Haynes v Harwood* [1935] 1 KB 146. See also *Baker v T.E. Hopkins & Son Ltd* [1959] 3 All ER 225. Cf. *Ogwo v Taylor* [1987] 3 All ER 961.

[23] *Ibid.* at 161–162.

[24] P.B.H. Birks, *An Introduction to the Law of Restitution* (1985), pp. 193 ff.

However, moral compulsion alone does not provide sufficient justification to grant the intervener a claim. After all, there are many instances in which we act because we feel morally compelled to do so, but where the law does not grant us a claim. Charitable donations, for example, will often be instigated by some form of moral compulsion, yet no one would argue that the law ought to allow restitution of all such donations.[25] It is no answer to say that in the latter type of case the intervener had an *animus donandi*. For that begs the question: if I give a pound to a beggar with a hungry and distressed child on his arm, did I have an *animus donandi* or was my intent (*animus*) vitiated because I felt morally compelled? And what if instead of giving money, I fed the beggar and his child and brought them to an inn? Thus, if 'moral compulsion' is to be our reason for granting a claim, we would have to draw a distinction between the kind of 'moral compulsion' that does negate consent, and the kind that does not.[26] To draw such a distinction would be all the more difficult if, as we must suspect, the difference is one of degree and not of principle.

Yet, what distinguishes necessitous interventions from other types of intervention (including charitable donations), is that the very nature of the emergency renders it impossible for the intervener to express his will (in so far as he has freely formed one) to the beneficiary. For, even though some interveners may be said to have been able to make up their mind freely, they do not have the opportunity to communicate their decision to the beneficiary. Such interveners may, like the good Samaritan, decide that they are willing to assist a wounded man, as well as bear the burden of all the expenses that will be incurred. However, as Thomson observed in a 1971 article, there are not only good and bad Samaritans, but also 'minimally decent Samaritans', 'very good Samaritans', and 'splendid Samaritans'.[27] Thus, I may decide that I am willing to help a fellow human being, but only on the *proviso* that my expenses will be reimbursed. I am in this respect not much different from a generous benefactor to charity, who insists on having a plaque put up in his honour. Indeed, it is theoretically possible that both of us acted under a similar degree of moral compulsion, and therefore that we acted equally 'voluntarily' or 'non-voluntarily'. Yet what distinguishes me from the generous donator is that the nature of the emergency in which I was involved made it impossible for me to negotiate with the beneficiary. Hence no matter how freely a necessitous intervener is able to form his will, the circumstances of an emergency will normally make it impossible for him to ensure that the rights and the duties he incurs are determined by this will. The charitable benefactor, on the other hand, does have the opportunity to communicate his will to the beneficiary. He may want to donate a large sum of money on the condition that he receives some kind of recognition, or he may want to give it unconditionally. Or, he may only be prepared to lend the money. Yet, because he can communicate and negotiate with the recipient

25 A. Burrows, *The Law of Restitution* (2nd edn 2002), p. 315.
26 P.B.H. Birks, *An Introduction to the Law of Restitution* (1985), pp. 173–4.
27 J.J. Thomson, 'A Defense of Abortion', (1971) 1 *Philosophy and Public Affairs* 47–66 at 62–64.

of his charity, he can do what the intervener in an emergency could not do: he can see to it that the rights and duties that he incurs are in accordance with his will.

The truth of the matter is therefore, that in the typical emergency intervention neither the beneficiary nor the intervener is in any real sense capable of self-determination. This is not a result of our legal system, but rather of the nature of emergency situations. The (unfortunate) course of events on the road from Jerusalem to Jericho rendered self-determination an impossibility for *both* the victim *and* the good Samaritan. It follows that any rule that we decide to apply to this type of case can be criticized on the basis that it will in some cases go against the will of individual parties. If we do not grant a claim, some interveners will argue that they would not have undertaken uncompensated intervention if they had been capable of self-determination in its true sense. Conversely, if we do grant a claim, some of those who were assisted will argue that they would not have compensated or reimbursed the intervener, let alone remunerated or rewarded him, of their own accord. In these circumstances, we should perhaps agree with Dagan that the law ought to adopt a rule that would represent the presumed preferences of the parties involved in at least a majority of cases. This could be a rule that entitles the intervener to claim reimbursement of his expenses. However, whichever rule of law is adopted, it would not – as Dagan appears to conclude[28] – be consistent with the beneficiary's right of self-determination. Instead, the very reason why the rule of law ought to determine the rights and duties of the parties involved in an emergency is that both are typically incapable of self-determination in its true sense.

[28] H. Dagan, 'In Defense of the Good Samaritan' (1999) 97 Michigan LR 1152–1200 at 1165.

10

The Continental Doctrine of '*Negotiorum Gestio*'[1]

This chapter contains an introductory account of the basic scope and meaning of the doctrine of *negotiorum gestio*. It should again be stressed that it is not here intended to describe the doctrine in all its details, nor to give a full report of the ways in which an intervener might recover in the continental systems here discussed. Instead, the purpose of this chapter is merely to illustrate how a general principle allowing necessitous interveners to recover – *negotiorum gestio* – operates within a modern legal system. Thus, this chapter does not contain any discussion of, for example, the intervener's possible claims in contract[2] or tort,[3] nor of the specific provisions in the German civil code entitling the finder of lost goods to reimbursement of his expenses as well as a reward ('*Finderlohn*').[4]

10.1 Historical Background

Earlier in this book, we touched upon the doctrine of *negotiorum gestio*. We described it there as being a Roman doctrine, concerned with the unsolicited management of the 'affairs' of another.[5] Little is known about the early history of *negotiorum gestio*, other than that it was probably introduced by the praetor.[6] The

[1] Kaser regards the term as '*unrömisch*' and prefers '*negotia gesta*'. M. Kaser, *Das Römische Privatrecht*, Vol I (2nd edn 1971), p. 586.

[2] See the French '*convention d'assistance*': *Civ.* 27 May 1959, *D* 1959, 524, on which H. and L. Mazeaud, *Rev.trim.dr.civ.* 1959, 735, and *Civ.* 1 December 1969, *D* 1970, 422. See for strong criticism of the notion of a *convention d'assistance* S. Hocquet-Berg, '*Remarques sur la Prétendue Convention d'Assistance*' *Gaz Pal* 1996 (*Doctrine*), 32–40.

[3] See A. Tunc, 'The Volunteer and the Good Samaritan' in J.M. Ratcliffe, (ed.), *The Good Samaritan and the Law* (1966), pp. 43–62 at pp. 52–53 and W. van Gerven, J. Lever and P. Larouche, *Cases, Materials and Text on National, Supranational and International Tort Law* (2000), pp. 463–464 and 733–734.

[4] §§ 970–971 *BGB*, on which see S.J. Stoljar, 'Negotiorum Gestio' in E. von Caemmerer and P. Schlechtriem (eds), *International Encyclopedia of Comparative Law*, Vol. X Restitution – Unjust Enrichment and Negotiorum Gestio (1984), ch. 17, pp. 97–98.

[5] See above p. 44.

[6] M. Wlassak, *Zur Geschichte der Negotiorum Gestio* (1879), p. 21.

edictal provision is said to have commenced as follows:

> If anyone has managed the affairs of another or has administered what were his affairs at the time of his death, I will grant a trial on this account.[7]

'Affairs' ('*negotia*') may originally have had a specific meaning. It has been argued that the Edict's purpose was to ensure the defence of absent parties at trial.[8] Yet, whatever its precise original scope, there is no doubt that by the classical period the doctrine applied to a wide variety of affairs. Examples include looking after a sick slave,[9] collection or payment of debts,[10] standing surety,[11] and buying slaves or land for another.[12]

In the event of a *negotiorum gestio*, the person whose affairs were managed was granted an *actio negotiorum gestorum (directa)*, while the *gestor* would have an *actio negotiorum gestorum contraria*. As we have seen, the *gestor* could be held liable with the *actio directa* for losses resulting from his failure to exercise due care. Also, he would have to account for his management and surrender any benefits that he received in relation to the intervention. Moreover, subject to what was said in Part I, Section 4.4, he was bound to complete the intervention he had embarked on. On the other hand, the *actio contraria* enabled him to sue for expenses incurred and losses suffered in the course of the intervention. While *negotiorum gestio* thus appears to have given rise to a bilateral relationship,[13] the requirements for the availability of the *actiones directa* and *contraria* were by no means identical.

The scope of the *actio directa* was wide. In principle anyone who intervened in the affairs of another could be held liable. Whether or not the intervener intended the other to benefit would have been immaterial. Indeed, Ulpian tells us that where the intervention was intentionally self-serving, there was all the more reason to hold the intervener liable under the *actio directa*.[14] It does, however, appear to have been required that the *gestor* was aware that he was intervening in the affairs of another.[15]

[7] *D.* 3.5.3.*pr.* (Ulpian): '*Si quis negotia alterius, sive quis negotia, quae cuiusque cum is moritur fuerint, gesserit: iudicium eo nomine dabo*'. See also O. Lenel, *Das Edictum Perpetuum* (2nd edn 1907), p. 100 (§ 35). It has been argued that '*alterius*' is an interpolation for '*absentis*': J. Partsch, *Studien zur Negotiorum Gestio I* (1913), pp. 10–14. *Contra*: H.H. Seiler, *Der Tatbestand der negotiorum gestio im römischen Recht* (1968), pp. 48–49.

[8] M. Wlassak, *Zur Geschichte der Negotiorum Gestio* (1879), pp. 40–41 and O. Lenel, *Das Edictum Perpetuum* (2nd edn 1907), p. 101 (§ 35). Cf. *D.* 3.5.1 (Ulpian). It is now widely believed that the doctrine has two further roots: *cura furiosi* and *procuratio omnium bonorum*, on which see H.H. Seiler, *Der Tatbestand der negotiorum gestio im römischen Recht* (1968), pp. 105–110, 263–275 and 314–315.

[9] *D.* 3.5.9.1 (Ulpian).

[10] *D.* 3.5.22 (Paul) and *D.* 3.5.5.11 (Ulpian).

[11] *D.* 3.5.4 (Ulpian) and *D.*3.5.45.*pr* (Africanus).

[12] *D.* 3.5.10 (Pomponius) and 3.5.45.*pr.* (Africanus).

[13] Albeit an *imperfectly* bilateral relationship: R. Zimmermann, *The Law of Obligations, Roman Foundations of the Civilian Tradition* (1996), p. 433.

[14] *D.* 3.5.5.5 (Ulpian). It is, however, suspected that the text may have been altered: H.H. Seiler, *Der Tatbestand der negotiorum gestio im römischen Recht* (1968), pp. 29–30.

[15] *D.* 3.5.18.3 (Paul) and *D.* 3.5.18.2 (Paul). But cf. *D.* 3.5.48 (Africanus). See H.H. Seiler, *Der Tatbestand der negotiorum gestio im römischen Recht* (1968), pp. 21–26.

When it came to the action by the *gestor* for his expenses – the *actio contraria* – a rather narrower approach was adopted. The *gestor* would only be granted the *actio contraria* in as far as he had managed another's affairs '*utiliter*' ('adequately' or 'usefully').[16] While the interpretation of *utilitas* was typically casuistic, it seems that it was not required that the intervention be strictly necessary.[17] It was sufficient if *ex ante* it appeared that the intervention would be of benefit to the person assisted.[18] Nor was it required that the intervention prove successful. Thus, we learn from Ulpian that where a sick slave died despite the best efforts of the *gestor*, he could still recover his expenses with the *actio contraria*.[19]

Yet, no matter how *utilis* the intervention, the predominant view was that a *gestor* could not avail himself of the *actio contraria* if he had acted contrary to the known wishes of the person assisted.[20] Moreover, the malicious and self-serving intervener would not be given the full benefit of the *actio contraria*. If he could recover at all, then it would be only to the extent that the defendant was enriched.[21] Finally, it should be noted that the *gestor* could not recover if he intended his services – or more precisely the resultant expenditure – to be a gift.[22]

What, then, were the policy considerations underlying the *actio contraria*? Throughout its history, its main purpose appears to have been to encourage intervention for the benefit of those who through absence or otherwise could not look after their own affairs. Originally, this policy may well have been aimed specifically at friends and relatives of the person assisted. The notions of friendship ('*amicitia*')[23] and affection ('*affectio*')[24] feature prominently in the Digest's casuistry.[25] Indeed, the many discussions on mistaken identity give reason to suspect that at one time it was essential that the *gestor* knew the person on whose behalf he intervened.[26] However, the same texts confirm that already by the time of Ulpian it no longer mattered whether or not he knew the person assisted. It is thus that the Emperor Justinian could state quite generally that the doctrine served to

16 *D.* 3.5.9.1 (Ulpian).

17 H.H. Seiler, *Der Tatbestand der negotiorum gestio im römischen Recht* (1968), pp. 53–54, with further references and R. Zimmermann, *The Law of Obligations, Roman Foundations of the Civilian Tradition* (1996), p. 442. Cf. *D.* 3.5.9.1 (Ulpian); *D.* 3.5.21 (Gaius); *D.* 3.5.26.*pr* (Modestinus); *D.* 3.5.45.*pr* (Africanus) and *C.* 2.18.2.

18 *D.* 3.5.26 (Modestinus).

19 *D.* 3.5.9.1 (Ulpian). See also *D.* 3.5.11.2 (Ulpian), *D.* 3.5.12 (Paul) and *D.* 3.5.21 (Gaius).

20 *D.* 3.5.7.3 (Ulpian) and *D.*3.5.30.4 (Papinian). Cf. however *C.* 2.18.24 and *D.*17.1.40 (Paul), as well as F. Schulz, '*Nachklassische Quaestionen in den justinianischen Reformgesetzen des Codex Justinianus*', (1930) 50 *ZSS* 212–248 at 238–247 and H.H. Seiler, *Der Tatbestand der negotiorum gestio im römischen Recht* (1968), pp. 86–93.

21 *D.* 3.5.5.5 (Ulpian). Cf. *D.*3.5.48 (Africanus). See also E. Zimmermann, *Die Lehre von der Stellvertretenden Negotiorum Gestio* (1876), p. 132.

22 *D.* 3.5.4 (Ulpian). See also R. Zimmermann, *The Law of Obligations, Roman Foundations of the Civilian Tradition* (1996), p. 439, footnote 52.

23 *E.g. D.*3.5.5.8 (Ulpian); *D.*3.5.30.2 (Papinian) and *D.*3.5.35 (Paul).

24 *D.* 3.5.3.9 (Ulpian).

25 See for more detail H.H. Seiler, *Der Tatbestand der negotiorum gestio im römischen Recht* (1968), pp. 38–46.

26 *D.* 3.5.5.1 (Ulpian); *D.*3.5.5.10 (Ulpian); *D.*3.5.44.2 (Ulpian).

encourage beneficial intervention on behalf of absentees:[27]

(. . .) It is from motives of convenience that this has been admitted, to prevent the entire neglect of the affairs of absent persons, who may be forced to depart in haste, without having entrusted the management to any one; and certainly no one would pay any attention to their affairs, unless he could recover by action any expenses he might be put to.[28]

10.2 France: 'Gestion d'affaires d'autrui'

The broad scope of the Roman *actio contraria* was regarded with some distrust by scholars of the natural law school. Grotius wrote that the action contained 'none of those foundations on which nature grounds an obligation'.[29] Similarly, Pufendorf held that ingratitude, while '*detestabile*',[30] should not be actionable in court.[31] It is not surprising,[32] then, to find that the 1794 Prussian code and the Austrian code of 1811 carefully limited the scope of application of the *actio contraria*. In principle, any unrequested intervention in the affairs of another would render the intervener – the *Geschäftsführer ohne Auftrag* – liable.[33] By contrast, the *Geschäftsführer* would only be entitled to recover for his expenses if his intervention was necessary to avert imminent loss.[34] If the intervention was merely useful rather than necessary, he would be able to recover up to the amount by which the person assisted had been enriched.[35]

However, Grotius's views did not go uncontested. In particular, there were those who thought of *negotiorum gestio* as a specimen of unjust enrichment, a doctrine that was firmly supported by natural lawyers. Von Cocceji, for example, said of *negotiorum gestio* that 'the foundation for a natural obligation is here clearly visible, for an obligation is always imposed on him who is made richer at the expense of another'.[36] Similar sentiments were expressed by Pothier, who stated that the

[27] That is not to say that absence of the person assisted was strictly required: see H.H. Seiler, *Der Tatbestand der negotiorum gestio im römischen Recht* (1968), pp. 47–51.

[28] *I.* III.XXVII.1: *(. . .) Idque utilitatis causa receptum est, ne absentium, qui subita festinatione coacti, nulli demandata negotiorum suorum administratione, peregre profecti essent, desererentur negotia: quae sane nemo curaturus esset, si de eo, quod quis impendisset, nullam habiturus esset actionem. (. . .)* Translation: Th.C. Sandars, *The Institutes of Justinian* (7th edn 1883), p. 386. Cf. *D.*44.7.5.*pr* (Gaius).

[29] H. Grotius, *De Iure Belli ac Pacis* (ed. 1646), p. 217 (*Lib.* II, *Cap.* X, § IX): '*nullum enim habet eorum fundamentorum ex quibus natura obligationem inducit*'. Grotius speaks of the '*actio negotiorum gestorum*', but it is clear from the context that he has the *actio contraria* in mind.

[30] S. von Pufendorf, *De Jure Naturae et Gentium* (edn 1688), p. 255 (*Lib.* III, *Cap.* III, § 17).

[31] *Ibid.* at p. 256 (*Lib.* III, *Cap.* III, § 17).

[32] R. Zimmermann, *The Law of Obligations, Roman Foundations of the Civilian Tradition* (1996), p. 435. See for a more detailed account of the influence of natural law theories on the Prussian code: H. Conrad, *Die geistigen Grundlagen des Allgemeines Landrechts für die preußischen Staaten von 1794* (1958), pp. 10 ff.

[33] §§ 228–229 I 13 *PrALR* and § 1035 *ABGB*.

[34] §§ 234–237 I 13 *PrALR* and § 1036 *ABGB*. Neither provision requires that the intervention be successful.

[35] §§ 231–233 and 241 I 13 *PrALR* and § 1037 *ABGB*.

[36] S. von Cocceji in H. von Cocceji, *Commentarii ad Hugonis Grotii de Jure Belli ac Pacis*, Vol II (ed. 1746), p. 93 (*ad Lib.* II, *Cap.* X, § IX): '*Fundamentum obligationis naturalis hic in aprico est, semper enim quis obligatur si locupletior factus est ex re aliena*'.

'foundation' of this quasi-contract was 'natural equity'.[37] Consequently, the French provision in the *Code civil* of 1804 is markedly broader than its Prussian and Austrian counterparts:

1375 The 'principal' ('*maître*') whose affairs have been well administered must perform the obligations which the manager ('*gérant*') has contracted in his name, indemnify him for all personal obligations that he took upon himself, and reimburse him for all the useful and necessary expenses which he incurred.[38]

The provision commences by confirming[39] that the '*gérant*' was given authority to create a legal relationship between the person assisted (the '*maître*') and third parties. Where a GP instructed a specialist surgeon to operate on his patient, it was held that the patient could not refuse to pay the surgeon's fees despite the fact that he had not agreed to be operated on by that particular surgeon. Article 1375 *C.civ.* conferred upon the GP an authority to act as the agent of his patient.[40] On the same principle one could arrange for urgent repairs to the house of an absent neighbour, thereby creating a valid contract between the neighbour and the person or company rendering the repair services.[41] Thus, the relationship resulting from a *gestion d'affaires* is akin to a contract of mandate.[42] Indeed, if and when the person assisted ratifies the intervention – and this can even be done tacitly – the predominant opinion is that the *gestion d'affaires* is turned retroactively into a mandate.[43]

The analogy with mandate is again apparent when it comes to the *gérant*'s right to indemnity and reimbursement of expenses. For like the mandatory, the *gérant* is in principle expected to perform his services gratuitously.[44] In the past, some of the lower courts allowed professional interveners to claim remuneration for services rendered under the heading of 'expenditure'.[45] However, in 1992 the *Cour*

[37] *R.J. Pothier, Traité du Contrat de Mandat* (edn 1821), p. 152 (Appendix, § 167): '*Ce quasi-contrat a pour fondement l'équité naturelle*'. Cf. also J. Domat, *Les loix civiles dans leur ordre naturel* (rev. edn 1745), p. 168 (*Livre* II, *Titre* IV, *pr.*): '*Et les Loix civiles invitent toute sorte de personnes à ce devoir; donnat à ceux qui prennent le soin des affaires des personnes absentes l'assurance que ce qu'ils auront fait raisonnablement sera confirmé, & qu'ils seront remboursez [sic] des deniers qu'ils auront fournis pour un emploi utile*'.

[38] **1375** *Le maître dont l'affaire a été bien administrée doit remplir les engagements que le gérant a contractés en son nom, l'indemniser de tous les engagements personnels qu'il a pris, et lui rembourser toutes les dépenses utiles ou nécessaires qu'il a faites.*

[39] It is uncertain whether such authority was conferred upon the *gestor* in Roman law: see E. Zimmermann, *Die Lehre von der Stellvertretenden Negotiorum Gestio* (1876), pp. 136 ff. and H.H. Seiler, *Der Tatbestand der negotiorum gestio im römischen Recht* (1968), pp. 61–72.

[40] *Civ.*8 February 1932, *Gaz Pal* 1932.1.733. See also *Civ.*17 May 1939, *Gaz Pal* 1939.2.245.

[41] H., L. and J. Mazeaud and F. Chabas, *Leçons de Droit Civil*, Part II, Vol I, *Obligations, Théorie Générale* (9th edn 1998), p. 810 (nr 679).

[42] G. Ripert and J. Boulanger, *Traité de Droit Civil*, Vol II (*Obligations*) (1957), p. 473.

[43] *Ibid.* at 815 (nr 691). *Contra*: G. Marty and P. Raynaud, *Droit Civil, Les Obligations*, Vol 1 (2nd edn 1988), p. 402 (nr 388).

[44] M. Planiol and G. Ripert, *Traité Pratique de Droit Civil Français* Vol VII (*Obligations*) (2nd edn 1954), p. 17.

[45] See M. Picard, '*La Gestion d'Affaires dans la Jurisprudence Contemporaine*', *Rev.trim.dr.civ.*1921, 419–467 at 458–461 and M. Planiol and G. Ripert, *Traité Pratique de Droit Civil Français* Vol VII (*Obligations*) (2nd edn 1954), p. 17, with further references.

de Cassation expressly disapproved of this practice. In the view of the Court, it would be incompatible with the altruistic nature of *gestion d'affaires* to grant remuneration.[46] Yet, it is generally accepted that the 'necessary expenses' of article 1375 *C.civ.* do include loss suffered by the *gérant* in the course of the intervention.[47] An illustration can be drawn from a 1988 case, in which a supermarket customer chased after a group of armed robbers. He managed to retrieve part of the loot, but was shot in the process. The *Cour de Cassation* upheld a decision in which the supermarket was held liable to compensate the intervener because the latter had, in chasing after the armed robbers, managed the supermarket's affairs.[48] In the event that the *gérant* is unfortunate enough to die in the course of the intervention, it has been decided that the *maître* must compensate his dependants.[49]

For a successful claim based on article 1375 *C.civ.*, the requirements are similar to those in Roman law. Firstly, the *gérant* needs to have had the intention to intervene in the affairs of another.[50] Someone who manages the affairs of another in the mistaken belief that they are his own cannot rely on the present doctrine.[51] It is not necessary, however, that the *gérant* manages affairs that belong exclusively to another. When a co-owner intervenes for the benefit of the joint property, he acts in the interest of the other co-owners as well as himself. This forms no impediment to his claim in *gestion d'affaires*. It has been suggested that the intervener needs to know the person he is acting for,[52] but this is not supported by the authorities.[53]

The intervention needs to have been undertaken 'voluntarily' or 'spontaneously'.[54] Interventions undertaken in the performance of contractual or legal obligations are in principle excluded.[55] This means that professional rescuers such as the police, the fire brigade, mountain rescue *etc.*, cannot normally rely on the doctrine of *gestion d'affaires*.[56] In a 1963 case before the *Cour d'Appel* of Paris, it was decided that the police could not recover expenses incurred while attending the scene of a traffic accident, because they had merely performed their public duty. By contrast, the breakdown service that had towed away the vehicle involved in the accident could recover as a *gérant d'affaires*, despite the fact that they had

[46] *Com.*15 December 1992, *Rev.trim.dr.civ.*1993, 579.

[47] *E.g.* M. Planiol and G. Ripert, *Traité Pratique de Droit Civil Français* Vol VII (*Obligations*) (2nd edn 1954), p. 16; G. Marty and P. Raynaud, *Droit Civil, Les Obligations*, Vol 1 (2nd edn 1988), p. 401 (nr 387) and H., L. and J. Mazeaud and F. Chabas, *Leçons de Droit Civil*, Part II, Vol I, *Obligations, Théorie Générale* (9th edn 1998), p. 815 (nr 690).

[48] *Civ.* 26 January 1988, *D* 1989, 405. Cf. *Civ.* 7 January 1971, *JCP* 1971.2.16670. See also H., L. and J. Mazeaud and F. Chabas, *Leçons de Droit Civil*, Part II, Vol I, *Obligations, Théorie Générale* (9th edn 1998), p. 815 (nr 690).

[49] *Civ.*16 November 1955, *JCP* 1956.2.9087.

[50] This follows from the wording of *art.* 1372 *C.civ.* ('*volontairement*').

[51] *Civ.*25 June 1919, *S* 1921.1.12. See for further references R. Bout, *Juris-Classeur Civil, Quasi-contrats, Gestion d'Affaires, artt.*1372–1375 *C.civ.* (1996), *Fasc.* 20, nr 22.

[52] *Tribunal d'Instance de Paris* 21 October 1970, *Gaz Pal* 1971.1.28.

[53] R. Bout, *Juris-Classeur Civil, Quasi-contrats, Gestion d'Affaires, artt.*1372–1375 *C.civ.* (1996), *Fasc.* 20, nrs 24–27.

[54] Art. 1372 *C.civ.*

[55] G. Marty and P. Raynaud, *Droit Civil, Les Obligations*, Vol 1 (2nd edn 1988), p. 393 (nr 380).

[56] *E.g. Cour d'Appel de Paris* 7 December 1963, *JCP* 1964.4.32. See also M. Riou, '*L'Acte de Dévouement*' *Rev.trim.dr.civ.*1957, 221–245 at 243–245.

acted on the instructions of the police. Unless these instructions amounted to a public command – and the court held they did not – the breakdown service should be regarded as merely having been informed of the opportunity for rescue, and therefore as having acted voluntarily.[57]

Meanwhile, it appears that performance of the criminal law duty to render assistance to those in danger – discussed in Part I[58] – does not negate the spontaneous character of the intervention. The case law includes numerous instances in which the doctrine has been applied in favour of private rescuers.[59]

Article 1375 *C.civ.* further requires that the affairs of the *maître* have been 'well administered'. This is interpreted as requiring that the intervention be 'useful' ('*utile*').[60] But whether an intervention is useful is assessed retrospectively at the moment at which the *gérant* made his decision to intervene. It follows that for an intervention to be useful, it need not have been successful.[61] In addition to being useful,[62] the courts have developed a requirement that the intervention be 'appropriate' ('*opportune*').[63] In principle, an intervention is not regarded as appropriate if it goes against the known wishes of the *maître*.[64] The courts have also used this requirement as a safeguard against unnecessary intervention, in particular in cases in which the *maître* was perfectly capable of looking after his own affairs. Indeed, the *Cour d'Appel* of Douai once stated that 'a management of affairs is not created unless the *maître* is absent or not in a state to be able to look after his own affairs'.[65] Yet, in 1970 the *Cour de Cassation* expressly rejected this view.[66] More recently, however, the *Chambre commerciale* of the *Cour de Cassation* indicated that for an intervention to be appropriate, it must at least appear to the intervener that the *maître* cannot look after his own affairs.[67]

Finally, it has been suggested that the *gérant*, like the Roman *gestor*, cannot recover if he intended the expenses resulting from his services to be a gift to the

[57] *Cour d'Appel de Paris* 7 December 1963, *JCP* 1964.4.32. Cf. *Surrey Breakdown Ltd v Knight* [1999] RTR 84, discussed below, Section 12.1.

[58] Section 4.2.

[59] *E.g. Tribunal Civil de Lille* 28 June 1955, *Gaz Pal* 1955.2.413 and *Civ.*16 November 1955, *JCP* 1956.2.9087. See for further references G. Marty and P. Raynaud, *Droit Civil, Les Obligations*, Vol 1 (2nd edn 1988), p. 394 (nr 381) and R. Bout, *Juris-Classeur Civil, Quasi-contrats, Gestion d'Affaires, artt.*1372–1375 *C.civ.* (1996), *Fasc.* 20, nr 57.

[60] G. Ripert and J. Boulanger, *Traité de Droit Civil*, Vol II (*Obligations*) (1957), p. 471.

[61] F. Terré, P. Simler and Y. Lequette, *Droit civil; Les Obligations* (8th edn 2002), nr 1041.

[62] It has been argued that the propriety of the intervention is not a separate requirement, but is instead incorporated in the requirement of usefulness, *e.g.*: B. Starck, H. Roland and L. Boyer, *Droit Civil, Les Obligations, Contrat* (6th edn 1998), p. 750 (nr 2139).

[63] *Civ.* 28 October 1942, *DC* 1943, 29; See also B. Petit's note on *Com.*12 January 1999, *JCP* 1999.2.10070, with further references.

[64] *Civ.*11 February 1986, *JCP* 1986.4.110. See also P. Lerebours-Pigeonnière's note on *Civ.* 28 October 1942, *DC* 1943, 29 at 30.

[65] *Cour d'Appel de Douai* 26 January 1953, *JCP* 1953.4.153. See also *Cour d'Appel de Lyon*, 13 March 1969, *D* 1970, *Som* 179.

[66] *Civ.* 22 June 1970, *JCP* 1970.2.16511.

[67] *Com.*12 January 1999, *JCP* 1999.2.10070. See more generally R. Bout, *Juris-Classeur Civil, Quasi-contrats, Gestion d'Affaires, artt.*1372–1375 *C.civ.* (1996), *Fasc.* 20, nr 104. Cf. H., L. and J. Mazeaud and F. Chabas, *Leçons de Droit Civil*, Part II, Vol I, *Obligations, Théorie Générale* (9th edn 1998), p. 809 (nr 675).

maître. In practice, however, the courts rarely hold that such an intention has been established.[68]

10.3 Germany: the Geschäftsführer ohne Auftrag

In nineteenth-century Germany, *negotiorum gestio* was much discussed, too much it has been suggested.[69] Not everyone supported the doctrine, especially since it was thought to be at odds with the will theory, then very much *en vogue*.[70] But in a country in which most leading legal scholars were Romanists, *negotiorum gestio* was bound to survive. In 1849, Ruhstrat submitted that the principles of *negotiorum gestio* were 'without doubt the only correct principles for all epochs of an advanced legal system'.[71] Some forty years later, Kohler wrote what was probably the most influential defence, turning the doctrine into a 'legal paradigm of human help'.[72] '*Negotiorum gestio*', he said, 'is a very desirable act of neighbourly assistance, very worthy of encouragement and promotion'.[73] It is not surprising, then, to find that the notion of altruism is at the heart of the modern German doctrine of *negotiorum gestio*, that is, '*Geschäftsführung ohne Auftrag*'. Nevertheless, the influence of the will theory remains discernible. For, as we shall see, the German code puts much emphasis on the actual or presumed wishes of the person assisted ('*Geschäftsherr*').[74]

The *BGB* defines *Geschäftsführung* as having been undertaken *for* another.[75] An intervener who acts in the mistaken belief that he is managing his own affairs, does not qualify as a *Geschäftsführer ohne Auftrag*.[76] If he does intend to act for another, it does not matter whether he knows this person, or indeed whether he is mistaken as to the identity of the person assisted.[77] Sometimes the intervener manages the affairs of more than one person. For example, where a man came to the assistance of a woman who had been attacked by a madman, it was held that he was not only managing her affairs, but also those of her husband, as well as those of his health

[68] R. Bout, *Juris-Classeur Civil, Quasi-contrats, Gestion d'Affaires, artt.*1372–1375 *C.civ.* (1996), *Fasc.* 20, nrs 37–46.

[69] J.P. Dawson, '*Negotiorum Gestio*: the Altruistic Intermeddler' (1961) 74 Harvard LR 817–865 and 1073–1129 at 821.

[70] See for example Reinhardt, as quoted in C.G. von Wächter, '*Beiträge zur Lehre von der Negotiorum Gestio*' (1837) 20 *AcP* 333–361 at 338.

[71] E. Ruhstrat, '*Beiträge zur Lehre von der Negotiorum Gestio*' (1849) 32 *AcP* 173–199 at 173.

[72] S.J. Stoljar, 'Negotiorum Gestio' in E. von Caemmerer and P. Schlechtriem (eds), *International Encyclopedia of Comparative Law*, Vol X Restitution – Unjust Enrichment and Negotiorum Gestio (1984), ch. 17, no. 18.

[73] J. Kohler, '*Die Menschenhülfe im Privatrecht*', (1887) 25 *Jahrbücher für die Dogmatik des heutigen römischen und deutschen Privatrechts* 1–141 at 43: '*die negotiorum gestio . . . ist . . . eine sehr begehrenswerthe, eine sehr unterstüßungs- und förderungswerthe Menschenhülfe*'.

[74] R. Zimmermann, *The Law of Obligations, Roman Foundations of the Civilian Tradition* (1996), pp 434–435. See also §§ 677–679 *BGB*.

[75] § 677 *BGB*.

[76] See also § 687 (1) *BGB*.

[77] § 686 *BGB*. See also P. Schlechtriem, *Schuldrecht, Besonderer Teil* (5th edn 1998), p. 286.

insurers (provided that healthcare for the wife was covered by the policy).[78] It is not necessary for the *Geschäftsführer* to manage affairs exclusively for another; the doctrine applies equally when he manages affairs partly for another and partly for himself.[79]

However, as the expression '*Geschäftsführung ohne Auftrag*' already indicates, the intervention must not have been authorized by a mandate. More generally, the intervener must not have been bound by contract to intervene on behalf of the *Geschäftsherr*.[80] Whether § 683 *BGB* applies to interventions in the performance of a public duty, is uncertain. The drafters of the code stated that the doctrine does not apply where the *Geschäftsführer* merely performs the duty of his office ('*Amtspflicht*').[81] On several occasions the *Bundesgerichtshof* has taken a different view of the matter. Thus, it decided that where a fire brigade was called upon to extinguish a forest fire that was caused by sparks from a locomotive, it could recover its expenses from the railway company despite the fact that it had a public duty to attend the fire. The railway company would have been liable for loss suffered by third parties as a result of the fire, so it had a direct interest in the fire brigade's intervention.[82] However, a majority of German academics now rejects the court's reasoning.[83] Indeed, even if we assume that it remains good law, it is doubtful whether the same reasoning would apply where the *Geschäftsherr* is not legally responsible for the danger that prompted the intervention. The better view is probably that these cases are exceptional in that they allow a departure from the strict requirements of *Geschäftsführung ohne Auftrag* in order to fill a lacuna in the German law of tort.

Meanwhile, it is generally agreed that performance of the criminal law duty to render assistance in an emergency[84] does not prevent the intervener from recovering as a *Geschäftsführer ohne Auftrag*.[85]

Once it has been established that an intervention 'qualifies' as a *Geschäftsführung ohne Auftrag*, as defined in the previous two paragraphs, the intervener will have both rights and duties.[86] His duties have already been investigated earlier in this

[78] *BGH* 7 November 1960, *NJW* 1961, 359. See also: Staudinger/Wittmann (1995), *Vorbem.*zu §§ 677 ff., *RdNr* 24.

[79] *MünchKomm* – Seiler (1997) § 677, *RdNr* 8.

[80] P. Schlechtriem, *Schuldrecht, Besonderer Teil* (5th edn 1998), p. 286.

[81] 2 *Motive zu dem Entwurfe eines Bürgerlichen Gesetzbuches* (1896), pp. 856–857. See also: B. Windscheid and Th. Kipp, *Lehrbuch des Pandektenrechts*, Vol 2 (9th edn 1906), p. 912, footnote 1.

[82] *BGH* 20 June 1963, *NJW* 1963, 1825, on which B.S. Markesinis, W. Lorenz and G. Dannemann, *The German Law of Obligations*, Vol I (1997), p. 752. See also: *RG* 26 April 1913, *RGZ* 82, 206 at 214, on which J.P. Dawson, '*Negotiorum Gestio*: the Altruistic Intermeddler' (1961) 74 Harvard LR 817–865 and 1073–1129 at 854; *BGH* 4 December 1975, *NJW* 1976, 619 and *BGH* 15 December 1975, *NJW* 1976, 748.

[83] See W. Schubert, '*Der Tatbestand der Geschäftsführung ohne Auftrag*' (1978) 178 *AcP* 425–455 at 444, with further references in footnote 74 and A. Ernst, *Schuldrecht, Besonderer Teil* (1999), pp. 244–245 with further references.

[84] Discussed above, Part I, Section 4.3.

[85] R. Zimmermann, '*Der Selbstmort als Gefährdungssachverhalt*' (1979) *FamRZ* 103–110 at 104 and J.P. Dawson, '*Negotiorum Gestio*: the Altruistic Intermeddler' (1961) 74 Harvard LR 817–865 and 1073–1129 at 1111.

[86] It has been argued that the duties of the *Geschäftsführer* will only arise if his intervention is in accordance with the interest and the actual or presumed will of the *Geschäftsherr*. If not, the former's

book.[87] His principal right – the right to reimbursement – is laid down in § 683 *BGB*, the first sentence of which runs as follows:

§ **683** If the undertaking of the management ('*Geschäftsführung*') is in accordance with the interest and the actual or presumed wishes of the 'principal' ('*Geschäftsherr*'), the manager ('*Geschäftsführer*') may demand reimbursement of his expenses as a mandatary. (. . .)[88]

Thus, the intervener's right to reimbursement is subject to two further conditions. Firstly, the intervention must have been in accordance with the interest of the *Geschäftsherr*. It is generally agreed that the latter's interest is assessed from an objective viewpoint;[89] the subjective will of both the intervener and the person assisted are in this respect irrelevant. If, for example, a mountain rescue team is called into action because a skier has gone missing, and it later turns out that the skier was perfectly safe – having stayed the night with a woman he had met on the *piste* – the rescue operation was not in the skier's interest.[90] Conversely, where someone's life is actually in danger, it is always in his interest to be saved, even if he does not want to be saved.[91] However, he who intervenes in an attempted suicide may fail to meet the second requirement set by § 683 *BGB*:[92] the intervention must not only be in the interest of the person assisted, but also in accordance with his actual or presumed will. Both of these are assessed retrospectively at the time of the intervention. By 'actual will' is meant the *Geschäftsherr*'s will as expressly articulated or otherwise clearly manifested. It is not necessary, however, for this will to have been communicated to the intervener.[93] His presumed will is established through an objective test. Here, the idiosyncratic wishes of an eccentric *Geschäftsherr* are not taken into account.[94] Yet, although this is not immediately

liability would have to be based on delict or unjust enrichment. *E.g.* Staudinger/Wittmann (1995), *Vorbem. zu* §§ 677 ff., *RdNr* 2. However, this view is at odds with the actual wording of § 677 *BGB* and will not here be followed. See *MünchKomm* – Seiler (1997), § 677, *RdNr* 43 and cf. 2 *Motive zu dem Entwurfe eines Bürgerlichen Gesetzbuches* (1896), p. 861.

[87] Part I, Section 4.4 *sub* 3.

[88] § 683 *BGB: Entspricht die Übernahme der Geschäftsführung dem Interesse und dem wirklichen oder dem mutmaßlichen Willen des Geschäftsherrn, so kann der Geschäftsführer wie ein Beauftragter Ersatz seiner Aufwendungen verlangen. (. . .)* Translation based on S.L. Goren, *The German Civil Code* (Rev. edn 1994)

[89] *E.g.* Staudinger/Wittmann (1995), *Vorbem. zu* § 677 ff., *RdNr* 47 and *MünchKomm* – Seiler (1997), § 683, *RdNr* 4;

[90] Example borrowed from H. Stoll, '*Rechtsfragen bei Hilfeleistung in vermeintlicher Not*' in H. Ehmann, W. Hefermehl and A. Laufs (eds), *Privatautonomie, Eigentum und Verantwortung* (1980), pp. 411–430 at 411. But cf. *LG Heidelberg* 15 December 1965, *VersR* 1968, 53 at 54. This does not, of course, exclude the possibility of a claim in delict.

[91] Cf. P. Schlechtriem, *Schuldrecht, Besonderer Teil* (5th edn 1998), p. 287.

[92] See on this specific issue: R. Zimmermann, '*Der Selbstmort als Gefährdungssachverhalt*' (1979) *FamRZ* 103–110. According to Zimmermann, the answer depends on the one hand on whether the suicide attempt was serious and not merely a 'cry for help', and on the other hand on whether the 'victim' was of sound mind. If the answer to both questions is affirmative, the intervener would have to resort to a claim in delict. *Contra*: Staudinger/Wittmann (1995), § 679, *RdNr* 10.

[93] *MünchKomm* – Seiler (1997), § 683, *RdNr 9*.

[94] Staudinger/Wittmann (1995), *Vorbem. zu* §§ 677 ff., *RdNr* 50 and *MünchKomm* – Seiler (1997), § 683, *RdNr* 10.

clear from the wording of § 683, the courts will only turn to the 'presumed will' of the *Geschäftsherr* if his actual will cannot be established.[95] If the owner of an ancient house informs his friends and family that he has decided to let his house fall into decay – thereby manifesting his actual will – the unwitting neighbour who makes urgent repairs to the roof of this house cannot recover under § 683 *BGB*.[96] Indeed, it is now commonly held that the *Geschäftsherr*'s actual will not only overrides his presumed will, but also – contrary to the word wording of § 683 – his (objective) interest. The obsessed collector who openly expresses his willingness to pay wildly excessive prices for certain items will therefore have to reimburse the intervener who kindly obliges him, despite the fact that this intervention is – at least from an objective viewpoint – hardly in his interest.[97] Meanwhile, the *BGB* decrees that the will of the *Geschäftsherr* is, by way of exception, to be disregarded if the intervention constitutes the performance of a duty of a *Geschäftsherr* in the public interest, or the performance of a statutory duty to provide maintenance that would otherwise not be performed.[98] Amongst the former type of duty are some of the *Verkehrs(sicherungs)pflichten* discussed earlier in this book.[99] For example, where a car had been involved in an accident and was subsequently, on request by the police, towed away by the plaintiff breakdown service, it was held that the plaintiff could recover against its owner, because the intervention constituted the performance of a *Verkehrspflicht* of the owner, in the interest of the public.[100]

Finally, it should be mentioned that in German law, too, the intervener will not be able to recover if he intended the expenses resulting from his intervention to be a gift.[101] However, this exception is – as in France – of little practical consequence.[102]

The above conditions having been met, § 683 *BGB* entitles the *Geschäftsführer* to 'reimbursement of his expenses' ('*Ersatz seiner Aufwendungen*'). This includes a right to be indemnified for personal liabilities incurred in the intervention.[103] Indeed, where the *Geschäftsführer* has in his own name entered into a contract for

[95] K. Larenz, *Lehrbuch des Schuldrechts*, Vol II/1 (13th edn 1986), p. 444 and Staudinger/Wittmann (1995), *Vorbem. zu* §§ 677 ff., *RdNr* 49 with further references.

[96] Example borrowed from J.P. Dawson, '*Negotiorum Gestio*: the Altruistic Intermeddler' (1961) 74 Harvard LR 817–865 and 1073–1129 at 1093.

[97] Example borrowed from A. Ernst, *Schuldrecht, Besonderer Teil* (1999), pp. 244–245. See also Staudinger/Wittmann (1995), *Vorbem. zu* §§ 677 ff., *RdNr* 49 with further references. *Contra*: K. Larenz, *Lehrbuch des Schuldrechts*, Vol II/1 (13th edn 1986), p. 444 (using the same example) and P. Schlechtriem, *Schuldrecht, Besonderer Teil* (5th edn 1998), p. 288.

[98] § 679 *BGB*.

[99] Part I, Section 4.3. See Staudinger/Wittmann (1995), § 679, *RdNr* 4 and P. Schlechtriem, *Schuldrecht, Besonderer Teil* (5th edn 1998), p. 288.

[100] *LG Limburg* 14 April 1965, *MDR* 1965, 742. See for more examples S.J. Stoljar, 'Negotiorum Gestio' in E. von Caemmerer and P. Schlechtriem (eds), *International Encyclopedia of Comparative Law*, Vol X Restitution – Unjust Enrichment and Negotiorum Gestio (1984), ch. 17, pp. 69–70 and *MünchKomm* – Seiler (1997), § 679, *RdNr* 7.

[101] § 685 *BGB*.

[102] *BGH* 6 December 1962, *BGHZ* 38, 302 provides a rare example, but this decision has received much criticism and it must be doubted whether it is still good law. See *MünchKomm* – Seiler (1997) § 685, *RdNr* 4 with further references.

[103] § 257 *BGB*.

the benefit of the *Geschäftsherr*, he can demand that the latter perform the contract for him.[104] However, unlike the French *gérant*, it is generally assumed that he does not have authority 'by operation of the law' to bind the *Geschäftsherr* directly towards third parties.[105]

The expenses incurred also include loss suffered as a result of the intervention.[106] A famous but controversial example is that of the car driver who swerved to avoid a child and was severely injured in the process.[107] The *Bundesgerichtshof* held that she had, by avoiding a collision, managed the affairs of the child and that the loss she suffered as a result was recoverable under the heading of 'expenses'.

Although *Geschäftsführung ohne Auftrag* is in principle gratuitous,[108] the courts do allow remuneration to those who intervened in the course of their profession. In assessing the size of the remuneration, the court takes regard of the customary charges within the profession.[109] However, if the intervener himself usually charges less than what is customary, this may be taken into account.[110]

[104] Staudinger/Wittmann (1995), § 683, *RdNr* 3.

[105] J. Denecke, *BGB-RGRK* (11th edn 1959), *Vorbem. zu* § 677, *Anm.* 1 and Staudinger/Wittmann (1995), *Vorbem. zu* §§ 677 ff., *RdNr* 60. *Contra*: K. Bertzel, '*Der Notgeschäftsführer als Repräsentant des Geschäftsherrn*' (1959) 158 *AcP* 107–150.

[106] *MünchKomm* – Seiler (1997), § 683, *RdNr* 18; Staudinger/Wittmann (1995), § 683, *RdNr* 5 and P. Schlechtriem, *Schuldrecht, Besonderer Teil* (5th edn 1998), p. 290.

[107] *BGH* 27 November 1962, *BGHZ* 38, 270.

[108] By analogy with the contract of mandate: § 662 *BGB*. See also B.S. Markesinis, W. Lorenz and G. Dannemann, *The German Law of Obligations*, Vol I (1997), p. 751.

[109] *E.g. BGH* 7 January 1971, *NJW* 1971, 609 at 612, on which B.S. Markesinis, W. Lorenz and G. Dannemann, *The German Law of Obligations*, Vol I (1997), p. 751 and *BGH* 15 December 1975, *NJW* 1976, 748 at 749. See for earlier examples J.P. Dawson, '*Negotiorum Gestio*: the Altruistic Intermeddler' (1961) 74 Harvard LR 817–865 and 1073–1129 at 1083.

[110] *BGH* 30 September 1993, *NJW* 1993, 3196.

11

The Position in English Law

11.1 The Traditional View: No Claim

In *Stovin v Wise*, Lord Hoffmann stated that 'except in special cases (. . .), English law does not reward someone who voluntarily confers a benefit on another'.[1] Indeed, the traditional view is that English law in principle denies the intervener a claim, be it for reward or for mere reimbursement of his expenses. Yet, as with the rule of no liability for nonfeasance, it proves surprisingly difficult to find any authority for this supposed principle. One case that is sometimes cited in support of the traditional view[2] is the 1793 case of *Nicholson v Chapman*.[3] There, timber belonging to Nicholson fell into the River Thames. The bailiff of the manor of Wimbledon, who stumbled upon the timber somewhere downstream, requested Chapman to carry the timber to a place of safety. When Nicholson sought to recover his timber, Chapman refused to hand it to him unless he was paid for his efforts. Nicholson then brought an action of trover. Eyre CJ held that Nicholson's action should succeed because Chapman had no lien over the timber:

> Principles of public policy support the lien in the case of salvage. Not only public policy and commercial necessity do not require that it should be established in this case, but very great inconvenience may be apprehended from it, if it were to be established. The owners of this kind of property, and the owners of craft upon the river which lie in many places moored together in large numbers, would not only have common accidents from the carelessness of their servants to guard against, but also the wilful attempts of ill-designing people to turn their floats and vessels adrift, in order that they might be paid for finding them.[4]

This would certainly seem to suggest that – in the opinion of Eyre CJ – the voluntary intervener should not be granted a claim, the argument used being that such a policy would be open to abuse, as discussed above, in Part II, Section 8.4. However, elsewhere in his judgment Eyre CJ appears to indicate that the law would entitle the intervener to 'some reasonable recompence' [sic]. Of the acts of finding and taking care of the thing found, he noted:

> This is a good office, and meritorious, at least in the moral sense of the word, and certainly intitles the party to some reasonable recompence from the bounty, if not from the justice of

[1] [1996] 3 All ER 801 at 819.

[2] *E.g.* C.G. Addison, *A Treatise on the Law of Contracts*, Vol I (2nd edn 1849), p. 67, footnote (*p*) and A. Burrows and E. McKendrick, *Cases and Materials on the Law of Restitution* (1997), p. 475 ff.

[3] (1793) 2 H Bl 254, 126 ER 536.

[4] *Ibid.* at 258–259.

the owner; and of which, if it were refused, a court of justice would go as far as it could go, towards enforcing the payment.[5]

This passage prompted Birks to remark that 'as for the simple obligation to repay expenses, *Nicholson v Chapman* had, if anything, rather favoured such a claim'.[6] However, towards the end of his speech, Eyre CJ suggested that 'perhaps it is better for the public that these voluntary acts of benevolence from one man to another, which are charities and moral duties, but not legal duties, should depend altogether for their reward upon the moral duty of gratitude'.[7]

Thus, depending on which part of the judgment one decides to rely, *Nicholson v Chapman* appears to provide support for both the proposition that the law does grant the intervener a claim, and the proposition that it does not. *Authority*, however, it provides for neither. After all, the court was merely concerned with the question whether or not Chapman should have a lien over the timber, not with whether he had a claim for reward or reimbursement.[8] It should also be noted that even if such a claim had been considered and rejected, *Nicholson v Chapman* would have to be distinguished from the 'typical' good Samaritan case, on the grounds that Chapman did not act out of benevolence, but because the bailiff told him to act.[9] It would have remained an open question whether Chapman would be entitled to claim his expenses from the bailiff (or his employer), who in turn might have been able to recover from Nicholson.

Perhaps the most famous case that is thought to deny voluntary interveners a claim is *Falcke v Scottish Imperial Insurance Co.*[10] A life insurance policy had been mortgaged on a number of occasions. Falcke was one of the mortgagees. The mortgagor and owner of the ultimate equity of redemption, Emanuel, had paid a premium in order to stop the policy from lapsing. When Falcke subsequently died, his executrix decided to enforce the security. However, Emanuel claimed that he had a lien on the policy and was entitled to repayment of the premium before Falcke or any of the other mortgagees were paid. The Court of Appeal decided that Emanuel was not entitled to such a lien and that the premiums should therefore be paid out to Falcke's executrix. In a famous speech, Bowen LJ stated that one man's efforts to preserve or benefit the property of another 'do not according to English law create any lien upon the property saved or benefited, nor,

[5] (1793) 2 H Bl 254, 126 ER 536 at 258.

[6] P.B.H. Birks, '*Negotiorum Gestio* and the Common Law' (1971) 24 CLP 110–132 at 111–112. See for a similar interpretation *Baker v Hoag*, 3 Barbour 203 (Sup. Ct of NY, 1848), at 206 and 208 *per* Parker J and S.J. Stoljar, *The Law of Quasi-Contract* (2nd edn 1989), p. 214.

[7] *Nicholson v Chapman* (1793) 2 H Bl 254, 126 ER 536.

[8] See F.D. Rose, 'Restitution for Inland Salvage', (1986) 102 LQR 185–191 at 186. The same is true of the earlier case of *Binstead v Buck* (1776) 2 Black W 1117, 96 ER 660, on which W.B. Williston, 'Agency of Necessity' [1944] 22 Can Bar Rev 492–508 at pp. 503–504.

[9] A point that was made by counsel for Nicholson, *Nicholson v Chapman* (1793) 2 H Bl 254, 126 ER 536 at 255: 'But it is clear that Chapman took the goods merely by the direction of the bailiff of the manor, and not with any view or motive to preserve them for the true owner, or to act in any manner for his benefit.' Cf. *Surrey Breakdown Ltd v Knight* [1999] RTR 84, discussed below, at pp. 265–267.

[10] (1886) 34 Ch D 234.

even if standing alone, create any obligation to repay the expenditure'.[11] Yet, there are several reasons why *Falcke* does not provide authority for the supposed principle of no claim for the voluntary intervener. Firstly, like *Nicholson v Chapman*, the case is concerned with the question whether the intervener should have a lien on the property he saved, not with whether he should have a claim for his expenditure. To grant Emanuel a lien would have been to allow him to 'jump the queue' of secured creditors. In so far as Bowen LJ's *dictum* concerns the simple claim to repay expenditure, it must therefore be regarded as *obiter*.[12] Secondly, on its facts *Falcke* must be distinguished from the typical case of necessitous intervention. Emanuel did not intervene to preserve the interests of another, but rather out of, as Birks put it, 'a self-oriented desire to preserve the value of his own interest'.[13] Also, and perhaps more importantly, nothing indicates that it would have been impossible or impracticable for Emanuel to contact Falcke or any of the other mortgagees in order to establish their wishes. Thus, even if we were to regard Bowen LJ's statements on the duty to repay expenditure as part of the *ratio decidendi* (*quod non*), *Falcke* can at most be said to provide authority for the proposition that an intervention which (partly) serves the intervener's own interest and in circumstances in which the intervener can easily communicate with the other parties whose interest he intends to preserve, does not give rise to a claim for reimbursement of his expenses.[14]

Finally, the decision of the House of Lords in *The Goring*[15] is sometimes quoted in support of the submission that English law does not grant the intervener a claim.[16] A small passenger vessel called *Goring* was seen drifting unmanned down a non-tidal stretch of the River Thames in the middle of the night. If it had not been for the fact that the three claimants attempted and eventually succeeded in hauling it to safety, the *Goring* might well have sustained considerable damage, as well as caused damage to a number of moored yachts. Accordingly, the claimants demanded to be remunerated for salvage services. The owners of the *Goring* moved for a strikeout, arguing that the Admiralty jurisdiction of the High Court was limited to tidal waters. Sheen J, however, found for the claimants. In his view, the policy argument on which the law of salvage is based should apply to emergencies in tidal and in non-tidal waters alike:

> If a ship or her cargo is in danger in non-tidal waters it is highly desirable, as a matter of public policy, that other ships should be encouraged to go to her assistance without hesitation. The fact that waters are non-tidal may greatly affect the degree of danger from which a ship is salved. But that goes to the amount of the salvage reward and not to the question whether the services attract any reward.[17]

[11] *Falcke v Scottish Imperial Insurance Co.* (1886) 34 Ch D 234 at 248.

[12] F.D. Rose, 'Restitution for Inland Salvage', (1986) 102 LQR 185–191 at 186; Lord Goff of Chieveley and G. Jones, *The Law of Restitution* (6th edn 2002), pp. 454–455.

[13] P.B.H. Birks, *An Introduction to the Law of Restitution* (1985), p. 195.

[14] Cf. *ibid.* at p. 195.

[15] [1988] 1 AC 831.

[16] P.B.H. Birks and C. Mitchell, 'Unjust Enrichment' in P.B.H. Birks (ed.), *English Private Law*, Vol II (2000), pp. 525–635 at p. 581.

[17] *The Goring* (CA) [1987] 1 QB 687, at 693.

However, this view did not find favour with a majority of the Court of Appeal. Reversing Sheen J's decision, the Court of Appeal held that the claimants had failed to establish a right to recover a salvage reward for services to vessels in non-tidal waters. Referring to both *Nicholson v Chapman* and *Falcke v Scottish Imperial Insurance Co.*, Gibson LJ stated that 'the common law has never recognised any general doctrine of necessitous intervention by a stranger'.[18] And, despite the fact that he dissented, Donaldson MR accepted that 'a claim for salvage remuneration, otherwise than by contract, is a cause of action unknown to the common law'.[19]

The decision of the Court of Appeal was upheld in the House of Lords.[20] Lord Brandon, with whom Lord Bridge and Lord Fraser agreed, was of the opinion that the action of salvage could not be extended to non-tidal waters by the process of judicial decision. 'If any such extension is to be made', he said, 'it must (. . .) be left to the legislature to make it'.[21] Yet, *The Goring* cannot be said to have established a principle of no recovery for voluntary interveners. After all, the question that was addressed by the courts merely concerned the claimants' entitlement to a reward.[22] Nothing was decided in respect of their potential entitlement to compensation or reimbursement of their expenses. This was acknowledged by Gibson LJ, who also hinted that in respect of expenses or other loss, voluntary interveners might well be entitled to recover:

> This case is not concerned with the restoration of property, or with the return of expenses laid out, or with compensation for injury or damages suffered. *In such cases the law has shown a ready ability to develop by analogy*. This case is concerned only with a claim to a reward under salvage law for services rendered.[23]

Indeed, *The Goring* does not altogether preclude the possibility of granting a reward to voluntary interveners. True, the House of Lords explicitly refused to extend the action of salvage to non-tidal waters. *A fortiori*, it must be assumed that an extension of the action of salvage to land is equally out of the question. Yet, this does not necessarily mean that a right to be rewarded could not be founded on a basis other than the law of salvage.[24] As we will see below,[25] the action of salvage entitles the salvor not only to a reward, but incorporates several additional rights, the most notable of which is a lien on the property that was salvaged. It is possible, therefore, that the claimants were refused a reward for their efforts, *not* because the general idea of rewarding voluntary interveners failed to find favour with their Lordships, but rather because it was thought undesirable to apply the specific provisions of the law of salvage more broadly than necessary. Support for this view

18 *The Goring* (CA) [1987] 1 QB 687, at 708.
19 *Ibid.* at 704.
20 *The Goring* (HoL), [1988] 1 AC 831.
21 *Ibid.* at 857.
22 See Lord Goff of Chieveley and G. Jones, *The Law of Restitution* (6th edn 2002), p. 456, footnote 81.
23 *The Goring* (CA) [1987] 1 QB 687, at 709–710 (emphasis added).
24 F.D. Rose, 'Restitution for the Rescuer' (1989) 9 OJLS 167–204 at 168–169. Cf. *The Tojo Maru* [1972] AC 242 at 268, *per* Lord Reid: 'On land a person who interferes to save property is not in law entitled to any reward'.
25 Section 11.9.

can be drawn from the judgment of Bingham LJ (as he then was):

> The law, happily, develops. If novelty were itself a sufficient objection, the claim of Mrs. Donoghue (or Miss M'Allister) might have been summarily struck out. But there is a special factor here. The plaintiffs have, by issue of their writ in rem, invoked the Admiralty jurisdiction of the High Court. Their claim, if sound, gives rise to a maritime lien and a right of arrest, appraisement, sale and so on. These are features special to the Admiralty jurisdiction of the High Court.[26]

11.2 Cases Where the Intervener has been granted a Claim

While there seems to be no authority for the supposed principle of denying voluntary interveners a claim, English law does not appear to contain a general principle that does grant interveners a claim.[27] True, the Roman doctrine of *negotiorum gestio* did find its way into Bracton's work on the laws and customs of England.[28] Also, there are many instances where the intervener is allowed to recover for his expenses; on occasion he is even rewarded. Yet, the courts have so far refrained from establishing a general principle. Instead, if and when they wished to grant the intervener a claim, the courts have generally preferred to resort to more conventional doctrines to achieve their aim. In the process these doctrines were often stretched beyond their natural limits. *Which* of the conventional doctrines were selected for such (ab)use, is very much a matter of historical accident. Up and until the late 19th century, it appears to have been the law of contract that was seen as best fit to provide the Samaritan with recovery of his expenditure.

Let us return to the case of *Nicholson v Chapman*.[29] Counsel for Chapman claimed that he was entitled to hold on to Nicholson's timber, because 'by the common law, every person who employs labour or skill on the goods of another without a special contract, is entitled to retain them till proper recompence is made'.[30] This general principle, they thought, could be derived from at least one of three legal doctrines. Firstly, they appealed to policy underlying the law of salvage. The law of salvage grants salvors a lien on the property they saved until payment has been made. Chief Justice Eyre, however, did not think that the law of salvage applied to this case, stating that taking care of goods left by the tide upon the banks of a navigable river could only in a 'vulgar sense be said to be salvage'.[31] Then, there was the doctrine of 'distress damage feasant'.[32] Under this doctrine, if any chattel was trespassing onto land, the owner of that land or another person with a sufficient interest in it could distrain the chattel until sufficient amends

[26] *The Goring* (CA) [1987] 1 QB 687, at 717.

[27] R.M. Jackson, *The History of Quasi-Contract in English Law* (1936), p. 124: 'the principle of *negotiorum gestio* does not exist in our law.'

[28] H. de Bracton, *De Legibus et Consuetudinibus Angliae* (G.E. Woodbine, ed., 1968), pp. 42b and 100b.

[29] (1793) 2 H Bl 254, 126 ER 536.

[30] *Ibid.* at 256.

[31] *Ibid.* at 257.

[32] On the history of which, see G.L. Williams, *Liability for Animals* (1939), pp. 7–25.

were tendered. Originally, this doctrine may have applied to animals only.[33] By the time of Charles I, it had also come to apply to inanimate objects, such as Nicholson's timber.[34] It is not clear whether distress was allowed for trespass *per se*, or only in cases where the trespass had resulted in damage. There was at least some authority that suggested that the mere encumbrance resulting from the presence of another person's animals or things on one's land was enough to justify distress damage feasant.[35] The purpose of the distress would presumably then be not to secure compensation of the damage (there was none), but to ensure payment of the costs of impounding and/or keep of the chattel.[36] However, Chief Justice Eyre must have been of the opinion that a mere trespass did not suffice. Accordingly, he held that the doctrine of distress damage feasant did not apply, the case before him not being one of 'damage-feasance'.[37]

Thirdly and lastly, counsel for Chapman sought to rely on the old law concerning 'franchises'. Franchises were privileges derived from the royal prerogative.[38] One such franchise was that of 'wreck'. At common law, the Crown was entitled to all unclaimed shipwrecks. This privilege could be – and was regularly[39] – granted by the Crown to lords of the manor and could also be acquired through prescription. Another franchise was that of 'estray'. A lord of the manor who had acquired the franchise of estray, would be entitled to take possession of all tame animals that strayed onto his land. Once he had taken possession, he was required to announce his 'find' on two market days in the nearest towns. If the owner did not claim his property within a year and a day, ownership in the stray animal would pass to the lord of the manor. If, on the other hand, the owner did turn up within the said period to claim his property, he would have to compensate the lord of the manor for the cost of looking after the animal.[40] This obligation would arise, regardless of whether the lord of the manor acted upon considerations of self-interest or

[33] G.L. Williams, *Liability for Animals* (1939), p. 26. It should be noted that the doctrine now no longer applies to animals: Animals Act 1971, s. 7(1).

[34] See *Arthur v Anker* [1996] 3 All ER 783 at 789 and 793–794, with further references.

[35] See for an extensive discussion on this issue G.L. Williams, *Liability for Animals* (1939), pp. 70–76 and *Arthur v Anker* [1996] 3 All ER 783 where it was decided that the remedy is only available if actual damage was suffered (Hirst LJ dissenting). It should be noted that – with regard to livestock – the rules laid down in section 4 of the Animals Act (1971) allow the landowner to recover for any expenses reasonably incurred in keeping livestock that has strayed onto his land, even if he has suffered no damage.

[36] See also *Sorrell v Paget* [1950] 1 KB 252 at 260, *per* Bucknill LJ.

[37] *Nicholson v Chapman* (1793) 2 H Bl 254, 126 ER 536 at 258.

[38] W. Blackstone, *Commentaries on the Laws of England*, Book 2 (1st edn 1766), p. 67. See also W. Cruise, *A Digest of the Laws of England respecting Real Property*, Vol 3 (3rd edn 1824), pp. 279 ff.

[39] S.A. Moore, *A History of the Foreshore and the Law Relating Thereto* (3rd edn 1888), pp. 22–23: (. . .) 'the franchise of wreck had been granted out by the King over the greater part of the coasts of the kingdom, but, nevertheless, in some places it was still in the Crown'. See also pp. 22 and 688–689, footnote (h).

[40] *Taylor and James' Case* (1607) Godb 150, 78 ER 91 at 151 *per* Cook CJ (reported under the name *Taylor v Jeanes* in Noy 144). See also *Pledall v Cosmore* (1621) 1 Roll Abr 879, c.5; *Henly v Walsh* (1705) 2 Salk 686, 91 ER 583 at 687, note and W. Cruise, *A Digest of the Laws of England respecting Real Property*, Vol 3 (3rd edn 1824), pp. 298–299.

altruism. It seems that – in any case by the beginning of the 17th century – similar rules had been adopted with regard to wreck.[41] The obvious problem for Chapman was, that even if the lord of the manor where Nicholson's timber was found (Wimbledon) had the franchises of both estray and wreck, the timber simply could not be said to be a wreck or a stray animal. The attempts by Chapman's legal representatives to argue that the lord of the manor of Wimbledon had a franchise that entitled Chapman to retain the timber until his expenses were paid for were therefore doomed to fail. Moreover, with regard to the franchise of estray it had been decided in 1607 that the lord of the manor could not delegate the powers that he had under the franchise to one of his tenants.[42] Had the lord of the manor had a franchise that entitled him to take charge of Nicholson's timber, it would therefore still have been doubtful whether Chapman could rely on this franchise.

Not convinced by any of the three lines of arguments that were put forward by counsel for Chapman, Eyre CJ duly found for the claimant. In his view Chapman's act amounted to nothing more than 'a mere finding and taking care of the thing found', which did not entitle him to any lien on the timber. However, with regard to the broader question of whether Chapman should be entitled to claim his expenses, he made the observation – cited earlier in this chapter – that 'a court of justice would go as far as it could go, towards enforcing the payment'.[43] A similar proposition can be found as early as 1530, in the second dialogue of St German's *Doctor and Student*. Arguing that someone who takes abandoned goods into custody should be allowed reimbursement of expenses, the student draws an analogy with finders:

> (. . .) yf any man (. . .) put the goodes in saufegarde to the vse of the owner: I thynk he doth laufully & that he shal be alowed for his reasonable expences in that behalf as he shalbe of goodes found/but that he shal haue no property in them no more than in godes found (. . .)[44]

Regrettably, neither St. German's student, nor the Chief Justice elaborated on the exact basis on which these reasonable expenses could be claimed. A footnote added by the reporter of *Nicholson v Chapman*, one Henry Blackstone, suggests that the basis was most likely to be an 'implied promise':

> It seems probable that in such a case, if any action could be maintained, it would be an action of *assumpsit* for work and labour, in which the Court would imply a special instance and request, as well as a promise.[45]

41 See *Sir Henry Constable's Case* (1601) 5 Co Rep 106a, 77 ER 218 at 108b.

42 *Taylor and James' Case* [1607] Godb 150, 78 ER 91 at 150 *per* Cook CJ.

43 *Nicholson v Chapman* (1793) 2 H Bl 254, 126 ER 536 at 258.

44 Chr. St. German, *Doctor and Student* (T.F.T. Plucknett and J.L. Barton, eds, 1974), p. 292 (ch. 51).

45 *Nicholson v Chapman* (1793) 2 H Bl 254 at 258, footnote (a). Cf. H. Finch, *Law, or a Discourse Thereof* (1678 edn), pp. 180–181, where it is suggested that cases of finding give rise to '(as it were) contracts in Law, though not arising from the special agreement of the parties'.

11.3 Contract: The Promise 'Implied in Law'

By 1793 there was nothing unusual about inferring a request or promise from the conduct of (one of) the parties, as where a man took a cloth to a tailor to be made into a gown, without specifically agreeing on the price. From his act of bringing the cloth to the tailor, it was inferred that he agreed to pay a reasonable price for the tailor's efforts.[46] It must be assumed that the same could apply to cases of necessitous intervention. That is not to say that any cry for help would immediately give rise to the inference of a promise to pay for the intervention. However, depending on the circumstances such an inference might have been appropriate. An illustration can be drawn from the modern case of *Upton-on-Severn RDC v Powell*,[47] where the defendant called the fire brigade to put out a fire at his farm. On the facts of the case, the Court of Appeal concluded that this request included an implied promise to pay for the brigade's services.[48] Yet, for an eighteenth century court to imply a promise where a service had been performed without a request or promise, must have been unusual, albeit not unheard of.[49] Indeed, even if the beneficiary had subsequently promised to reimburse or reward the intervener for his unrequested intervention, this promise was not regarded as binding because 'a meer voluntary curtesie will not have a consideration to uphold an *assumpsit*'.[50] However, in a small class of cases, an action of *assumpsit* was allowed despite the absence of both request and express promise. Here, the contractual relationship was not based on agreement between the parties, but was imposed by the courts: 'implied in law'. Most of the few cases in point appear to have involved the unrequested performance by one party of another's duty.

A. Performance of Another Person's Duty: Burying the Dead

In common law, it was the first duty of an executor or administrator to bury the deceased.[51] Naturally, the burial had to be suitable to the rank and circumstances of the deceased.[52] It must be assumed that this was a public duty,[53] hence not enforceable in private law. After all, the aggrieved party was no longer in a position to bring a lawsuit. Yet, it appears to have been a well established principle that anyone – even a complete stranger – was entitled to perform this duty in the executor's

46 *The Six Carpenters' Case* (1611) 8 Co Rep 146a, 77 ER 695 at 147a.

47 [1942] 1 All ER 220.

48 See for a more detailed discussion P. Mitchell, 'A Ratio Decidendi for Upton-on-Severn Rural District Council v Powell', (1997) 12 Journal of Contract Law 76–86.

49 W. Blackstone, *Commentaries on the Laws of England*, Book 3 (1768), pp. 161–165. See for a historical outline R.M. Jackson, *The History of Quasi-Contract in English Law* (1936), pp. 39 ff.

50 *Lampleigh v Brathwait* (1615) Hob 105, 80 ER 255 at 106. Cf. Ch. Viner, *A General Abridgment of Law and Equity*, Vol I (1746), pp. 279 ff. (Actions [of *Assumpsit*], Q).

51 J. Comyns, *A Digest of the Laws of England* (5th edn 1822), p. 462 (Administration, C1).

52 W. Blackstone, *Commentaries on the Laws of England*, Book 2 (1st edn 1766), pp. 507–508.

53 *Rees v Hughes* [1946] 1 KB 517 at 523, *per* Scott LJ.

stead, and recover from the estate.[54] Thus, in the 1829 case of *Rogers v Price*[55] the executor of a deceased man was held liable upon an implied *assumpsit* 'for work and labour as an undertaker and materials furnished for the funeral'. Baron Garrow set out the policy considerations that supported this decision:

> The common principles of decency and humanity, the common impulses of our nature, would direct everyone, as a preliminary step, to provide a decent funeral, at the expense of the estate.[56]

In at least one case, the intervener was allowed to recover for other costs as well as the cost of the funeral. In *Shallcross v Wright*,[57] the deceased had died of a highly contagious fever. On the advice of a physician, the bed and furniture in the room in which he died were burnt, and all people were removed from the house, 'fumigated, cleansed and whitewashed' and put up in a nearby hotel. Lord Langdale held that all these acts were necessary for the safety of the persons in the house, as well as for the protection of the entire neighbourhood and allowed the plaintiff to recover all costs upon an implied contract.

When the deceased was a married woman, the duty to bury her used to fall upon the husband.[58] Where someone took upon him the burial of another's wife, he could recover from the husband on an implied *assumpsit*.[59] The 1788 case of *Jenkins v Tucker*[60] left some doubt as to whether one could only recover if one was 'the proper person to interfere'. However, the subsequent cases of *Ambrose v Kerrison*[61] and *Bradshaw v Beard*[62] confirmed that even a stranger could recover, provided that he did not aim to prevent the husband from performing the last duty to his wife's remains.

It is not entirely clear whether a father was legally responsible for the burial of his deceased children. In 1628 Jones J stated that he thought that a father was at common law bound to do so,[63] and this appears to have been the predominant view.[64] If this is correct, it must be assumed that anyone who buried a child on behalf of its father was allowed to recover for his expenses upon an *assumpsit* implied in law. The earliest authoritative decision to that effect is said to date from 1656, but the reports are inconclusive.[65]

[54] Ch. Viner, *A General Abridgment of Law and Equity*, Vol XI (1753), p. 207 (Executors, B.a 24). See also *Tugwell v Heyman* (1812) 3 Camp 298, 170 ER 1389.

[55] (1829) 3 Y & J 28, 148 ER 1080.

[56] *Ibid.* at 34.

[57] (1850) 12 Beav 558, 50 ER 1174.

[58] *Rees v Hughes* [1946] 1 KB 517 at 523–524, *per* Scott LJ.

[59] *Bertie v Lord Chesterfield* (1722) 9 Mod 31, 88 ER 296.

[60] (1788) 1 H Bl 90, 126 ER 55.

[61] (1851) 10 CB 776, 138 ER 307.

[62] (1862) 12 CBNS 344, 142 ER 1175.

[63] *Besfich v Coggil* (1628) Palmer 559 at 560, 81 ER 1219.

[64] *R. v Vann* (1851) 2 Den 325, 169 ER 523 and *Clarke v London General Omnibus Co.* [1906] 2 KB 648 at 659, *per* Lord Alverstone CJ. However, doubts were expressed by Farewell LJ, *ibid.* at 663.

[65] In *Hunt v Wotton* (1679) T Raym 259, 83 ER 133, Montague CB and Atkyns B refer to *Church v Church* (1656) as authority for this proposition. However, according to Baker a statement to that effect appears in no report of that case. See J.H. Baker, 'The Use of Assumpsit for Restitutionary Money Claims' in E.J.H. Schrage, *Unjust Enrichment* (2nd edn 1999), pp. 31–57 at p. 43, footnote 66.

As far as the burial of married women is concerned, the above cases are now no longer thought to be good law. After all, the combined effect of the Married Women's Property Act 1882 and the Law Reform (Married Women and Tortfeasors) Act 1935 has put married women in the same position as unmarried women or men. In accordance with the cases discussed in the first paragraph of this subsection, the costs of her burial should be recovered from her estate. Yet, from whom should the person who buried a married woman recover if it turns out that her estate does not contain sufficient funds? The answer to this question was deliberately left open in the case of *Rees v Hughes*.[66]

B. Performance of Another Person's Duty: Looking After the Poor?

Under old poor law,[67] parish officers were bound to take care of the so-called 'casual poor'. If a pauper fell ill and was in want of medical care, he was considered 'as casual poor wherever his infirm and indigent body was found, and he had a claim on the parish where he was so found to have his necessities provided for by them'.[68] In a cluster of cases in the first half of the nineteenth century, voluntary interveners who had looked after a pauper were allowed to recover their expenses upon an implied *assumpsit* from the parish in which the pauper had fallen ill. It has been suggested by Professor Burrows that these cases are 'most obviously explained as [examples of] restitution for necessity'.[69] It is doubtful, however, whether necessity alone was enough to support the intervener's claim in any of these cases.

In the first of these cases, *Simmons v Willmott*,[70] a pauper had been thrown from a cart and severely bruised. He was brought to the plaintiff's house, where he was kept and attended by a nurse for ten days. The plaintiff sought to recover the cost of keep, as well as the money he had paid to the nurse from the parish in which the accident had occurred. Lord Eldon allowed the claim, stating:

It comes to this point. Was the person relieved, within the description of casual poor? If he was, the parish-officers are bound to take care of him: a common person would not; but if

[66] [1946] 1 KB 517 at 527, *per* Morton LJ. A possible argument in favour of the view that the husband would continue to be subsidiarily liable, can be derived from the 1722 case of *Bertie v Lord Chesterfield*. There, the wife of the late Earl of Caernarvon had been granted a settlement of 'separate maintenance', of which she could dispose by will. When she died, her executor, one Mr Bertie, employed an undertaker to bury the Countess. Initially Bertie had intended to recover the cost of burial from the estate of the Countess, but when it emerged that she had 'given away more than she had to dispose', he brought a claim against the estate of the late Earl. The Court of Chancery held that the estate of the late Earl was liable to pay the expenses of burying the wife, 'because the plaintiff took nothing of her estate by being made executor, for she gave away the whole in legacies'. *Bertie v Lord Chesterfield* (1722) 9 Mod 31, 88 ER 296 at 32.

[67] The old poor law was abolished in section 1 of the National Assistance Act 1948.

[68] *Lamb v Bunce* (1815) 4 M & S 275, 105 ER 836 at 277, *per* Lord Ellenborough CJ. This duty was made statutory in the Poor Law Amendment Act 1834, s. 54.

[69] A. Burrows, *The Law of Restitution* (2nd edn 2002), p. 311.

[70] (1800) 3 Esp 91, 170 ER 549.

a common person does take care of him, on the liability of the parish-officers, I think he has a right to recover against them.[71]

Regrettably, Lord Eldon did not specify the requirements for being allowed such recovery. Burrows speculated that it was the 'pressure' of the pauper's 'immediate want' that was the decisive factor, and concluded that the case is one of restitution for necessity.[72] But the pauper's emergency is mentioned at no point in the judgment. Indeed, the facts of the case suggest a different analysis. It was established at trial that the plaintiff had sent a messenger to the parish officers to inform them of the state of affairs. Moreover, the overseer who received the message had directed the messenger to 'go to the beadle' (a parish officer of lower rank) 'and also desired him[73] to assist in taking care of the man'.[74] In the eyes of a nineteenth century judge, these communications may well have amounted to an actual request and promise, inferred from the conduct of the parties rather than implied 'in law'. Thus, it remains doubtful whether a similar claim would have been granted in a case in which no communication had taken place between intervener and parish.

The same is true in respect of the 1815 case of *Lamb v Bunce*.[75] In that case a surgeon attended a pauper with the knowledge of the overseer. Mere silence, of course, would not normally be interpreted as a request. However, even in modern English law silence can exceptionally amount to a request. For example, where there has been an ongoing course of dealing between the parties, silence may by implication amount to an acceptance.[76] That was precisely the case here: the plaintiff was generally employed to attend the poor of the defendant parish. Add to that the fact that during the period of attendance the overseer frequently visited the pauper at his sickbed, and a request is inferred without too much difficulty. '[W]hen the parish officer visited the pauper according to his duty', Lord Ellenborough CJ said, 'and knew that the plaintiff who was generally employed for the poor was in attendance upon him, and did not repudiate his attendance, he in effect commanded it'.[77]

A case that is perhaps more difficult to explain in terms of promises inferred from the conduct of the parties, is *Tomlinson v Bentall*.[78] A poor woman had broken her thigh in an accident in the parish of Heybridge. She was refused medical attendance in that parish and after much dispute – and four hours of carting the poor woman back and forth in the middle of the night – she was eventually brought to her home parish of Malden. There, she was attended by the plaintiff surgeon, who sought to recover his fee by bringing an action of *assumpsit* against the parish of Heybridge. Counsel for the defendants objected that they had never

[71] *Ibid.* at 93. [72] A. Burrows, *The Law of Restitution* (2nd edn 2002), p. 311.
[73] It remains unclear whether 'him' refers to the messenger or to the beadle.
[74] *Simmons v Willmott* (1800) 3 Esp 91, 170 ER 549 at 92.
[75] (1815) 4 M & S 275, 105 ER 836.
[76] G.H. Treitel, *The Law of Contract* (10th edn 1999), p. 31 with further references.
[77] *Lamb v Bunce* (1815) 4 M & S 275, 105 ER 836 at 277.
[78] (1826) 5 B & C 738, 108 ER 274.

promised to pay for the medical care. The court upheld the plaintiff's action of *assumpsit*. Yet, it is rather difficult to discern a request in this case. Indeed, the defendants by their dishonourable behaviour had made it abundantly clear that they did not intend to be held responsible for the poor woman. Perhaps the true basis of the judgment was a policy concern that the parish should not be able to benefit from its officers' wrongdoing by their refusal to perform their duty:

> The accident having happened to the pauper in the parish of Heybridge, it was the duty of the officers of that parish to provide medical assistance for her there. (. . .) I think they could not, by removing her elsewhere, shift upon other people that burden which the law cast upon themselves.[79]

Yet, whatever the precise basis, the mere fact that the medical assistance was given in circumstances of emergency or necessity is unlikely to have sufficed.[80] Unless there was a blatant refusal by the parish to perform its duty, a request by the parish, whether express or inferred from the conduct of the parish officers, appears to have been required if the intervener's claim was to be sustained. This was confirmed in *Paynter v Williams*,[81] in which Bayley B stated:

> The legal liability of the parish does not give anyone who chooses to attend a pauper and supply him with medicines a right to call on them for payment. It is their duty to see that a proper person is employed, and they are to have an option who the medical man shall be.[82]

In 1930, the responsibility for the welfare of the poor was transferred from the parishes to local authorities under the control of the Ministry of Health.[83] The cases discussed in this subsection are therefore no longer authoritative.

C. Performance of Another Person's Duty: a General Principle?

In the United States of America, the courts drew upon the burial cases to formulate a general principle. Thus, in the 1906 case of *Mathie v Hancock*, Rowell CJ stated that 'when an obligation is imposed by law upon one to do an act because of an interest in the public to have it done, and that one fails to do it, he who does do it, expecting compensation, may recover therefor of him on whom the obligation is imposed'.[84] In England, attempts had been made to provoke the adoption of a

[79] (1826) 5 B & C 738, 108 ER 274, at 748–749, *per* Holroyd J.

[80] Burrows again classifies *Tomlinson* as a case of 'necessity': A. Burrows, *The Law of Restitution* (2nd edn 2002), p. 311. So too P.B.H. Birks, 'In Defence of Free Acceptance' in A. Burrows (ed.), *Essays on the Law of Restitution* (1991), pp. 105–146 at p. 117 and footnote 54.

[81] (1833) 1 C & M 810, 149 ER 626 (Exch).

[82] *Ibid.* at 819.

[83] R.D. Steele, *The National Assistance Act 1948* (1949), p. 3 with further references.

[84] *Mathie v Hancock* 78 Vt 414, 63 Atl 143 at 144 (Sup. Ct of Vermont, 1906). See also *Manhattan Fire-Alarm Co. v Weber* 22 Misc Rep 729, 50 NYS 42 (Sup. Ct of NY, 1898); *Keith v De Bussigney* 179 Mass 255, 60 NE 614 at 615 (Sup. Jud. Ct of Massachusetts, 1901) and W.A. Keener, *A Treatise on the Law of Quasi-Contracts* (1893), p. 346. Cf. also American Law Institute, *Restatement of the Law of Restitution* (1937), § 115 and F.C Woodward, *The Law of Quasi Contracts* (1913), p. 310 (§ 193).

similarly broad principle. In *Urmston v Newcomen*[85] Attorney-General Sir John Campbell expressed the view that 'if a party be bound to perform an act, and neglect it, another party performing it for him acquires a right of action against him'.[86] However, the court could not be tempted to adopt a generalization of this kind, and instead decided the case on its particular facts.

In the absence of evidence to the contrary, it would appear that those who voluntarily performed another person's legal duty, could not recover in *assumpsit*. The same was generally held in respect of obligations that were not imposed by the law, but were created by contract or otherwise.[87] In the words of Swinfen Eady J: 'If A voluntarily pays B's debt, B is under no obligation to repay A (. . .) and in this respect I can see no difference between the discharge of a statutory liability and the discharge of a contractual liability'.[88] Yet, there is at least one case in which an exception to this rule appears to have been recognized, where the contractual obligation of another was performed in circumstances of emergency. In *Waters v Weigall* a house that was rented by the plaintiff was damaged in a storm. According to the plaintiff it was his landlord who was bound to repair the house. However, because the house was in want of immediate repair, the plaintiff decided to make the necessary repairs himself. The Court of Exchequer held that the plaintiff could deduct the cost of these repairs from his rent, provided that the landlord was indeed bound to make the repairs, and that the plaintiff was 'right in expending this sum in repairs for him'.[89] The Court does not appear to have distinguished between cases where someone performed the obligation of another, purely for the benefit of that other, and cases such as the one it was considering, where performance would benefit both parties involved.

D. Preserving Another's Life or Property: Recovery on the Basis of an Implied Promise?

In cases where one person had voluntarily intervened to preserve another person's life or property, some American courts again made liberal use of the doctrine of implied promises. In *Reeder v Anderson's Adm'rs*,[90] for example, the 'finder' of a runaway slave was allowed an action on the basis of an 'implied undertaking' by the owner 'to (at least) indemnify any person who shall, by the expenditure of time

[85] (1836) 4 A & E 899, 111 ER 1022. [86] *Ibid.* at 903.

[87] See also *Reason v Wirdnam*, (1824) 1 Car & P 434, (1927) 171 ER 1262, *per* Park J: 'I am clearly of the opinion, that, if a person takes a journey to become bail for another, he cannot maintain an action against such person, for his trouble or loss of time in such a journey; because, he does not undertake the journey as work or labour, or as a person employed by the defendant; but he does it as his friend, and to do him a kindness'.

[88] *Re National Motor Mail-Coach Co. Ltd* [1908] 2 Ch 515 at 520. See also *ibid.* at 523, *per* Cozens-Hardy MR and *Tappin v Broster* (1823) 1 Car & P 112, 171 ER 1124. An exception to this principle had been allowed where someone discharged debt in order to preserve his own goods; *Exall v Partridge* (1799) 8 TR 308, 101 ER 1405. Cf. also *Owen v Tate* and *The Zuhal K and Selin*, discussed below, Section 11.7. [89] *Waters v Weigall* (1795) 2 Anst 575, 145 ER 971, at 576.

[90] 4 Dana 193 (Ky Ct of Apps, 1836).

and money, contribute to a reclamation of the lost property'.[91] However, recovery was only allowed where the intervener had performed his services with the intention to charge for them. And, in the absence of evidence to the contrary, it was presumed that where someone voluntarily intervened to preserve another man's property, he did so gratuitously.[92] A similar position was adopted in cases involving the preservation of life and limb. In principle, the presumption was that the act of saving another constituted a gratuitous service. However, where the intervener was a doctor or a nurse, this presumption was reversed. Thus, it was said that 'if a physician administered to a man deprived of his senses by a dangerous blow', 'he would certainly be bound to make reasonable remuneration, though incapable at the moment of making an actual request'.[93]

In England, the doctrine of implied promises was applied much more restrictively. As far as the preservation of another's property is concerned, application of the doctrine appears to have been confined to instances where there was a pre-existing relationship between the intervener and the beneficiary. The best-known case in point is perhaps *Great Northern Rly v Swaffield.*[94] There, the plaintiff Railway Company was allowed to recover the cost of stabling a horse, which had not been picked up upon arrival by its owner. It should be noted at the outset that the basis of this decision is not altogether clear. The speech of Pollock B contains references to cases of 'agency of necessity',[95] but these may have been invoked merely by way of analogy.[96] Kelly CB does seem to have based his decision on the doctrine of agency of necessity, but Piggott B adopted implied contract reasoning. The speech of Amphlett B is in this respect inconclusive.

Pollock B stressed that in his view, the claimant had been bound under the contract of carriage to look after the defendant's horse. 'If there were that duty without the correlative right' he said, 'it would be a manifest injustice'.[97] It must be assumed that if the claimant had been a mere bystander, he would not, according to Pollock B, have had a legal duty to intervene and consequently no right to recover. By contrast, Kelly CB, Pigott B, and Amphlett B made no mention of the stationmaster's contractual duties. Indeed, Pigott B stated that the plaintiffs 'were bound, *from ordinary feelings of humanity*, to keep the horse safely and feed him',[98] that the expense was 'rightly incurred' and that 'there was, under these circumstances, an implied contract by the defendant entitling the plaintiff to recover the

[91] 4 Dana 193 (Ky Ct of Apps, 1836) at 193. See also *Meekins v Simpson* 176 NC 130, 96 SE 894 (Sup. Ct of N.C., 1918) and *Chase v Corcoran* 106 Mass 286 (Sup. Ct of Mass., 1871).

[92] *Bartholomew v Jackson* 20 Johns 28, 11 Am Dec 237 (Sup Ct of NY, 1822).

[93] *Richardson v Strong* 35 NC 106 at 108, *per* Ruffin CJ, 55 Am Dec 430 (Sup. Ct of N.C., 1851). See also F.C Woodward, *The Law of Quasi Contracts* (1913), p. 315 (§ 201) with further references.

[94] (1874) LR 9 Ex 132.

[95] *Ibid.* at 136, *per* Kelly CB and at 138, *per* Pollock B.

[96] A. Burrows, *The Law of Restitution* (2nd edn 2002), p. 306 and A. Burrows and E. McKendrick, *Cases and Materials on the Law of Restitution* (1997), p. 502.

[97] *Ibid.* at 137–138. Amphlett B, at 139, appears to have agreed with this view. It should be noted that neither Pollock B, nor indeed Amphlett B or Kelly CB, gave a clear indication of the legal basis upon which the claimant could recover.

[98] *Ibid.* at 137. Cf. *ibid.* at 139, *per* Amphlett B.: 'a matter of common humanity'.

amount from him'.[99] This could be taken to imply that interveners who perform a moral, rather than a legal duty should equally be allowed to recover. However, Pigott B did stress that in failing to collect the horse, the defendant had brought about the situation of necessity. In any case, in so far as Pigott B intended to lay down a general principle allowing necessitous interveners to recover, his remarks are clearly *obiter*.

Cases in which the intervener was allowed to recover on an implied promise for costs incurred in preserving another person's life or good health are equally rare. In the absence of an express agreement on the matter, even doctors do not seem to have been allowed to charge for their services. The fact that the services of doctors were here traditionally thought of as being of a purely honorary character,[100] may explain why the English courts did not follow their American counterparts in this respect. The only general category of cases where recovery was allowed appears to be where necessaries had been provided to the mentally incapacitated. In the 1842 case of *Williams v Wentworth*, it was successfully argued that where necessaries were provided to a 'lunatic', the law should imply a contract in the same way as it did 'as against a husband, for necessaries supplied to his wife'.[101] There is at least one case, where a similar claim was granted to someone who looked after a drunkard suffering from *delirium tremens*.[102]

E. The Decline of the Implied Contract Theory

The *crux* of contractual obligations is, and always has been, 'agreement'. And one can only speak of agreement – in any meaningful sense – if there has been some form of communication between the parties. This communication can be verbal or through conduct. In exceptional cases one can even communicate through silence. The typical case of necessitous intervention, however, involves no communication at all. To imply, then, a request or promise 'in law' amounts *de facto* to the imposition of contractual obligations where there is in truth no contract.[103] It should be of no surprise, then, that the courts have long abandoned the use of contracts implied in law. This development was set in motion in the second half of the nineteenth century. In 1852, the Common Law Procedure Act ended the need for 'fictitious and needless statements' in the claimant's pleadings. More particularly, it was decreed that 'the statement of promises which need not be proved, as

99 *Ibid.* at 137 (emphasis added).

100 *Chorley v Bolcot* (1791) 4 TR 317 at 318, 100 ER 1014, *per* Lord Kenyon CJ. See also C.G. Addison, *A Treatise on the Law of Contracts*, Vol I (2nd edn 1849), p. 67.

101 *Williams v Wentworth* (1842) 5 Beav 325 at 327, 49 ER 603. See also *Re Rhodes* (1890) 44 Ch D 94 and Lord Goff of Chieveley and G. Jones, *The Law of Restitution* (6th edn 2002), pp. 462–464 with further references. See for a discussion of a husband's liability for necessaries supplied to his wife Part II, Section 11.4 'Agency of Necessity', Subsection A.

102 *West Ham Union v Pearson* (1890) 62 LT 638. Cf. *Gore v Gibson* (1845) 13 M & W 623, 153 ER 260 at 627, *per* Alderson B.

103 Cf. P.B.H. Birks, *Unjust Enrichment* (2003), pp. 229–235.

promises in *indebitatus* counts' should be omitted.[104] To stress the distinction between the real and the merely fictitious implied promise, an increasing number of authors decided to adopt the Roman term 'quasi-contract' to denote the promise implied in law.[105] Some appear to have thought that Frederick Pollock was one of the first in England to advocate this re-categorization.[106] In truth, Pollock had been preceded by others, amongst whom someone he described as being 'devoid of any historical sense and seldom well informed or accurate in the details of either English or Roman law': John Austin.[107] In a footnote to one of his published lectures, Austin wrote:

> Quasi-contracts, or contracts *quasi* or *uti*, ought to be distinguished carefully from tacit or implied contracts. A tacit or implied contract is a genuine contract. (. . .) But a quasi-contract is not a genuine convention, and, by consequence, is not a genuine contract. In the language of English jurisprudence, facts or events which are contracts *quasi* or *uti*, are styled *implied contracts*, or *contracts which the law implies*: that is to say, contracts *quasi* or *uti*, and implied or tacit contracts, are commonly or frequently confounded by English lawyers.[108]

However, in a minority of influential textbooks the 'contracts implied in law' continued to be treated of as genuine contracts well into the twentieth century.[109] The same disparity can be discerned in the case law of the time. In the 1890 case *Re Rhodes*, Cotton and Lindley LJJ expressed their dissatisfaction with the implied contract terminology.[110] Lindley LJ appears to have preferred the Roman phrase '*obligationes quasi ex contractu*'[111] – perhaps unsurprisingly so, as he happened to be Pollock's former 'master in the law'.[112] Similar sentiments were expressed in the late thirties and early forties by Scott LJ,[113] Lord Wright[114] and Lord Atkin.[115] Indeed, it was said that Lord Atkin's speech in the 1941 case of *United Australia Ltd v Barclays Bank Ltd* 'finally killed the notion that the fictitious contract still

[104] Common Law Procedure Act 1852, s. 49.

[105] The Roman terminology had been used in the courts before, albeit very occasionally and not always in its present meaning. *E.g. Le Mason v Dixon* (1628) W 173, 82 ER 92; *City of London v Goree* (1676) 3 Keb 677, 84 ER 947 and *Boson v Sandford* (1691) 3 Salk 203, 91 ER 777.

[106] *E.g.* F.C Woodward, *The Law of Quasi Contracts* (1913), p. 6 (§ 4); W.S. Holdsworth, *A History of English Law*, Vol III (3rd edn 1923), p. 424, footnote 9 and P.B.H. Birks, *Unjust Enrichment* (2003), p. 230.

[107] F. Pollock, 'Has the Common Law Received the Fiction Theory of Corporations?', (1911) 27 LQR 219–235 at p. 223, footnote 2. See also C.H.S. Fifoot, *Pollock and Maitland* (1971), p. 13 with further references.

[108] J. Austin, *The Province of Jurisprudence Determined* (2nd edn 1861), p. 306, footnote. See also F. Pollock, *Principles of Contract* (1876), p. 28 and W.R. Anson, *Principles of the English Law of Contract* (1879), pp. 321 ff.

[109] *E.g.* A.E. Randall, *Principles of the Law of Contracts* (7th edn 1921), pp. 43 ff. and W.A. Macfarlane and G.W. Wrangham, *Chitty's Treatise on the Law of Contracts* (18th edn 1930), pp. 41 ff.

[110] *Re Rhodes* (1890) 44 Ch D 94 at 105 and 107.

[111] *Ibid.* at 107.

[112] See the dedication on one of the first pages of F. Pollock, *Principles of Contract* (1876).

[113] *Morgan v Ashcroft* [1938] 1 KB 49 at 74–76.

[114] *Brook's Wharf and Bull Wharf Ltd v Goodman Brothers* [1937] 1 KB 527 at 545 and later in *Fibrosa Spolka Akcyjna v Fairbairn Lawson Combe Barbour Ltd* [1943] AC 32 at 61–64. See also his article in the Cambridge Law Journal, (1938) 6 CLJ 305–326.

[115] *United Australia Ltd v Barclays Bank Ltd* [1941] AC 1 at 27–29.

survive[d]'.[116] While even after that date some within the judiciary continued to use the old language,[117] a majority of judges, as well as academic scholars, has since come to reject the implied contract theory.[118]

11.4 'Agency of Necessity'

Traditionally, the law of agency was regarded as part of the law of contract.[119] And, although that is now no longer thought to be correct,[120] many of the theories developed with regard to the law of contract are reflected in the law of agency. While the 'promise implied in law' haunted the law of contract, a similar concept filtered into the law of agency: the 'authority implied in law', or 'authority of necessity'.[121] The resulting doctrine is commonly referred to as 'agency of necessity', and was developed in three different types of cases: cases involving married women, shipmasters, and acceptors for honour.

A. Agency of Married Women (and their Children?) in Respect of Necessaries

Until the late nineteenth century, a married woman was incapable of entering into contracts or indeed of owning property. However, she could act as her husband's agent.[122] This would normally require the authority of her husband, whether express, implied in fact, or apparent.[123] Yet, where a married woman made a contract for 'necessaries', the courts raised a presumption that the required authority had been given. While the earliest cases of this kind may have employed implied contract language, 'implying' a direct request by the husband to any third party to provide his wife with necessaries,[124] the issue eventually came to be thought of as one of agency.[125] It was presumed that the husband, being obliged to maintain his

116 J.H. Munkman, *The Law of Quasi-Contracts* (1950), p. 9.

117 *E.g. Re Diplock* [1948] Ch 465 at 480.

118 Most explicitly Lord Browne-Wilkinson in *Westdeutsche Bank v Islington* [1996] 2 WLR 802 at 833. But cf. S. Hedley, *Restitution: Its Division and Ordering* (2001).

119 C.G. Addison, *A Treatise on the Law of Contracts*, Vol II (2nd edn 1849), pp. 669–670; J.H. Munkman, *The Law of Quasi-Contracts* (1950), p. 76 and Lord Goff of Chieveley and G. Jones, *The Law of Restitution* (6th edn 2002), p. 451.

120 Lord Goff of Chieveley and G. Jones, *The Law of Restitution* (6th edn 2002), p. 452 and F.M.B. Reynolds, *Bowstead and Reynolds on Agency* (17th edn 2001), pp. 3–4.

121 F.M.B. Reynolds, 'Agency and Representation' in P.B.H. Birks (ed.), *English Private Law*, Vol II (2000), pp. 163–221 at 184.

122 A.W.B. Simpson, *A History of the Common Law of Contract* (1975), pp. 545–549.

123 See for the distinction between these different types of authority F.M.B. Reynolds, *Bowstead and Reynolds on Agency* (17th edn 2001), p. 1.

124 *E.g. Dent v Scott* (1648) Aleyn 61, 82 ER 916. See J.H. Baker, 'The Use of Assumpsit for Restitutionary Money Claims' in E.J.H. Schrage, *Unjust Enrichment* (2nd edn 1999), pp. 31–57 at pp. 45–46 with further references.

125 *Manby v Scott* (1663) 1 Mod 124, 86 ER 781. See J.H. Baker, 'The Use of Assumpsit for Restitutionary Money Claims' in E.J.H. Schrage, *Unjust Enrichment* (2nd edn 1999), pp. 31–57 at p. 46.

wife, had given his wife authority to acquire necessaries.[126] After all, 'she is "bone of his bone, flesh of his flesh," and no man did ever hate his own flesh so far as not to preserve it'.[127] Where the husband and wife lived together, the presumption could be rebutted by proof that the husband had prohibited his wife from pledging his credit. It could be argued that the wife's authority in such cases was implied 'in fact', not 'in law'.[128] However, in cases where the husband had wrongfully deserted his wife, the presumption of authority was held to be irrebuttable. Thus, in *Bolton v Prentice*[129] the defendant had for no apparent reason refused his wife access to the marital home, and had forbidden the claimant to 'ever trust[ing] her again'. More generally, he had declared that he would no longer maintain his wife, nor pay anyone who did. Nevertheless, Prentice was held liable in *assumpsit* for the cost of the necessaries that were provided to his wife by Bolton, because as a wrongdoer he had 'no right to prohibit anybody'.[130] The deserted wife had thus become her husband's 'agent of necessity'.[131]

For the tradesman who provided a deserted wife with his merchandise, the road to recovery was nevertheless an uncertain one. The law would only raise an implied authority in respect of 'necessaries'. While there is little doubt that food, drink and medical care came under this heading,[132] the 'necessity' of other articles or services depended on the lifestyle that the husband had chosen for himself and his wife.[133] Thus, while an ordinary woman may not have required ball dresses and riding outfits, they were held to be part of the necessary apparel of the wife of a 'gentleman of property, the son of a baronet, a deputy lieutenant and magistrate of his county'.[134] As a general rule, it was for the plaintiff to establish that the articles or services he supplied were necessary to the woman in question.[135] The presumption of authority was rebutted if the wife committed an act of adultery.[136] In *Govier v Hancock*, the defendant husband had brought his mistress into his marital home, had treated his wife with 'great cruelty' and had finally turned her out of doors. Away from home, his wife committed adultery too. The court held that the defendant was liable for the necessaries provided to his wife after he had wrongfully turned her away, though not for those provided to her after she had committed adultery.[137] Whether the provider of the

[126] *Etherington v Parrot* (1703) 1 Salk 118, 91 ER 110; W. Selwyn, *An Abridgment of the Law of Nisi Prius*, Vol I (2nd edn 1810), p. 287 and J. Chitty, *The Law of Contracts* (3rd edn 1841), pp. 160–161 with further references.

[127] *Manby v Scott* (1663) 1 Mod 124, 86 ER 781 at 128 *per* Hyde J.

[128] *Debenham v Mellon* (1880) 6 App Cas 24 at 31–32, *per* Lord Selborne LC and at 36, *per* Lord Blackburn.

[129] (1744) 2 Strange 1214, 93 ER 1136.

[130] *Ibid.* at 1214. See also *James v Warren* (1706) Holt KB 104, 90 ER 956.

[131] *Eastland v Burchell* (1878) 3 QBD 432 at 436, *per* Lush J.

[132] *Hunt v De Blaquiere* (1829) 5 Bing 550, 130 ER 1174 at 559, *per* Park J and *Harrison v Grady* (1865) 13 LT 369 at 370, *per* Erle CJ.

[133] *Phillipson v Hayter* (1870) LR 6 CP 38 at 42, *per* Willes J.

[134] *Morgan v Chetwynd* (1865) 4 F & F 451, 176 ER 643.

[135] *Phillipson v Hayter* (1870) LR 6 CP 38 at 42, *per* Willes J.

[136] *Manby v Scott* (1663) 1 Mod 124, 86 ER 781 at 129 *per* Hyde J and *Atkyns v Pearce* (1857) 2 CBNS 763, 140 ER 616.

[137] *Govier v Hancock* (1796) 6 TR 603, 101 ER 726.

necessaries *knew* that the wife had committed adultery appears to have been thought irrelevant.[138]

The above doctrine was abolished by section 41(1) of the Matrimonial Proceedings and Property Act 1970. However, it is possible that the doctrine continues to have some bearing on cases in which necessaries are provided to children. There is little doubt that a married woman's necessaries could incorporate the victuals or clothes for her children.[139] Also, although a contract made by a child is generally voidable, a child must at common law pay a reasonable price for the necessaries it contracted for and received.[140] But is a child capable of acting as an agent of necessity for his or her father? In the 1836 case of *Urmston v Newcomen*, it was argued that the obligation to reimburse necessaries 'must be as strong in the case of a child as in that of a wife'.[141] Yet, it is uncertain whether at common law a father was legally obliged to maintain his children.[142] The question was left open in *Urmston v Newcomen*, but claims against the father were rejected in both *Mortimore v Wright*[143] and *Shelton v Springett*.[144] However, neither of these cases was concerned with the equivalent of a deserted wife, *i.e.* an abandoned child. If a local authority takes an abandoned child under the age of sixteen into its care, it can recoup its expenses from the child's parents under the Children Act 1989, section 29.[145] It is at least arguable that a similar right should befall private individuals who come to the assistance of an abandoned child, on the basis that the child acted as an 'agent of necessity' for his parents.[146] Support for this view can be drawn from the American case of *Greenspan v Slate*,[147] where the parents declined to provide their daughter with medical aid after she had broken her foot. One Dr Greenspan looked after her, and then sought to recover his professional fees from the child's parents. The Supreme Court of New Jersey allowed the claim, stating that the needs of a child must be 'just as great or even greater' than the needs of a wife.[148]

B. The Shipmaster's Agency of Necessity

The relationship perhaps most commonly associated with the doctrine of agency of necessity is that between the shipmaster on the one hand, and the ship owner or cargo owner on the other.

138 See also *Atkyns v Pearce* (1857) 2 CBNS 763, 140 ER 616 at 767, *per* Cockburn CJ.

139 See *Atkyns v Pearce* (1857) 2 CBNS 763, 140 ER 616 and *Phillipson v Hayter* (1870) LR 6 CP 38.

140 M. Bacon, *A New Abridgment of the Law*, Vol III (1740), pp. 132–134 ('Infancy and Age' (I), 1.) with further references; *Nash v Inman* [1908] 2 KB 1 and The Sale of Goods Act 1979, s. 3(2).

141 (1836) 4 A & E 899 at 903, 111 ER 1022.

142 See *Nichole v Allen* (1827) 3 C & P 36 at 37, 172 ER 312 *per* Lord Tenterden CJ and *Bazeley v Forder* (1868) LR 3 QB 559 at 564, *per* Blackburn J. for an affirmative answer. However, see for the opposite view *Mortimore v Wright* (1840) 6 M & W 482, 151 ER 502 and *Bazeley v Forder* (1868) LR 3 QB 559 at 565, *per* Cockburn CJ. Cf. also W. Blackstone, *Commentaries on the Laws of England*, Book 1 (1765), p. 437, where it is suggested that a father was only bound to provide necessaries to his children in so far as they were unable to work, 'the penalty on refusal being no more than 20 s. a month'.

143 (1840) 6 M & W 482, 151 ER 502.

144 (1851) 11 CB 452, 138 ER 549.

145 Cf. National Assistance Act 1948, s. 42 and Child Support Act 1991, ss. 1 and 4.

146 See also Lord Goff of Chieveley and G. Jones, *The Law of Restitution* (6th edn 2002), p. 465.

147 12 NJ 426, 97 Atl 2nd 390 (Sup. Ct of NJ, 1953).

148 *Ibid.* at 399.

The relationship between the ship owner and the master was one of (contractual) agency. The master was entrusted with the everyday management of the ship, and was given authority to bind its owners to every lawful contract made by him 'relative to the usual employment of the ship'.[149] And, since it was not uncommon during sea voyages to be confronted with a variety of unforeseen events, it was inferred that the master had authority to do all that was necessary for the ship to reach its destination.[150] Examples include engaging an engineer to make repairs,[151] borrowing money for the ship's provisions[152] and – perhaps more unusually – procuring legal counsel to defend oneself against a malicious charge of murder.[153] If the master incurred any expenses in the course of exercising his authority, he could recover these from the ship owner.[154] Like the agency itself, this correlative entitlement to indemnity was contractual, whether it was upon an express or an implied term.[155]

However, by way of contrast with this general authority, the shipmaster was in circumstances of 'absolute necessity' given an 'extraordinary' authority to pledge, hypothecate, sell,[156] or contract for salvage of the ship and/or its cargo.[157] In the Rolls of Oleron – the fountainhead of maritime law – this extraordinary authority was termed a 'power' as opposed to the general 'mandate' that the master was given by the owners.[158] In so far as the ship was concerned, one could argue that this power could just as well have been derived from the master's actual authority to do all that was necessary to reach the port of destination.[159] However, the same

[149] J.H. Abbott (ed.), *A Treatise of the Law Relative to Merchant Ships and Seamen* (5th edn 1827), pp. 90–91.

[150] *Edwards v Havill* (1853) 14 CB 107, 139 ER 45 at 109. See also J.H. Abbott (ed.), *A Treatise of the Law relative to Merchant Ships and Seamen* (5th edn 1827), p. 102, G. St Clair Pilcher and O.L. Bateson, *Maclachlan on Merchant Shipping* (7th edn 1932), p. 106 and *The Unique Mariner* [1978] 1 Lloyd's Rep 438 at 449.

[151] *The Flecha* (1854) 1 Sp Ecc & Add 438, 164 ER 252.

[152] *Edwards v Havill* (1853) 14 CB 107, 139 ER 45.

[153] *The James Seddon* (1866) LR 1 A & E 62.

[154] G. St Clair Pilcher and O.L. Bateson, *Maclachlan on Merchant Shipping* (7th edn 1932), p. 108 with further references.

[155] F.M.B. Reynolds, *Bowstead and Reynolds on Agency* (17th edn 2001), p. 274.

[156] In *Benzen v Jeffries* (1698) 1 Ld Raym 152, 91 ER 999 it was suggested that a master did not have the power to sell the ship. However, the later cases of *Robertson v Clarke* (1824) 1 Bing 445, 130 ER 179 and *Hunter v Parker* (1840) 7 M & W 322, 151 ER 789 confirm that a master did have this power where, as a result of irreparable damage to the ship, there was no prospect of her reaching her destination.

[157] G. St Clair Pilcher and O.L. Bateson, *Maclachlan on Merchant Shipping* (7th edn 1932), p. 110; W. Welwod, *An Abridgement of all Sea-Lawes* (1613), pp. 25–26 (Tit. VIII). For the historical background, see W.S. Holdsworth, *A History of English Law*, Vol VIII (1903), pp. 248 ff. and L.J.W. Aitken, 'Negotiorum gestio and the Common Law: A Jurisdictional Approach', (1988) 11 Sydney LR 566–598 at pp. 585 ff. The master's authority to contract for salvage on behalf of the ship- and/or cargo owner was recognized in article 6 of the International Convention on Salvage 1989 and has now become law under the Merchant Shipping Act 1995, s. 224(1).

[158] L.J.W. Aitken, 'Negotiorum gestio and the Common Law: A Jurisdictional Approach', (1988) 11 Sydney LR 566–598, p. 588.

[159] F.M.B. Reynolds, *Bowstead and Reynolds on Agency* (17th edn 2001), p. 127 and A. Mandaraka-Sheppard, *Modern Admiralty Law* (2001), p. 692. Cf. *The Unique Mariner* [1978] 1 Lloyd's Rep 438 at 449.

could not be said with regard to the cargo. There was usually no pre-existing agency relationship between the shipmaster and the cargo owner. The shipmaster's authority to pledge, hypothecate, sell or contract for salvage of the cargo must therefore have been derived from a newly created agency; an agency created 'by the general policy of the law'.[160]

Over the years, several requirements have been developed for the creation of such an 'agency of necessity'. First and foremost, there must have been a situation of absolute necessity. Some of the earlier cases and treatises on the subject suggest that a 'twofold' necessity is required: *e.g.* a 'physical' need to borrow money to repair the ship, as well as an absolute necessity to obtain this money through hypothecation of the ship or cargo.[161] If the money could have been obtained in any other way, the second limb of the 'twofold' necessity requirement would not have been satisfied, and the master would not have had authority to hypothecate. However, later cases adopt a more casuistic and arguably more sophisticated approach. In *Australasian Steam Navigation Co. v Morse*,[162] Sir Montague Smith submitted that it must be 'in a mercantile sense' necessary to take the measures that would be taken by a 'wise and prudent man'. Thus, even if it is possible to dry and repack a cargo of wool, a master may be justified in selling it, if the cost of drying and repacking exceeds the value of the wool.[163] Similarly, it was stated by Lindley LJ in *Phelps, James & Co. v Hill*[164] that 'by "possible" and "necessary" is meant "reasonably possible" and "reasonably necessary"'.[165]

Yet, even when confronted with such a situation of 'necessity', the master will only be granted authority 'by operation of the law' if he could not have obtained actual authorization from the ship- or cargo owner. Again, some cases appear to have adopted a rather rigid approach, requiring that communication was absolutely impossible.[166] However, in the famous 1801 case of *The Gratitudine*,[167] it had already been indicated that the master was 'not in all cases to wait till he [heard] from a distant country'.[168] An early attempt to formulate a more concrete test was made in 1842 by Patteson J, who suggested that the true requirement was that it was impossible to communicate 'without very great prejudice and delay'.[169] In later cases the requirement tended to be formulated in more general terms: the

160 *The Gratitudine* (1801) 3 C Rob 240, 165 ER 450 at 258, *per* Sir William Scott.

161 G. St Clair Pilcher and O.L. Bateson, *Maclachlan on Merchant Shipping* (7th edn 1932), pp. 41 and 110; R. Lowndes, *The Law of General Average* (1873); F.P. Maude, C.E. Pollock and G. Bruce, *A Compendium of the Law of Merchant Shipping*, Vol I (4th edn 1881), pp. 158 and 564; *The Karnak* (1869) LR 2 PC 505 at 512, *per* Sir William Erle and *Atlantic Mutual Insurance Co. v Huth* (1880) 16 Ch D 474 at 481, *per* Cotton LJ.

162 (1872) LR 4 PC 222.

163 *Ibid.* at 230–231.

164 [1891] 1 QB 605.

165 *Ibid.* at 610–611. See also *China Pacific S.A. v Food Corporation of India* (HoL) [1982] AC 939 at 965, *per* Lord Simon.

166 *Wilson v Millar* (1816) 2 Stark 1, 171 ER 553 at 4, *per* Lord Ellenborough and *Prager v Blatspiel, Stamp & Heacock Ltd* [1924] 1 KB 566 at 571, *per* McCardie J.

167 (1801) 3 C Rob 240, 165 ER 450.

168 *Ibid.* at 262, *per* Sir William Scott.

169 *Johns v Simons* (1842) 2 QB 425, 114 ER 168 at 430. See also *The Karnak* (1869) LR 2 PC 505 at 513, *per* Sir William Erle.

impossibility to be 'conveniently communicated with',[170] or the 'practical'[171] or 'commercial'[172] impossibility to communicate. And, having considered the modern authorities, it was more recently held by the Court of Appeal in *The Choko Star*,[173] that a relationship of agency of necessity will only arise if 'it is not reasonably practicable to communicate with the cargo owners or to obtain their instructions'.[174] It follows that actions that go against the express instructions of the ship- or cargo owner will normally not be regarded as falling within the master's authority.[175]

A third requirement, in addition to 'necessity' and 'impossibility to communicate', is that the master must have acted *bona fide* in the interest of the ship- and/or cargo owners. Although the concept of '*bona fides*' or 'good faith' features in many nineteenth century cases, it is not always clear whether it was regarded as a separate condition, or merely as an aspect of the requirement of 'necessity'. However, the two had been recognized as distinct requirements already in 1824 by Lord Gifford CJ.[176] The same view appears to have been adopted by the Privy Council in *Tronson v Dent*,[177] and was confirmed by McCardie J in *Prager v Blatspiel, Stamp & Heacock Ltd*:[178] '*bona fides* was essential in addition to actual necessity'.[179]

By way of fourth and final[180] requirement, it has been suggested that the action taken by the shipmaster must have been reasonable and prudent in the circumstances.[181] In truth, however, it is difficult to see how this requirement could be distinguished from the general requirement of necessity. After all, if the action of the shipmaster was not reasonable and prudent, how can it be said to have been 'necessary'?[182]

These requirements having been met, the agent of necessity could bind his 'principal' as if he were their contractual agent. His authority, though not actual, arose by operation of the law. And like his contractual counterpart, the agent of necessity was given a right to be reimbursed for any expenses he had incurred in the course of his agency. This right was expressly recognized by the Privy Council in *Cargo ex Argos*:[183]

> (. . .) a duty is cast on the master in many cases of accident and emergency to act for the safety of the cargo, in such a manner as may be best under the circumstances in which it

[170] *Beldon v Campbell* (1851) 6 Exch 886 at 890, *per* Parke B.
[171] *Springer v Great Western Rly Co.* [1921] 1 KB 257 at 265, *per* Bankes LJ.
[172] *Ibid.* at 268, *per* Scrutton LJ.
[173] [1990] 1 Lloyd's Rep 516.
[174] *Ibid.* at 525, *per* Slade LJ.
[175] W.B. Williston, 'Agency of Necessity' [1944] 22 Can Bar Rev 492–508 at pp. 499–500 and F.M.B. Reynolds, *Bowstead and Reynolds on Agency* (17th edn 2001), p. 128 with further references.
[176] *Robertson v Clarke* (1824) 1 Bing 445, 130 ER 179 at 450.
[177] (1853) 8 Moore PC 419, 14 ER 159 at 452, *per* Sir John Patteson.
[178] [1924] 1 KB 566.
[179] *Ibid.* at 572–573.
[180] F.M.B. Reynolds, *Bowstead and Reynolds on Agency* (17th edn 2001), p. 128 add to their list of requirements that the principal must have been 'competent'. For present purposes this requirement can safely be ignored.
[181] Lord Goff of Chieveley and G. Jones, *The Law of Restitution* (6th edn 2002), p. 451 and *The Choko Star* [1990] 1 Lloyd's Rep 516 at 525, *per* Slade LJ.
[182] Cf. *The Australia* (1859) Swab 480, 166 ER 1226.
[183] (1873) LR 5 PC 134.

may be placed; and (. . .), as a correlative right, he is entitled to charge its owner with the expenses properly incurred in doing so.[184]

C. The Acceptor for Honour

A third doctrine, also originally developed in the Courts of Admiralty,[185] is concerned with the so-called 'acceptor for honour (*supra protest*)'. Where a bill of exchange had not been accepted, anyone – including a stranger – could keep the credit of the bill alive by accepting it for the honour of a person liable on the bill, usually the drawer.[186] Provided that the bill had been protested for non-acceptance,[187] the acceptor for honour would be entitled to recover from the party for whose honour he had accepted the bill.[188] The doctrine became statutory through the Bills of Exchange Act 1882.[189]

As with many doctrines that were developed in the admiralty courts, a civil law influence was here clearly discernable. In the eyes of the continental jurists, acceptance for honour was closely related to, or even a specimen of *negotiorum gestio*.[190] It is hardly surprising, then, to find English scholars explaining the subject in terms of quasi-contract, or more particularly quasi-mandate. Thus, Beawes stated that the acceptor for honour 'hath his redress and remedy on the person for whose honour he accepted it, who is obliged to indemnify him, *as if* he had acted entirely by his directions'.[191] Having established an analogy with the contract of mandate, it is only a small step to categorize the acceptor for honour as an agent of necessity. Yet, whether acceptance for honour is indeed an example of agency of necessity is rather doubtful. Nineteenth century speeches by Parke B[192] and Lord Esher MR[193] would appear to support an affirmative answer. However, most modern authors treat the two as separate, though perhaps related doctrines.[194] The most potent objection to the classification of the acceptor for honour as an agent of necessity is that his intervention does not create any legal relationship between the person

184 *Ibid.* at 165, *per* Sir Montague Smith. See also *Petrinovic & Co. Ltd v Mission Française des Transports Maritimes* (1942) 71 Lloyd's List LR 208 at 222, *per* Atkinson J and *China Pacific S.A. v Food Corporation of India* (HoL) [1982] AC 939 at 965, *per* Lord Simon, with further references.

185 L.J.W. Aitken, 'Negotiorum gestio and the Common Law: A Jurisdictional Approach', (1988) 11 Sydney LR 566–598 at p. 569.

186 Ch. Viner, *A General Abridgment of Law and Equity*, Vol IV (1748), p. 251 (Bills of Exchange, L).

187 See for further requirements A.G. Guest, *Chalmers and Guest on Bills of Exchange, Cheques and Promissory Notes* (1998), pp. 543–544.

188 W. Beawes, *Lex Mercatoria Rediviva* (1752), p. 420.

189 Ss. 65–68.

190 L.J.W. Aitken, 'Negotiorum gestio and the Common Law: A Jurisdictional Approach', (1988) 11 Sydney LR 566–598 at pp. 578–580 with further references.

191 W. Beawes, *Lex Mercatoria Rediviva* (1752), p. 420 (emphasis added). See also the *Supplement to Viner's Abridgment*, Vol I (1799), p. 563 (Bills of Exchange, L 4).

192 *Hawtayne v Bourne* (1841) 7 M & W 595, 151 ER 905 at 599.

193 *Gwilliam v Twist* [1895] 2 QB 84 at 87.

194 *E.g.* H.G. Hanbury, *The Principles of Agency* (2nd edn 1960), p. 45; S.J. Stoljar, *The Law of Quasi-Contract* (2nd edn 1989), p. 174, footnote 112 and Lord Goff of Chieveley and G. Jones, *The Law of Restitution* (6th edn 2002), pp. 461–462. Cf. G.H. Treitel, 'Agency of Necessity', (1954) 3 Univ of Western Australia LR 1–12 at 1 and G.L.H. Fridman, *The Law of Agency* (7th edn 1996), p. 135.

for whose honour he accepts and the holder of the bill. In so far as it is an example of agency, acceptance for honour is exclusively concerned with the internal relationship between the so-called agent and his 'principal'.[195] Also, it could be questioned whether there is true 'necessity' involved in the case of the acceptor for honour. Rather than a threat to property or life and limb, all that is at stake here is the principal's honour.[196] And where the shipmaster and the provider of necessaries to a deserted wife needed to establish that their intervention was necessary, the necessity of an acceptance for honour appears to have been assumed. In any case, the Bills of Exchange Act 1882[197] does not mention 'necessity' as a separate requirement.

Although acceptance for honour used to be commonplace,[198] it is now, in practice, obsolete.[199]

D. A General Doctrine of Agency of Necessity?

The three categories of cases that we have considered can hardly be said to form a homogeneous group. While the first two categories are concerned with true agency – the agent of necessity creating a legal relationship between the 'principal' and third parties – we have seen that it is doubtful whether the case of the acceptor for honour involves true agency reasoning. On the other hand, both the shipmaster and the acceptor for honour act in accordance with the interests and presumed wishes of their supposed principals, where the deserted wife acts to preserve her own interests, and sometimes even contrary to her husband's express wishes.[200] It should be of no surprise, then, that the judiciary has tended to shy away from reducing the principles developed in these three categories to one, comprehensive doctrine. In the 1895 case of *Gwilliam v Twist*,[201] for example, Lord Esher MR opined that 'this doctrine of authority by reason of necessity is confined to certain well-known exceptional cases, such as those of the master of a ship or the acceptor of a bill of exchange for the honour of the drawer'.[202] Arguably, however, the doctrine of agency of necessity had already been extended to cases involving land carriers before Lord Esher voiced this opinion. As we have seen,[203] some of the judges in *Great Northern Rly v Swaffield*[204] appear to have adopted agency reasoning. Later cases confirm the extension of the doctrine to land carriers.[205] It is these

[195] F.M.B. Reynolds, *Bowstead and Reynolds on Agency* (17th edn 2001), p. 128.

[196] G.L.H. Fridman, *The Law of Agency* (7th edn 1996), p. 135.

[197] Ss. 65–68.

[198] J.M. Holden, 'Bills of Exchange During the Seventeenth Century', (1951) 67 LQR 230–248 at 242.

[199] A.G. Guest, *Chalmers and Guest on Bills of Exchange, Cheques and Promissory Notes* (1998), p. 543 and W. and R. Hedley, *Bills of Exchange and Bankers' Documentary Credits* (4th edn 2001), p. 144.

[200] S.J. Stoljar, *The Law of Quasi-Contract* (2nd edn 1989), p. 210.

[201] [1895] 2 QB 84.

[202] *Ibid.* at 87. But cf. the speeches by Smith and Rigby LJJ at 87–89. See also *Buxton v Snee* (1748) 1 Ves Sen 154, 27 ER 952 and *Hawtayne v Bourne* (1841) 7 M & W 595 at 599, *per* Parke B.

[203] See above, Part II, Section 11.3, Sub-section D.

[204] (1874) LR 9 Ex 132.

[205] *Sims & Co. v Midland Rly Co.* [1913] 1 KB 103 at 112, *per* Scrutton J, confirmed by the Court of Appeal in *Springer v Great Western Rly Co.* [1921] 1 KB 257.

cases that prompted McCardie J to state that 'agency of necessity is not confined to shipmaster cases and to bills of exchange'.[206] But when he attempted to take the issue one step further by formulating a general principle – in his view a 'broad and useful one'[207] – his attempt was nipped in the bud by Scrutton LJ in *Jebara v Ottoman Bank*.[208] Scrutton LJ drew a distinction between cases where there was already an existing relationship of agency, and cases where there was no such pre-existing agency, 'as in the case of a finder of perishable chattels or animals'.[209] To the former type of case, the doctrine of agency of necessity could readily apply. The same could not be done without difficulty to the latter type of case. Having discussed Eyre CJ's judgment in *Nicholson v Chapman*, his Lordship concluded that he could not expand the doctrine to cases where there was no pre-existing agency.[210]

This distinction has since been criticized on the basis that where the shipmaster acts on behalf of the cargo owners – one of the classic examples of agency of necessity – there is no 'pre-existing agency'.[211] It has also been pointed out that his Lordship's reliance on *Nicholson v Chapman* was misplaced, as that case was concerned with a lien rather than a claim for reimbursement of expenses.[212] Add to that the fact that the Court of Appeal's decision in *Jebara* was reversed by the House of Lords,[213] and it becomes very tempting to dismiss Scrutton LJ's view as being altogether irrelevant.

Yet, it cannot be denied that a distinction similar to that drawn by Scrutton LJ still survives today.[214] There are innumerable instances where the doctrine of agency of necessity has been applied to cases where there was some pre-existing relationship between intervener and his 'principal'. This pre-existing relationship need not be one of agency: examples include bailment,[215] a contractual relationship other than agency[216] and, probably, the relationship of master and servant.[217] By contrast, there are very few cases where no pre-existing relationship can be discerned. A rare example is the 1852 admiralty case of *The Cynthia*.[218] On her way from Tampica to Liverpool, the crew of *The Cynthia* mutinied and murdered the master and boatswain. When the vessel arrived in the port of Campeachy, the

206 *Prager v Blatspiel, Stamp & Heacock Ltd* [1924] 1 KB 566 at 569. 207 *Ibid.* at 570.

208 [1927] 2 KB 254. 209 *Ibid.* at 271. 210 *Ibid.* at 271.

211 G.H. Treitel, 'Agency of Necessity', (1954) 3 Univ of Western Australia LR 1–12 and R. Powell, *The Law of Agency* (2nd edn 1961), p. 414.

212 W.B. Williston, 'Agency of Necessity' [1944] 22 Can Bar Rev 492–508 at pp. 503–505.

213 *Ottoman Bank v Jebara* [1928] AC 269.

214 See also S.J. Stoljar, *The Law of Quasi-Contract* (2nd edn 1989), p. 209.

215 *Coldman v Hill* [1919] 1 KB 443 at 456, *per* Scrutton LJ and *China Pacific S.A. v Food Corporation of India* (HoL) [1982] AC 939 at 965, *per* Lord Simon. Cf. *Sachs v Miklos* [1948] 2 KB 23 at 35–36, *per* Lord Goddard CJ and *Munro v Willmott* [1949] 1 KB 295 at 297, *per* Lynskey J. Today, a bailee of uncollected goods is by statute entitled to sell them, provided that he has taken reasonable steps to communicate with the bailor: Torts (Interference with Goods) Act 1977, s. 12.

216 *Kemp v Pryor* (1802) 7 Ves Jun 240, 32 ER 96 at 247, *per* Lord Eldon. Cf. *Cornwal v Wilson* (1750) 1 Ves Sen 509, 27 ER 1173.

217 *Poland v John Parr & Sons* [1927] 1 KB 236 at 240, *per* Bankes LJ, at 244, *per* Scrutton LJ and at 245, *per* Atkin LJ. 218 (1852) 20 LT (OS) 54.

British consul took control of it, appointed a new master and hypothecated the ship for the purchase of stores and necessaries. It was objected that this hypothecation was invalid, because only the master could hypothecate the ship in circumstances of necessity. This objection failed to impress Dr Lushington, who held that 'in justice and in equity, [he] ought not to pronounce against the validity of the bond'.[219] It should be noted that, while there was no pre-existing relationship between the consul and the owners of the ship, the consul was not in every sense a 'mere bystander': his position imposed upon him, as Dr Lushington put it, a duty 'to preserve and protect the property of British owners'.[220] Apart from *The Cynthia*, there are perhaps one or two reported cases in which the doctrine has been applied despite the fact that there was no pre-existing relationship.[221] Suffice it to say that these cases represent the exception, rather than the rule.

11.5 Bailment

If a thing be lent to a man for fun,
Or because it wants to have something done,
Or popped to pay off a troublesome dun,
Or for any reason under the sun
Delivered in trust to anyone,
Or to get repaired or for sale meant;
Whatever the cause of the trust may be
He who owns the thing is bailor, you see,
And he who gets it is called bailee,
And the business between them is a bailment.[222]

The term 'bailment' is believed to be derived from the French verb *bailler*, meaning 'to deliver'.[223] Any voluntary parting with possession of a chattel will normally result in bailment. Unsurprisingly, therefore, a variety of legal relationships is categorized under the heading of 'bailment'. In the 1703 case of *Coggs v Bernard*, Chief Justice Holt identified six different 'sorts of bailment', all of which corresponded to contracts in Roman law, most notably deposit (*depositum*), loan for use (*commodatum*), and pledge (*pignus*).[224] Yet, whether bailment is part of the law of contract is a question that has been subject of ample dispute. Leaving the early law aside,[225] the predominant view up and until the end of the nineteenth

[219] (1852) 20 LT (OS) 54, at 55. [220] *Ibid.*

[221] *White v Troups Transport* [1976] CLY 33 and *Surrey Breakdown Ltd v Knight* [1999] RTR 84. Both cases are discussed below, Part II, Section 12.1.

[222] D.F. de l'Hoste Ranking, *The Law of Agency and the Law of Bailment* (2nd edn 1904), p. 31, which attributes the poem to a 'clever little book' called *Legends of Leading Cases*.

[223] W. Blackstone, *Commentaries on the Laws of England*, Book 2 (1766), p. 452.

[224] *Coggs v Bernard* (1703) 2 Ld Raym 909, 92 ER 107 at 912–913.

[225] See for the position in early law W.S. Holdsworth, *A History of English Law*, Vol III (3rd edn 1923), pp. 336 ff.

century appears to have been that bailment, if not a contract in itself,[226] was at least based on a contract.[227] Thus, Sir William Jones in his famous *Essay on the Law of Bailments*, defined bailment as:

(. . .) a delivery of goods in trust, on a contract expressed or implied, that the trust shall be duly executed, and the goods redelivered, as soon as the time or use, for which they were bailed, shall have elapsed or be performed.[228]

When it came to defining the duties of bailor and bailee, the Roman law doctrine drawn upon by Chief Justice Holt in *Coggs v Bernard* continued to be clearly discernable. For example, the borrower/bailee in a loan for use, like the borrower in *commodatum*,[229] would have to look after the chattel with the utmost diligence, and would be liable even for the slightest neglect.[230] He must not use it except insofar as that use was permitted by the terms of the bailment. If his use exceeded these terms, he would be liable for all the damage incurred during the period of misuse.[231] Finally, he had to redeliver the chattel to the lender/bailor at the appointed time and place, and in proper condition.[232] The obligations of the lender, on the other hand, were few and far between. His main duty was to warn the borrower against defects in the chattel.[233] In case of a loan for a fixed term, the lender might also have to allow the borrower peaceful possession of the chattel until the term expired.[234] However, for present purposes the most important obligation concerned the so-called *impensae* ('expenses'). In Roman law, the borrower in *commodatum*, and indeed the depositee in *depositum* as well as the pledgee in *pignus*, were contractually entitled to recover from the owner all exceptional expenses incurred in looking after the thing borrowed, deposited or pledged.[235] And, although there is very little authority on this issue,[236] there is some evidence that a similar obligation may have found its way into the English law of bailment.

In *China Pacific S.A. v Food Corporation of India*[237] the defendants had chartered a vessel, *The Winson*, for the carriage of a cargo of their wheat from the

[226] See for an example of this view *R. v Ashwell* (1885) 16 QBD 190 at 223, *per* Lord Coleridge CJ.

[227] See N.E. Palmer, *Bailment* (2nd edn 1991), p. 19 with further references.

[228] W. Jones, *An Essay on the Law of Bailments* (1781), p. 117.

[229] *D.* 13.6.18 (Gaius).

[230] *Coggs v Bernard* (1703) 2 Ld Raym 909, 92 ER 107 at 915, *per* Holt CJ. Cf. N.E. Palmer, *Bailment* (2nd edn 1991), pp. 665–668 and *D.* 13.6.5.5–6 (Ulpian).

[231] *Coggs v Bernard* (1703) 2 Ld Raym 909, 92 ER 107 at 915, *per* Holt CJ and *Isaack v Clark* (1614) 2 Bulstr 306, 80 ER 1143 at 309, *per* Dodderidge J. Cf. *D.* 13.6.5.7 (Ulpian).

[232] N.E. Palmer, *Bailment* (2nd edn 1991), pp. 674 and 676. Cf. *D.* 13.3.1 (Ulpian) and *D.* 13.6.5.*pr.* (Ulpian).

[233] N.E. Palmer, *Bailment* (2nd edn 1991), pp. 631 ff. with further references.

[234] M. Bacon, *A New Abridgment of the Law*, Vol I (1736), pp. 240–241 (Tit. *Bailment, sub* C). However, Bacon was relying on the case of *Lee v Atkinson* (1609) Yelv 172, 80 ER 114, which was in fact a case of hiring, not loan for use. For a more thorough discussion of this issue, see N.E. Palmer, *Bailment* (2nd edn 1991), pp. 658–665 and *idem*, 'Bailment' in P.B.H. Birks (ed.), *English Private Law*, Vol II (2000), pp. 357–406 at p. 383 with further references. For Roman law, see *D.* 13.6.17.3 (Paul).

[235] See for *commodatum D.* 13.6.18.2 (Gaius), for *depositum D.* 16.3.5.*pr.* (Ulpian) and *D.* 16.3.23 (Modestinus) and for *pignus D.* 13.7.8.*pr.* (Pomponius).

[236] W.W. Buckland and A.D. McNair, *Roman Law and Common Law* (1936), p. 209.

[237] [1982] AC 939.

United States of America to India. In the course of the voyage *The Winson* stranded on the North Danger Reef in the South China Sea. A day later, a Lloyd's standard form of salvage agreement was signed on behalf of both the ship owners and the owners of the cargo, the defendants. The salvors, the plaintiffs in the action, performed salvage services for approximately two months, but eventually had to abandon the operation owing to fighting in the vicinity between the armed forces of North and South Vietnam. By then, they had managed to save almost half of the cargo of wheat, which they had carried to Manila and for which they had arranged suitable storage accommodation. Besides bringing the usual claims for salvage, the salvors sought to recover the costs of storage from the owner of the cargo. Counsel for the salvors argued that the salvors had become bailees of the cargo, and that 'where a bailee incurs reasonable expenses as a bailee he is entitled to recover those expenses (. . .) from the bailor'.[238] The Court of Appeal accepted the former, but not the latter proposition. Megaw LJ, with whom Bridge and Cumming-Bruce LJJ agreed, expressed the view that, in the absence of a contractual entitlement, a bailee could only recover expenses that had been incurred in the course of an emergency. By the time that the cargo had arrived in Manila, it could not be said that there was still a situation of emergency or necessity. Therefore, the salvors were not allowed to recover for the expenses they had incurred in off-loading and storing the cargo.[239] However, on appeal this decision was unanimously overturned by the House of Lords. The two main speeches were by Lord Diplock and Lord Simon. Lord Simon commenced by accepting that there is no general right of a bailee to be reimbursed expenses incurred in fulfilling his duty to safeguard bailed goods. His Lordship then proceeded by stating that there are exceptions to this general rule, and that 'agency of necessity' is by no means the only one. In his Lordship's view, the case before him warranted such an exception because of the following specific circumstances:

> (1) the contract of bailment was a commercial one; (2) it came to an end when the salved goods were brought to a place of safety, which, it has been the common assumption, was the entry into the port of Manila (. . .); (3) the bailee then continued in possession as a gratuitous bailee; (4) he incurred reasonable expenses in safeguarding and preserving the goods, to the benefit of the bailor; (5) the bailor stood by, knowing that the bailee was so acting to his (the bailor's) benefit.[240]

By way of exception to the general rule, the plaintiffs were allowed to recover on the basis of the specific circumstances of the case. Especially the fifth and last circumstance mentioned by Lord Simon – that the bailor knowingly allowed the bailee to incur expenses on his behalf – could prove to be a considerable hurdle for other bailees attempting to recover their expenses. However, the speech with which the majority of their Lordships expressed agreement was that of Lord

238 *China Pacific S.A. v Food Corporation of India* (CA) [1980] 3 All ER 556 at 562.

239 *Ibid.* at 562–3, *per* Megaw LJ.

240 *China Pacific S.A. v Food Corporation of India* (HoL) [1982] AC 939 at 964.

Diplock, not that of Lord Simon. And unlike Lord Simon, Lord Diplock does not appear to have found it necessary to limit the scope of the decision to the specific circumstances of the case. The plaintiffs had been bailees for the defendants throughout the entire period in question, albeit that what was initially a bailment for valuable consideration (under the contract of salvage) later became gratuitous.[241] Yet, even a gratuitous bailee owes his bailor a duty to take care of the bailed goods as a man of ordinary prudence would take care of his own property. 'And if he fulfils that duty', his Lordship stated, 'he has, in my view, a correlative right to charge the owner of the goods with the expenses reasonably incurred in doing so'.[242] The fact that Lord Diplock used these general terms in advocating the bailee's 'correlative right' to recovery, should not be taken to mean that his Lordship intended this right to be free of restrictions. Two restrictions are immediately apparent: the bailee can only recover those expenses that were incurred 1) reasonably and 2) in the fulfilment of his duty. The Court of Appeal had indicated that inability to communicate with the bailor was also required.[243] Lord Diplock expressly rejected this view, stating that 'inability to communicate with the owner of the goods is not a condition precedent to the bailee's own right to reimbursement of his expenses'. His Lordship acknowledged that in this respect a bailee was in a more favourable position than an agent of necessity.[244] However, it must be assumed that, like the agent of necessity, a bailee cannot recover when he acts contrary to the express wishes of the bailor.[245]

Thus, *China Pacific S.A. v Food Corporation of India* provides some authority for the proposition that a bailee who, by preserving the bailed goods, voluntarily confers a benefit upon the bailor, is entitled to be reimbursed for his expenses in doing so. As long as the contractual analysis of bailment is maintained, the consequences of this proposition are limited. For, although the bailor may not exactly have agreed to reimburse the bailee for the expenses made on his behalf, it was he who voluntarily appointed the bailee to look after his property. A mere stranger, therefore, would not be able to call upon the law of bailment in order to compel an owner of goods to pay for a benefit bestowed upon him.[246]

Yet, in recent years the contractual analysis of bailment has gone out of favour. On historical grounds, it has been argued that bailment cannot be defined in terms of contract, because bailment is a much older concept than contract.[247] This is, of course, a *non sequitur*. After all, 'contract' is a term of classification, and as such can very well cover concepts that existed before the term itself was

[241] *Ibid.* at 964, *per* Lord Simon. *Contra*: F.D. Rose, 'From bailment to Bailment', [1982] 2 LMCLQ 200–209 at 208.

[242] *China Pacific S.A. v Food Corporation of India* (HoL) [1982] AC 939 at 960.

[243] *China Pacific S.A. v Food Corporation of India* (CA) [1980] 3 All ER 556 at 563, *per* Megaw LJ.

[244] *China Pacific S.A. v Food Corporation of India* (HoL) [1982] AC 939 at 962.

[245] See for a more detailed discussion of the case N.E. Palmer, *Bailment* (2nd edn 1991), pp. 584–591.

[246] *China Pacific S.A. v Food Corporation of India* (HoL) [1982] AC 939 at 961.

[247] A.R. Carnegie, 'Bailment and Contract in English Law Today', (1966) 3 Adel LR 7.

introduced.[248] More importantly, the division of the law of obligations into separate categories, one of which is 'contractual', is a Roman invention and as such predates bailment. A more potent objection against the contractual analysis, however, is that some of the modern cases appear to indicate that agreement is not a condition for the creation of bailment.[249] Of particular interest are those cases that suggest that a finder of lost goods becomes a bailee for the owner. Technically, of course, cases of finding could not be said to constitute 'bailment', for the simple reason that the lost goods were never delivered to the finder. In the medieval law of detinue the distinction was not immediately apparent: a bailor could bring the count of 'detinue *sur bailment*' against his bailee, but the bailment was not traversable.[250] Therefore, the same count could have been brought against anyone who unlawfully detained another's chattels,[251] including the finder.[252] The emergence of a separate count of 'detinue *sur trover*'[253] – in which the plaintiff alleged that he had lost and the defendant had found the chattel in question – initially resulted in no more than a theoretical division between cases of bailment and cases of finding. For like bailment, the trover in 'detinue *sur trover*' was not traversable.[254] Hence, a count of detinue *sur trover* could have been successfully brought against finders and bailees alike. However, the mere presence of these two different forms of detinue clearly indicates that – if not on a procedural then at least on an intellectual level – one did not regard finders and bailees as one and the same. Moreover, a speech by Fitzherbert J in 1535 attached some practical consequences to the distinction. For where a bailee lost possession of the chattels, he was in principle still liable in detinue. A finder – it seems – was not.[255] 'Therefore', Fitzherbert J stated,

[248] *E.g.* the term 'autobiography' is thought to have been coined by Robert Southey in the early nineteenth century. Yet, this does not mean that Caesar's *De Bello Gallico* cannot be described as being autobiographical.

[249] And, for English law, that bailment does not require consideration: A.R. Carnegie, 'Bailment and Contract in English Law Today', (1966) 3 Adel LR 7 at 8. See for other arguments N.E. Palmer, *Bailment* (2nd edn 1991), pp. 19–31.

[250] *Wagworth v Halyday* YB Trin 29 Edw III (1354), fo. 38; *Somerville v Anon* YB Hil 11 Hen IV (1410), fo. 50, pl. 27; YB Mich 18 Hen VIII (1526), fo. 3, pl. 15 and R. Brooke, *La Graunde Abridgement*, Book 1 (1573), p. 235 ('*Detinue de biens*') pl. 50.

[251] *Lyndeseye v Suth*, YB Mich 6 Edw II (1312), SS Vol 34, 166 at 167; *Thornhill v Anon.* YB Hil 17 & 18 Edw III (1344), RS 510 at 514–516 and YB Hil 11 Hen IV (1410), fo. 46, pl. 20. See also W.S. Holdsworth, *A History of English Law*, Vol III (3rd edn 1923), pp. 324–327 and Th.F.T. Plucknett, *A Concise History of the Common Law* (5th edn 1956), p. 374 with further references.

[252] The earliest suggestion to this effect dates from 1294: YB 22 Edw I (1294), RS 466–468.

[253] Also referred to as 'detinue *per inventionem*': *Carles v Malpaz* YB Trin 33 Hen VI (1455), fo. 26–27, pl. 12, where it was stated by Littleton that this count was a 'new found Haliday'. See also O.W. Holmes, *The Common Law* (1882), p. 169, footnote 1.

[254] J.W. Salmond, *The Law of Torts* (1st edn 1907), p. 287 and D.J. Ibbetson, *A Historical Introduction to the Law of Obligations* (1999), p. 107.

[255] M. Bacon, *A New Abridgment of the Law*, Vol I (1736), p. 243. See also the 'extract from a book on pleading' cited in J.H. Baker and S.F.C. Milsom, *Sources of English Legal History* (1986), p. 356; the speech of Dyer CJ in an anonymous 1572 case cited at p. 273 of the same work; *Vandrink and Archers Case* (1589/1590) 1 Leon 221 at 223, *per* Anderson J and *Mulgrave v Ogden* (1591) Cro Eliz 219, 78 ER 475. *Contra*: J. Story, *Commentaries on the Law of Bailments* (4th edn 1846), pp. 92–96 (§§ 85–87).

'it is a good plea in a writ of detinue, if the plaintiff counts on a bailment, for the defendant to say that he found the goods and delivered them to John Style before the action was brought'.[256] Relying on this speech, Fifoot concluded that 'detinue *sur bailment* and detinue *sur trover* became an inevitable antithesis'.[257]

If further evidence is needed for the proposition that finders were not until recently regarded as bailees, it can be drawn from the law of larceny. A finder who appropriated the goods he had found, could not be guilty of the crime of 'larceny as a bailee', under section 3 of the Larceny Act 1861.[258] Today however, this rule does not survive. A finder who appropriates lost goods is now covered by section 3(1) of the Theft Act 1961, regardless of whether he became a bailee or not. A similar fate befell the supposed rule that a finder does not owe the owner an affirmative duty of care with regard to the lost goods. In his *Doctor and Student,* St. German wrote that a finder should at least be liable if he lost the chattel through 'wylfull neclygence'.[259] Similarly, it was suggested in the 1614 case of *Isaack v Clark* that a finder of goods 'ought to keep them safely', and would be answerable to an action on the case for his 'ill and negligent keeping'.[260] An even broader duty was advocated, albeit *obiter*, by Donaldson LJ in *Parker v British Airways Board.* There, his Lordship stated that a finder who has taken a lost chattel into his control has an obligation both to 'care for it' and to 'take such measures as in all the circumstances are reasonable to acquaint the true owner of the finding and the present whereabouts of the chattel'.[261] It could of course be argued that this duty results merely from the finder's voluntary undertaking and that the applicable doctrine is tort law, not the law of bailment.[262] However, the majority of modern authors now appears to accept that finding gives rise to a form of bailment, despite the fact that no delivery, in the proper sense of the word, has taken place. Whereas Story midway through the nineteenth century rather tentatively suggested that finding could be qualified as '*quasi* deposit',[263] the Earl of Halsbury half a century later confidently stated that a finder was to be regarded as a depositary.[264] Likewise, in the leading work on the modern law of bailment, Palmer submits that

[256] YB Pas 27 Hen VIII (1535), fo. 13, pl. 35. Translation taken from J.H. Baker and S.F.C. Milsom, *Sources of English Legal History* (1986), p. 273.

[257] C.H.S. Fifoot, *History and Sources of the Common Law* (1949), p. 34. See also F. Pollock and F.W. Maitland, *The History of English Law before the Time of Edward I,* Vol II (2nd edn 1898), p. 175.

[258] *R. v Matthews* (1873) 12 Cox CC 489. See also *Merry v Green* (1841) 7 M & W 623, 151 ER 916 at 630, *per* Parke B.; *R. v Thurborn* (1848) 1 Den 387, 169 ER 293 at 395, *per* Parke B. (mistakenly reported under the name of *R. v Wood* in (1849) 3 Cox CC 453) and, most recently, *Thompson v Nixon* [1966] 1 QB 103 at 109–110, *per* Sachs J.

[259] Chr. St. German, *Doctor and Student* (T.F.T. Plucknett and J.L. Barton, eds, 1974), pp. 260–261 (ch. 38).

[260] (1614) 2 Bulstr 306, 80 ER 1143 at 312, *per* Coke CJ.

[261] [1982] 1 QB 1004 at 1017.

[262] See for such an argument P.H. Winfield, *The Law of Quasi-Contracts* (1952), pp. 29–30. In *Gilchrist Watt & Sanderson v York Products* [1970] 3 All ER 825 the point was left undecided. Cf. for a different reading of that case N.E. Palmer, *Bailment* (2nd edn 1991), p. 33 and A.P. Bell, *Modern Law of Personal Property in England and Ireland* (1989), p. 90.

[263] J. Story, *Commentaries on the Law of Bailments* (4th edn 1846), p. 92 (§ 85).

[264] The Earl of Halsbury, *The Laws of England,* Vol I (1907), p. 529. *Contra*: T. Hadden, 'Larceny by Finding – How Not to Reform the Law', [1965] CLJ 173–175 at 175.

'it seems acceptable now to characterise finding as a case of bailment'.[265] If finding does indeed constitute bailment, it could be argued that the finder not only has the duties, but also a 'correlative right' to reimbursement of expenses, as advocated for bailees in general by Lord Diplock in *China Pacific S.A. v Food Corporation of India*.[266] After all, Lord Diplock himself had, some fifteen years earlier, used the term 'bailment by finding'.[267] English case law, however, is without an authoritative decision on the matter.

11.6a Tort: 'Danger Invites Rescue'

In most of the cases discussed up to this point, the necessity that prompted the intervention could not be attributed to an identifiable defendant. It was not clear why Mr Nicholson's timber had fallen into the Thames, nor could anyone tell how *The Goring* had ended up drifting down that river. And while the mutinous crew of *The Cynthia* can rightly be said to have acted wrongfully, suing them was not a realistic option. Yet, when confronted with a case in which it is possible to identify both a wrongful act, and a wrongdoer with sufficiently 'deep pockets', the intervener might be able to recover through a claim in tort. Indeed, the very case with which we commenced involves a situation of necessity that resulted from wrongdoing. We must then ask ourselves: 'if the good Samaritan were able to identify the individuals who had "wounded" the man he rescued, and "stripped him of his raiment", could he bring a claim against them in tort?' Indeed, if it emerged that the rescuee had negligently brought himself in the situation of danger, would he be liable to compensate the good Samaritan?

These issues do not appear to have been considered by Commonwealth courts until the end of the nineteenth century. The American courts were amongst the first to do so. In *Eckert v Long Island Rly Co.*,[268] the plaintiff's husband spotted a toddler on the defendants' railroad track, with a train fast approaching. He managed to get to the child in time to rescue it, but was himself killed in the attempt. The Court of Appeals of New York State found for the plaintiff, holding that her husband 'owed a duty of important obligation to this child to rescue it from his extreme peril' and was not himself contributorily negligent in risking his life. *Eckert* was the first in a string of American cases allowing the rescuer an independent claim in negligence.[269] The most well-known of these is probably *Wagner v International Rly Company*.[270] In the course of a train journey, one of the cars

[265] N.E. Palmer, *Bailment* (2nd edn 1991), p. 32. See also A.P. Bell, *Modern Law of Personal Property in England and Ireland* (1989), p. 90.

[266] In E. Beal, *The Law of Bailments* (1900), pp. 97–98 it was tentatively suggested that this was indeed the law. *Contra* Lord Hailsham of St Marylebone (ed.), *Halsbury's Laws of England*, Vol 2 (4th edn 1973), p. 838 (§ 1811), footnote 9.

[267] *Morris v C.W. Martin & Sons Ltd* [1966] 1 QB 716 at 731–732.

[268] 43 NY 502, 3 Am Rep 721 (Ct of App. of NY, 1871).

[269] A.L. Goodhart, 'Rescue and Voluntary Assumption of Risk', (1934) 5 CLJ 192–203 at p. 196.

[270] *Wagner v International Rly Company* 232 NY 176, 133 NE 437 (Ct of App. of NY, 1921).

violently lurched and threw off Herbert Wagner. His cousin Arthur went to look for him, lost his footing and was himself injured. The New York Court of Appeals found the International Railway Company liable for Arthur's loss, Cardozo J famously stating:

Danger invites rescue. The cry of distress is the summons of relief. The law does not ignore these reactions of the mind in tracing conduct to its consequences. It recognizes them as normal. It places their effects within the range of the natural and probable. The wrong that imperils life is a wrong to the imperiled victim; it is a wrong also to his rescuer.

Meanwhile, there were relatively few English decisions on the matter. In one 1884 case, the Queen's Bench Division had allowed a claim by the widow of a coal miner who had attempted to rescue a fellow workman, but was himself killed by the poisonous gases in the mine.[271] But this case appears to have been forgotten almost immediately after it was decided.[272] More promising was the 1924 case of *Brandon v Osborne Garrett & Co.*,[273] in which a wife was injured in aiding her husband who had been hit by fallen glass. Swift J found for the plaintiff, but made much of the fact that she had acted 'instinctively'. This led one commentator to argue that a deliberate rescue attempt, as opposed to an instinctive intervention, would constitute a *novus actus interveniens* and thus break the chain of causation.[274] Ten years later, a similar view appears to have been adopted by Scrutton LJ. Discussing an example of a man who injured himself in trying to stop a bolted horse, his Lordship said:

A man is under no duty to run out and stop another person's horse, and, if he chooses to do an act the ordinary consequence of which is that damage may ensue, the damage must be on his own head (. . .). This is sometimes put on the legal maxim volenti non fit iniuria; sometimes it is put that a new cause has intervened between the original liability, if any, of the owner of the horse which has run away.[275]

However, this view would not prevail. Within a year the courts would be confronted with a case involving a policeman who had been injured in an attempt to stop bolting horses: *Haynes v Harwood.* On behalf of the defendants it was argued that the plaintiff's injuries were the result of his own voluntary act in trying to stop the horses.[276] But this argument failed to convince Finlay J, who opined that 'a wrong-doer cannot be heard to say that a man is the author of his own misfortune because, acting in pursuance of a moral duty, he attempts to deal with the situation created by the wrong'.[277] Finlay J accordingly found for the plaintiff. This judgment was affirmed on appeal, where the above passage by Scrutton LJ was

271 *Roebuck v Norwegian Titanic Company* (1884) 1 TLR 117.

272 W.V.H. Rogers, *Winfield and Jolowicz on Tort* (16th edn 2002), p. 859, footnote 7.

273 [1924] 1 KB 548.

274 W.T.S. Stallybrass, *Salmond on the Law of Torts* (7th edn 1928), pp. 38–39. Cf. also W.A. Macfarlane and G.W. Wrangham, *Clerk & Lindsell on Torts* (8th edn 1929), pp. 136–137, where it is suggested that the intervention must have been 'of involuntary character'.

275 *Cutler v United Dairies (London) Ltd* [1933] 2 KB 297 at 303.

276 *Haynes v Harwood* [1934] 2 KB 240 at 243.

277 *Ibid.* at 250.

CONSTABLE AVERTS DANGER BY STOPPING RUNAWAY HORSE.

questioned.[278] Also, it was added that for the plaintiff's action to succeed, his intervention need not have been instinctive or on the spur of the moment.[279]

It was of course not suggested in *Haynes v Harwood* that any loss suffered in a rescue attempt would be recoverable. One obvious limitation is that pure

[278] *Haynes v Harwood* (CA) [1935] 1 KB 146 at 158, *per* Greer LJ, at 162–163, *per* Maugham LJ and at 167, *per* Roche LJ. [279] *Ibid.* at 158–159, *per* Greer LJ and at 164, *per* Maugham LJ.

economic loss is generally not recoverable in negligence.[280] This means that reimbursement of expenses cannot normally be achieved through a claim in negligence. Moreover, liability is subject to the issues of remoteness and contributory negligence. Thus, where an intervener was injured because he tripped while running to the scene of a fire, it was held that his damage was not reasonably foreseeable and hence too remote.[281] And, where the risks involved in a rescue attempt are disproportionately high, an intervener may be guilty of contributory negligence if he embarks on the rescue. Given the pressure and urgency of the situation in which many rescuers find themselves, a court will not easily be persuaded that the rescuer was negligent.[282] Indeed, in *Baker v T.E. Hopkins & Son, Ltd.*[283] a claim was allowed despite the fact that the rescue was wholly unsuccessful and the rescuer died in the course of the attempt. Willmer LJ warned that it was 'fatally easy to be wise after the event' and stressed that the rescuer was entitled to be judged 'in the light of the situation as it appeared to him at the time'.[284] But in a 1917 case before the Supreme Court of Illinois, a man was found to have been contributorily negligent in trying to stop a runaway horse in an empty street. 'There is no evidence', Cartwright J said, 'that there was any one in the roadway or any person in the slightest danger from the horse'.[285] To risk one's life in these circumstances was disproportionate and therefore negligent. That is not to say that the principle of 'danger invites rescue' only applies where human life is at stake. An attempt to save property may be justified.[286] Whether this is so depends largely on the degree of danger and the value of the property.

Because the rescuer's right is independent from that of the primary victim,[287] the principle applies with equal force to cases where the victim himself has negligently created the danger that threatens his life or property. As far as property is concerned, confirmation can be found in *Salmon v Seafarer Restaurants Ltd.*[288] In *Salmon*, the defendants forgot to switch off a chip fryer at their restaurant, and a fire broke out. During the attempt to extinguish the fire, the plaintiff fireman sustained injuries. Woolf J, sitting in the Queen's Bench Division, applied the 'principles disclosed by the "rescue cases" '[289] and allowed the plaintiff's claim. *Salmon* was later approved by the House of Lords in *Ogwo v Taylor*.[290]

It had already been established a couple of years earlier, that the same principles apply to cases where the defendant negligently endangers his own life. In *Harrison v British Rly Board*,[291] the defendant attempted to board a train while it was moving

280 D. Howarth, *Textbook on Tort* (1995), pp. 267–273 with further references.

281 *Crossley v Rawlinson* [1982] 1 WLR 369.

282 *Harrison v British Rly Board* [1981] 3 All ER 679 at 686, *per* Boreham J.

283 [1959] 1 WLR 966. 284 *Ibid.* at 984.

285 *Devine v Pfaelzer* 277 Ill 255, 115 NE 126 (Sup. Ct of Ill. 1917). Cf. *Cutler v United Dairies (London) Ltd* [1933] 2 KB 297 and A.L. Goodhart, 'Rescue and Voluntary Assumption of Risk', (1934) 5 CLJ 192–203 at p. 200.

286 *Hyett v Great Western Rly Co.* [1948] 1 KB 345. See also F.D. Rose, 'Restitution for the Rescuer' (1989) 9 OJLS 167–204 at 179, with further references.

287 *Videan v British Transport Commission* [1963] 2 QB 650 at 669, *per* Lord Denning MR.

288 [1983] 1 WLR 1264.

289 *Ibid.* at 1272. 290 [1987] 3 All ER 961. 291 [1981] 3 All ER 679.

out of the station. The plaintiff was a guard on this train. He attempted to help the defendant onto the train, but was pulled off in the process and was injured. For the defendant it was argued that he owed no duty towards himself, and hence no duty towards the potential rescuer.[292] This argument was rejected by Boreham J, who said:

> Why should the defendant, who, by lack of reasonable care for his own safety, creates a dangerous situation which invites rescue, be in a better position than he who creates a similar situation by lack of reasonable care for another's safety? I can think of no reason, nor has any been suggested to me.[293]

It follows that where someone intervenes in a suicide attempt, he should be able to recover for loss suffered as a result of the intervention. The reason being, *not* that the rescuee owed himself a duty not to endanger his own life, but rather that he owed the intervener a duty not to create a situation in which the latter would feel bound to intervene, thereby running the risk of being harmed himself.[294]

11.6b Tort: The Principle of *Hunt v Severs*[295]

Somewhat similar to the rescue cases are those cases in which a friend or relative intervenes to take care of the victim *after* the accident. The voluntary carer is not a rescuer. 'Rescue' implies an immediate emergency, which leaves the rescuer little choice but to intervene. The voluntary carer, however, enters the scene after the emergency has passed. He decides to take care of the victim of his own free will, and his action thus constitutes a *novus actus interveniens*. Yet, where the intervener is the parent of the victim, he or she may be under a legal duty to provide care. Could it not be said that in such a case the expenses incurred by the carer are linked by an unbroken chain of causation to the act of the wrongdoer? Before the introduction of the Matrimonial Proceedings and Property Act 1970, that was exactly the position adopted by the courts in respect of husbands who took care of their injured wives.[296]

However, the existence of an independent claim by a parent was expressly denied by the Court of Appeal in *Donnelly v Joyce*.[297] In *Donnelly*, the infant plaintiff was seriously injured in a road accident caused by the defendant's negligence. The plaintiff's mother gave up her part-time job in order to look after her child. Counsel for the defendant argued that the plaintiff's mother, and she only, could recover for the loss she had suffered by giving up her employment.[298] The plaintiff should not be allowed to claim for someone else's loss. The Court of Appeal,

[292] *Ibid.* at 684. [293] *Ibid.* at 685.

[294] R. Wellmann, *Der Aufwendungsersatz des Geschäftsführers ohne Auftrag in der Rechtsprechung der anglo-amerikanischen Gerichte* (1959), p. 157 and D. Fleming, 'Knights Errant and the Law' (1982) 41 CLJ 33–36 at p. 36. *Contra*: *Saylor v Parsons* 98 NW 500 (Sup. Ct of Iowa 1904) at 502, *per* Ladd J.

[295] Cf. Road Traffic Act 1988, s. 157.

[296] *Best v Samuel Fox & Co. Ltd* [1952] AC 716 at 733, *per* Lord Goddard; *Kirkham v Boughey* [1958] 2 QB 338 at 342, *per* Diplock J and *Gage v King* [1961] 1 QB 188.

[297] [1974] 1 QB 454. [298] *Ibid.* at 455–456.

however, rejected this view. In the opinion of the Court, the plaintiff could not properly be said to be claiming for someone else's loss merely because someone else had provided for the plaintiff's needs. The plaintiff's loss was not the expenditure of money to pay for the nursing attention, but instead 'the need (. . .) for those nursing services, the value of which for the purposes of damages (. . .) is the proper and reasonable cost of supplying those needs'.[299] 'The corollary of this proposition', the Court said, 'is that, unless at any rate some very special circumstances exist, (. . .) the provider has no direct cause of action against the wrongdoer'.[300]

For twenty years, *Donnelly* was the leading authority. However, its reign was ended by the House of Lords in 1994, in *Hunt v Severs*.[301] The facts of *Hunt v Severs* may appear confusing, in that it was the tortfeasor himself who provided care to the plaintiff, who was his wife. Thus, it seemed that the plaintiff was suing her husband for the cost of services that he was already providing to her free of charge. The true issue was, of course, whether they could recover the value of these services from his insurer. For the defendant, it was argued that the service he provided gratuitously to the plaintiff was itself a form of compensation. Hence, if he were also required to pay for the cost of care, he would in fact be compensating her twice for the same loss.[302] The Court of Appeal accepted 'the thrust' of this argument, but nevertheless found for the plaintiff. In the view of the Court, it was not realistic in the present case to regard the defendant as paying twice[303] – the underlying consideration presumably being that the defendant's insurer was paying the damages. The decision of the Court of Appeal was however reversed by the House of Lords.[304] In a groundbreaking speech, Lord Bridge first turned the clock back twenty years, expressing the view that the cost of care was *not* loss suffered by the plaintiff, as was held in *Donnelly v Joyce*, but loss suffered by the person rendering the services. 'Once this is recognised', his Lordship said, 'it becomes evident that there can be no ground in public policy or otherwise for requiring the tortfeasor to pay to the plaintiff, in respect of the services which he himself has rendered (. . .)'.[305] With regard to cases in which the plaintiff sues for the cost of services rendered by persons other than the tortfeasor, his Lordship opined that the plaintiff should hold the damages he received on trust for the voluntary carer.[306]

The decision of the House of Lords in *Hunt v Severs* has been widely criticized.[307] However, Lord Bridge's proposition that it is in fact the voluntary carer's loss that is in issue, has escaped relatively unscathed.[308] Indeed, this proposition has

[299] *Ibid.* at 462. [300] *Ibid.* [301] [1994] 2 WLR 602.

[302] *Hunt v Severs* (CA) [1993] QB 815 at 818. See also *Hayden v Hayden* [1992] 1 WLR 986 at 1005, *per* Parker LJ. [303] *Ibid.* at 830.

[304] *Hunt v Severs* (HoL) [1994] 2 WLR 602. [305] *Ibid.* at 611. [306] *Ibid.*

[307] *E.g.* D. Kemp, 'Voluntary Services Provided by Tortfeasor to his Victim' (1994) 10 LQR 524–526; P. Matthews and M. Lunney, 'A Tortfeasor's Lot is not a Happy One?' (1995) 58 MLR 395–404; A. Reed, 'A Commentary on *Hunt v Severs*' (1995) 15 OJLS 133–140 and S.E. Degeling, *Victims and carers; liabilities in tort and unjust enrichment* (1998) (Unpublished thesis, University of Oxford).

[308] But see L.C.H. Hoyano, 'The Dutiful Tortfeasor in the House of Lords' (1995) 3 Tort LR 63–75 at pp. 66–69.

since been endorsed in a 1999 Law Commission Report,[309] which also included a recommendation for the Government to impose upon the successful plaintiff a personal obligation to account for damages for past care to the person who has provided that care.[310] Thus, it is clear that in the present legal climate the voluntary carer, like the rescuer, is looked upon favourably. The rescuer can bring a direct action against the tortfeasor; the voluntary carer has to depend upon the primary victim to recover 'his' loss for him. Meanwhile, it should of course be remembered that the law of negligence is of no avail to those who take care of, or rescue, victims of 'bad fortune' or of wrongdoers who cannot be identified or are insolvent. Moreover, pure economic loss is not recoverable through a claim in negligence.

11.6c: Tort: Quantum Damages

A more indirect avenue through which the courts have sometimes allowed interveners to recover for some or all of the expenses of their intervention, is by reducing their liability for loss caused in the course of the intervention. In the salvage case of *The Tojo Maru*, Lord Reid considered the following example:

> Suppose a house is on fire. It contains a valuable collection of, say, china. There is little or no hope of saving the collection but a passer-by, with or without the consent of the owner, goes in and brings most of the collection to safety. But owing to some gross negligence on his part some of the china is smashed. On land a person who interferes to save property is not in law entitled to any reward. But it would be most unjust in my view if, although he benefited the owner by saving the bulk of the property, he were held liable for his negligence in destroying the rest.[311]

Few would deny that to hold the intervener liable for the loss of the broken china would – in these circumstances – be manifestly unjust. Yet, however unjust it may be, it appears to be the law. True, in cases of this kind a court would probably be reluctant to find that the intervener acted negligently. But sometimes such a finding cannot be avoided.[312] Some courts might then be willing to accept an argument that the intervener's conduct – no matter how negligent it may have been – did not *cause* the loss. After all, is it not true that 'but for' the intervener's conduct – when taken as one, ongoing act – the china would have been destroyed anyway? Yet, while this argument might seem convincing if the circumstances were such

[309] Law Commission Report No. 262, *Damages for Personal Injury: Medical, Nursing and other Expenses; Collateral Benefits* (1999), p. 43 (para. 3.46–47). See for application of the principle *Evans v Pontypridd Roofing Ltd* [2001] EWCA Civ 1657.

[310] *Ibid.* at p. 49 (para. 3.62). Cf. also Law Commission Consultation Paper No. 144, *Damages for Personal Injury: Medical, Nursing and other Expenses* (1996) at pp. 61–62 (para. 3.56–58), where it was suggested to give the carer a direct right of action against the tortfeasor.

[311] *The Tojo Maru* [1972] AC 242 at 268.

[312] *Ibid.* at 268.

that the china was broken while it was still in the burning house, it would be much more difficult to maintain if the china was negligently broken after it had been brought to safety. There can be no doubt that a third party would incur liability for damaging goods that were successfully rescued by an intervener.[313] To then allow the intervener to escape such liability would *de facto* amount to allowing him to set-off the benefit he conferred against the loss that was caused by his carelessness.[314] And, as was admitted by Lord Reid, 'there is little or no authority for such a principle'.[315]

However, to accept such a principle would not have been completely unprecedented. One area of the law where the defendant has traditionally been allowed to set-off the benefit he conferred against the damage he caused is concerned with the wrongful interference with another's chattels. Amongst the earliest examples of such wrongs was detinue.[316] An action of detinue would have been available against a defendant who had acquired a chattel lawfully, but then wrongfully detained it: '*iniuste detinet*'. Thus, the most common use of the action of detinue was by bailors against their bailees.[317] Yet, as was observed earlier in this chapter,[318] finders also came to be liable in detinue, eventually leading to a separate count of 'detinue *sur trover*'. In the 15th century, a new form of action emerged: the action of 'conversion', also referred to as the action of 'trover' (not to be confused with 'detinue *sur trover*').[319] This action was based on the defendant's wrong in 'converting' the chattels to his own use, 'conversion' being such a broad notion, that the action would eventually spill over into areas that had previously belonged to the exclusive territory detinue, and indeed trespass.[320]

Although the action of conversion can be said to have had some proprietary characteristics,[321] it lay for damages.[322] Detinue was of a more proprietary character. It lay primarily for recovery of the chattel itself, but if the defendant refused to return it, damages were awarded instead.[323] The principles upon which damages

313 This was accepted by counsel for the salvors in *The Tojo Maru* [1972] AC 242, at 261.

314 R. Bagshaw, 'The duties of care of emergency service providers', [1999] LMCLQ 71–92 at 76.

315 *The Tojo Maru* [1972] AC 242 at 268. Indeed, to allow a set-off but no claim would be 'unjust and unsubtle': P.B.H. Birks, 'Restitution for Services' (1974) 27 CLP 13–36 at 35. *Contra*: J.A. Weir, 'Doing Good by Mistake – Restitution and Remedies' (1973) 71 CLJ 23–28 at 26.

316 J.W. Salmond, *The Law of Torts* (1st edn 1907), p. 285.

317 W.S. Holdsworth, *A History of English Law*, Vol III (3rd edn 1923), p. 324 and Th.F.T. Plucknett, *A Concise History of the Common Law* (5th edn 1956), p. 364.

318 See above, Part II, Section 11.5, p. 140.

319 See on the development of the action of conversion J.W. Salmond, *The Law of Torts* (1st edn 1907), pp. 286–288 and D.J. Ibbetson, *A Historical Introduction to the Law of Obligations* (1999), pp. 108–110.

320 See the notes under *Wilbraham v Snow* (1669) 2 Wms Saund 47, 85 ER 624 at 642–643 and D.J. Ibbetson, *A Historical Introduction to the Law of Obligations* (1999), pp. 108–109.

321 D.J. Ibbetson, *A Historical Introduction to the Law of Obligations* (1999), pp. 110–111.

322 M. Bacon, *A New Abridgment of the Law*, Vol I (1736), p. 2 (Damages, A), and footnote (b).

323 *Calwodelegh v John* YB Hil 18 Edw IV (1479), fo. 23, pl. 5 (name does not appear in the Yearbook, but is taken from J.H. Baker and S.F.C. Milsom, *Sources of English Legal History* (1986),

in either of these actions were assessed remain to a large extent concealed.[324] This is a result of the fact that the assessment of damages used to fall within the discretionary power of the jury, with hardly any judicial control.[325] Yet, in the nineteenth century some basic rules would emerge. As general rule, the measure of damages for conversion was the full value of the chattel,[326] the 'value of the chattel' normally being the value at the time of the conversion.[327] Thus, where the defendant had made improvements to the chattel, the resulting increase in value was not included in the damages. In *Reid v Fairbanks*[328] the defendants had converted the plaintiffs' ship. At the time of conversion the ship was in an unfinished state. Well aware that the plaintiffs disputed their title to the ship,[329] the defendants completed her at considerable expense. Counsel for the plaintiffs argued that his clients should be allowed to demand the value of the ship with all its improvements. The court, however, was of the opinion that the plaintiffs were not 'justly entitled' to the value of the improvements, and that 'no jury would give such damages'.[330] Maule J. explained:

> It may be that the wrong-doer, who acquires no property in the thing he converts, acquires no lien for what he expends upon it; (...) But it does not follow, that, if the owner brings trover, he is to recover the full value of the thing in its improved state. The proper measure of damages, as it seems to me, is the amount of pecuniary loss the plaintiffs have sustained by the conversion of their ship.

To which Jervis CJ added:

> That is, what she was really worth when the defendants converted her: the plaintiffs have lost the value of the vessel before the defendants began to lay out money upon her.[331]

A similar position was adopted where the defendant incurred expenses to make the converted goods saleable.[332] Thus, most cases in point involve expenses that resulted

p. 526); *Paler and Bartlet v Hardyman* (1605) Yelv 71, 80 ER 49 and *Peters v Heyward* (1623) Cro Jac 682. See also M. Bacon, *A New Abridgment of the Law*, Vol I (1736), p. 2 (Damages, A), footnote (b).

324 D.J. Ibbetson, *A Historical Introduction to the Law of Obligations* (1999), p. 57.

325 M. Bacon, *A New Abridgment of the Law*, Vol I (1736), p. 4 (Damages D 1) and Th. and H.D. Sedgwick, *A Treatise on the Measure of Damages* (6th edn 1874), p. 588–589.

326 See for conversion *Cook v Hartle* (1838) 8 Car & P 568, 173 ER 621 and F. Pollock, *The Law of Torts* (1887), pp. 291–292 and for trespass *de bonis asportatis* J.D. Mayne, *A Treatise on the Law of Damages* (1856), p. 220 and Th. and H.D. Sedgwick, *A Treatise on the Measure of Damages* (6th edn 1874), p. 663.

327 *Mercer v Jones* (1813) 3 Camp 477, 170 ER 1452, *per* Lord Ellenborough; *France v Gaudet* (1871) LR 6 QB 199 at 203, *per* Mellor J and *Solloway v McLaughlin* [1938] AC 247 at 257–258, *per* Lord Atkin. *Contra*: *Greening v Wilkinson* (1825) 1 Car & P 626, 171 ER 1344, *per* Abbott CJ. See for an elaborate account of the authorities *Kuwait Airlines Corp v Iraqi Airways Co* [2001] 3 WLR 1117, at 1232–1245, *per* Brooke LJ. The same general rules are said to have applied to trespass *de bonis asportatis*: J.W. Salmond, *The Law of Torts* (1st edn 1907), p. 332.

328 (1853) 13 CB 692, 138 ER 1371.

329 *Ibid.* at 715.

330 *Reid v Fairbanks* (1853) 13 CB 692, 138 ER 1371 at 729, *per* Jervis CJ.

331 *Ibid.* at 729. See also H. McGregor, *McGregor on Damages* (16th edn 1997), pp. 919–922 with further references.

332 *Munro v Willmott* [1949] 1 KB 295 at 299, *per* Lynskey J. See also a host of mining cases, discussed in H. McGregor, *McGregor on Damages* (16th edn 1997), pp. 922–929 with further references.

in a corresponding and readily discernable increase in the value of the chattel. Nevertheless, it is possible – though by no means certain – that similar deductions were made for expenses that were necessary, *not* to increase the value of the chattel, but to maintain its value as it was at the date of conversion. In *Davis v Oswell*, Parke B. appears to have suggested that the costs of keeping a horse were deductible.[333]

It has often been said that the method of assessing damages in conversion was the same in detinue.[334] However, whether this is correct, is doubtful.[335] Detinue was much more proprietary in character than conversion. And, where conversion was a single wrongful act, detinue was a continuing wrong, from the first refusal to return the goods to the date of the judgment.[336] When successful, an action in detinue would traditionally result in a judgment for the return of the chattel or its value, as well as payment of damages for its detention.[337] 'This', said Mellish LJ in *Re Scarth*, 'gave the defendant the choice whether he would give up the goods or pay the money'.[338] In 1854 the introduction of the Common Law Procedure Act brought a significant change; in section 78 of that Act, the courts were enabled to make a positive order for the return of the goods, if they saw fit to do so. In the 1892 case of *Peruvian Guano Co. v Dreyfus Brothers & Co.*[339] Lord Macnaghten hinted that a court would be reluctant to exercise this discretion if the plaintiff refused to reimburse the defendant's reasonable expenses. His Lordship said:

> I am not aware of any authority upon the point, but I should doubt whether it was incumbent upon the Court to order the defendant to return the goods *in specie* where the plaintiff refused to make fair and just allowance (...)[340]

However, this statement does not appear to have found favour with the Privy Council in *Glenwood Lumber Co. v Phillips*,[341] where it was said that 'it would not be right to impose on [the plaintiff] the obligation of paying [the defendants] the expenses of their wrongful act as a condition of recovering (...) his property'.[342] More recently, Lord Denning MR sided with Lord Macnaghten and said that 'no court would order [the chattel's] delivery unless compensation was made for the improvements'.[343]

A similar uncertainty surrounds those cases where the judgment assumed its more traditional form and left it to the defendant to either return the goods or pay

333 *Davis v Oswell* (1837) 7 Car & P 804, 173 ER 351.

334 *E.g.* J.D. Mayne, *A Treatise on the Law of Damages* (1856), p. 220; The Earl of Halsbury, *The Laws of England*, Vol XXVII (1913), p. 909, footnote (r) and *Sachs v Miklos* [1948] 2 KB 23 at 38, *per* Goddard LJ.

335 *General and Finance Facilities Ltd v Cooks Cars (Romford) Ltd* [1963] 1 WLR 644 at 649, *per* Diplock LJ.

336 *General and Finance Facilities Ltd v Cooks Cars (Romford) Ltd* [1963] 1 WLR 644 at 648, *per* Diplock LJ.

337 See the 'note', dated approximately 1530, in J.H. Baker and S.F.C. Milsom, *Sources of English Legal History* (1986), p. 402 and *General and Finance Facilities Ltd v Cooks Cars (Romford) Ltd* [1963] 1 WLR 644, at 650, *per* Diplock LJ.

338 *Re Scarth* (1874) 10 Ch App 234 at 235.

339 [1892] AC 166.

340 *Ibid.* at 176.

341 [1904] AC 405.

342 *Ibid.* at 412, *per* Lord Davey.

343 *Greenwood v Bennett* [1973] 1 QB 195 at 201.

their equivalent value. It appears to have been accepted as a general rule that the value of the chattel was assessed at the date of the judgment.[344] In principle, therefore, the plaintiff in detinue would receive not only the value of the goods he lost, but also the added value of any improvements that might have been made to the goods by the defendant.[345] However, in *Glenwood Lumber Co. v Phillips*[346] Lord Davey remarked *obiter* that the defendant's expenses incurred in making improvements 'might properly, but would not necessarily, be taken into account in estimating the alternative damages'.[347] And in *Munro v Willmott*[348], after some markedly unconventional reasoning, Lynskey J. arrived at a similar result.[349] Further support can be drawn from a 1971 report by the Law Reform Committee, which stated:

(...) where goods have acquired an increased value as a result of acts of the defendant, it is clear that, as a general rule, the plaintiff cannot, either in conversion or in detinue, recover such increase as part of the value or as damages (...)[350]

This report was followed some six year later by the introduction of the Torts (Interference with Goods) Act 1977. This Act covers conversion[351] and – in s. 2 – abolishes detinue. In s. 6(1), it contains a special provision with regard to improvements made by the defendant:

If in proceedings for wrongful interference against a person (the '"improver") ') who has improved the goods, it is shown that the improver acted in the mistaken but honest belief that he had good title to them, an allowance shall be made for the extent to which, at the time as at which the goods fall to be valued in assessing damages, the value of the goods is attributable to the improvement.

One of the most remarkable features of this provision is that it requires a 'mistaken but honest belief' on the part of the improver that he had 'good title' to the goods. This requirement does not appear to feature in the case law that preceded the Act,[352] nor was it recommended by the Law Reform Committee. Indeed, in *McGregor on Damages* the introduction of a requirement of good faith has been criticized as being 'a backward step'.[353] Nevertheless, the requirement stands and as such closes the door to voluntary interveners like the good Samaritan. After all, he who voluntarily intervenes for the benefit of another is by definition aware of the fact that he does not have 'good title' to the goods.

[344] *Rosenthal v Alderton and Sons Ltd* [1946] 1 KB 374.

[345] In the event that the plaintiff sued not only for the goods themselves, but also for any other loss resulting from the detention, the defendant may have been allowed to deduct his expenses under the latter head of damages.

[346] [1904] AC 405.

[347] *Ibid.* at 412.

[348] [1949] 1 KB 295.

[349] *Ibid.* at 298.

[350] Law Reform Committee, *Eighteenth Report (Conversion and Detinue)* (1977), p. 30 (§ 89).

[351] Tort (Interference with Goods) Act 1977, s. 1(a).

[352] H. McGregor, *McGregor on Damages* (16th edn 1997), p. 921. However, the presence of good faith on the part of the defendant/improver seems to have played an important role in *Peruvian Guano Co. v Dreyfus Brothers & Co.* [1892] AC 166 at 177. Cf. also The Earl of Halsbury, *The Laws of England*, Vol XXVII (1913), p. 911 (nr 1605).

[353] H. McGregor, *McGregor on Damages* (16th edn 1997), pp. 921–922.

11.7 Unjust Enrichment

The decline of the implied contract theory left a doctrinal no man's land. Most of the vacant ground has since been occupied by the law of unjust enrichment. It is only natural, then, to expect that in so far as the necessitous intervener used to be able to recover upon a promise implied in law, he would now be able to recover in unjust enrichment. Thus, many textbooks on restitution now assume that someone who buries another can recover his expenses from the estate in unjust enrichment: the 'enrichment' being the fact that the estate saved an otherwise unavoidable expenditure,[354] and the 'unjust' factor being something along the lines of 'moral compulsion'[355] or a policy of encouraging intervention.[356] However, there appear to be no modern cases in which an intervener has been allowed the cost of burial in unjust enrichment. Indeed, given the modern methods of communication it seems unlikely that such cases will come before the courts again. Cases involving the provision of necessaries to minors or the mentally incapacitated are now covered by the Sale of Goods Act 1979. Section 3(2) of that Act entitles anyone who provides necessaries to minors, the mentally disabled or drunkards to recover a 'reasonable price'.

One and perhaps the only area in which the courts have had occasion to employ unjust enrichment terminology in respect of voluntary interveners, is concerned with the payment of another's debt. As we have seen in Section 11.3 of Part II, the conventional position was that 'if A voluntarily pays B's debt, B is under no obligation to repay A'.[357] However, this position has been eroded, first in *Owen v Tate*[358] and subsequently in *The Zuhal K and Selin.*[359]

In *Owen v Tate,*[360] the plaintiff voluntarily guaranteed the defendants' debt. Having been called upon and honoured the guarantee, the plaintiff sought indemnity from the defendant. The plaintiff argued that he was legally compelled to pay, and could thus recover under the restitutionary doctrine of 'legal compulsion'. For the defendant it was argued that there was no reason to distinguish between a voluntary payment of another's debt, and – as in the present case – a voluntary assumption of an obligation to pay, followed by payment. This would seem to be correct. 'Restitutionary consequences ought not to be affected by the machinery which the intervener happens to have used, whether immediate payment or promise followed by payment.'[361] The Court of Appeal agreed with the defendant and disallowed the claim, albeit *per incuriam.*[362] However, both

354 P.B.H. Birks, *An Introduction to the Law of Restitution* (1985), p. 118.

355 *Ibid.* at pp. 197–198.

356 *E.g.* A. Burrows, *The Law of Restitution* (2nd edn 2002), p. 315 and P.B.H. Birks and C. Mitchell, 'Unjust Enrichment' in P.B.H. Birks (ed.), *English Private Law*, Vol II (2000), pp. 525–635, p. 580.

357 *Re National Motor Mail-Coach Co. Ltd* [1908] 2 Ch 515 at 520, *per* Swinfen Eady J. See above, p. 123.

358 [1975] 2 All ER 129.

359 [1987] 1 Lloyd's Rep 151.

360 [1975] 2 All ER 129.

361 P.B.H. Birks and J. Beatson, 'Unrequested Payment of Another's Debt' (1976) 92 LQR 188–212 at p. 209. *Contra*: A. Burrows, *The Law of Restitution* (2nd edn 2002), p. 284.

362 See footnote 367, below, and the corresponding part of the main text.

Scarman and Stephenson LJJ indicated that if the guarantee had been given in circumstances of necessity, the plaintiff might have been allowed recovery. Scarman LJ stated:

> If without an antecedent request a person assumes an obligation or makes a payment for the benefit of another, the law will, as a general rule, refuse him a right of indemnity. But if he can show that in the particular circumstances of the case there was some necessity for the obligation to be assumed, then the law will grant him a right of reimbursement if in all the circumstances it is just and reasonable to do so.[363]

The decision in *Owen v Tate* has been widely criticized.[364] However, the principle formulated by Scarman LJ was adopted and applied in *The Zuhal K and Selin*.[365] There, the plaintiff guarantors were granted indemnity after discharging the defendants' liability to the owners of a damaged cargo of grapefruits. The plaintiffs had argued, *inter alia*, that they had been asked to act as guarantors by a third party with ostensible authority from the defendants. This was accepted by the court, and that should have been a sufficient basis to allow the plaintiffs' claim. However, Sheen J went on to refer to Scarman LJ's speech in *Owen v Tate*, and concluded that in the present case 'it was reasonably necessary in the interest of the shipowners that the guarantee should be given' and that 'it is clearly just and reasonable that a right of reimbursement should arise'.[366]

Both *Owen v Tate* and *The Zuhal K and Selin* are open to criticism. The predominant opinion is that the plaintiff guarantors in both cases should have been allowed to recover, but that to arrive at that result no recourse to a supposed doctrine of necessity was required. A variety of alternative avenues has been suggested, the most straightforward of which is the Mercantile Amendment Act 1856. Section 5 of that Act entitles any guarantor subrogation to the creditor's rights, whether the guarantee was given voluntarily or not. Had the plaintiffs in either case invoked that Act, any discussion of the relevance of necessity would have been superfluous.[367] However, this should not distract us from the wider issues at stake. The fact is that the courts in both cases *did* conclude that necessity could be a justification for recovery. Even if there are other possible bases for recovery, the speeches in *Owen v Tate* and *The Zuhal K and Selin* at least indicate a willingness to accept 'necessity' as an 'unjust factor' within the law of unjust enrichment. The formula adopted by Scarman LJ covers guarantors as well as those who pay another's debt immediately. Yet, it is difficult to see why the law should distinguish between the payment of another's debt, and the conferring of any other type of

363 *Owen v Tate* [1975] 2 All ER 129 at 135. See also *ibid.* at 136, *per* Stephenson LJ. Cf. *Re A Debtor* [1937] Ch 156 at 166, *per* Greene LJ and *Anson v Anson* [1953] 1 QB 636 at 646, *per* Pearson J.

364 *E.g.* W.R. Cornish 'Interveners and Unjust Enrichment' (1975) 38 MLR 563–566; P.B.H. Birks and J. Beatson, 'Unrequested Payment of Another's Debt' (1976) 92 LQR 188–212 and A. Burrows, *The Law of Restitution* (2nd edn 2002), pp. 282–286.

365 [1987] 1 Lloyd's Rep 151.

366 *Ibid.* at 156.

367 P. Watts, 'Guarantees Undertaken Without the Request of the Debtor', [1989] LMCLQ 7–10 at p. 10.

benefit.[368] In the United States, the *Restatement of the Law of Restitution* also allows a claim to the intervener who saves another's life, health, property or credit. The *Restatement* requires that the intervention was done 'unofficiously' and without an intent to charge.[369] The time may not be far off when the English courts, too, extend the doctrine of unjust enrichment to cases of necessitous intervention. Yet, whether the law of unjust enrichment provides the right tools to deal with situations of necessitous intervention remains to be seen. This question will be addressed in the next chapter.

11.8 Equitable Analogies

In the view of Bowen LJ, the supposed principle that 'liabilities are not to be forced upon people behind their backs'[370] applied to law and equity alike.[371] Nevertheless, on occasion voluntary interveners have been able to recover in equity, where they probably would have failed at law.

One such instance concerns loans made to infants, the mentally incapacitated or married women for necessaries. While those who provided necessaries could recover at law, those who loaned money for that purpose could not.[372] The *ratio* of this distinction being, that women and infants might waste the money: 'it may be borrowed for necessaries, but laid out and spent at a tavern'.[373] Yet, if and to the extent that the money was used to purchase necessaries, equity would place the lender in the position of the person who provided the necessaries. In the leading case of *Harris v Lee*,[374] a married woman had twice been given the 'foul distemper'[375] by her husband. She came to town to be cured, and borrowed 30 pounds to pay for her treatment and other necessaries. It was held that, while the lender could not recover at law, he could stand in the place of the doctors, tradesmen *etc.* who had provided the necessaries, and recover against the husband.[376] Some have termed this doctrine 'subrogation in equity'.[377] It has been suggested that subrogation could equally be granted in cases of the type of *Owen v Tate* and *The Zuhal K and Selin*.[378] Perhaps anyone who voluntarily pays off another's debt should be enti-

368 A. Burrows, *The Law of Restitution* (2nd edn 2002), pp. 285–286.

369 American Law Institute, *Restatement of the Law of Restitution* (1937), §§ 113–117.

370 *Falcke v Scottish Imperial Insurance Co.* (1886) 34 Ch D 234 at 248.

371 *Ibid.* at 250.

372 *Earle v Peale* (1712) 1 Salk 386, 91 ER 336. See also J. Chitty, *The Law of Contracts* (3rd edn 1841), pp. 151 and 169 with further references.

373 *Earle v Peale* (1712) 1 Salk 386, 91 ER 336 at 387, *per* Parker CJ.

374 (1718) 1 P Wms 482, 24 ER 482.

375 Probably a euphemism for syphilis.

376 *Ibid.* at 483. See also *Jenner v Morris* (1861) 3 De G F & J 45, 45 ER 795; *Marlow v Pitfeild* (1719) 1 P Wms 558, 24 ER 516 (infant) and *Re Beavan* [1912] 1 Ch 196 (mentally incapacitated).

377 *E.g.* J.H. Munkman, *The Law of Quasi-Contracts* (1950), p. 78 and S.J. Stoljar, *The Law of Quasi-Contract* (2nd edn 1989), p. 167.

378 *E.g.* W.R. Cornish 'Interveners and Unjust Enrichment' (1975) 38 MLR 563–566 at p. 565 and Lord Goff of Chieveley and G. Jones, *The Law of Restitution* (6th edn 2002), pp. 131 and 432.

tled to be subrogated to the creditor's rights.[379] Suffice it to say that there are as yet no English cases in which this view has been accepted.[380]

A second equitable doctrine that might be said to allow certain interveners to recover concerns the position of the trustee who has voluntarily intervened for the benefit of the trust. Until recently, it was the starting-point in English law that a trustee is bound to act gratuitously, no matter how onerous the duties he has taken upon himself. However, it has long been established that a trustee is entitled to reimburse himself for all expenses properly incurred out of the trust property.[381] This rule, which has been statutory since 1859,[382] applies not only to express trustees, but to implied and constructive trustees as well.[383] Its *ratio* was aptly formulated by Kekewich J in *Rowley v Ginnever*:[384]

> The rule of equity is universal, and is expressed in the words of the maxim, 'He that seeks equity must do equity.' If you insist upon a man performing his duties as trustee and making over property as trustee, you must treat him as a trustee throughout, and you cannot expect him to perform his duties without at the same time exonerating him from expenditure incurred which benefits the property of which he is the trustee.[385]

The trustee's right to reimbursement is a right against the trust estate. By way of exception a claim has been allowed against the beneficiary, most notably where the beneficiary was also the settlor of the trust and had personally requested the trustee to accept the trust. The true basis of this claim is, however, an implied contract rather than the equitable doctrine here in issue.[386]

Besides reimbursement of expenses, the courts have on occasion used their 'inherent jurisdiction' to order that the trustee be remunerated. Again, this power is said to derive from the principle that he who seeks equity must do equity.[387] By way of policy argument, it has been added that in some cases remuneration of the trustee would promote the 'good administration of trusts'.[388] However, because until recently the office of trustee was – as a general rule – gratuitous, the courts have been reluctant to exercise this discretionary power. But where the trustee's duties turned out to be much more burdensome than could have been anticipated when he or she accepted office, courts have occasionally been persuaded to order remuneration. One such case

[379] *Re Cleadon Trust Ltd* [1939] 1 Ch 286 would appear to stand in the way of this solution. But cf. W.R. Cornish 'Interveners and Unjust Enrichment' (1975) 38 MLR 563–566 at 565–566 and S.J. Stoljar, *The Law of Quasi-Contract* (2nd edn 1989), p. 169.

[380] See however for a discussion of some North American cases C. Mitchell, *The Law of Subrogation* (1994), pp. 103–104.

[381] *Worrall v Harford* (1802) 8 Ves Jun 4, 32 ER 250 at 8, *per* Lord Eldon.

[382] Law of Property Amendment Act 1859, s. 31. A similar provision can be found in the Trustee Act 1893, s. 24, the Trustee Act 1925, s. 30(2) and now in the Trustee Act 2000, s. 31.

[383] Trustee Act 1925, ss. 30(2) and 68(17).

[384] [1897] 2 Ch 503.

[385] *Ibid.* at 507. Cf. *Re Chapman* (1895) 72 LT 66.

[386] *Fraser v Murdoch* (1881) 6 App Cas 855 at 872–873, *per* Lord Blackburn. See also D.J. Hayton, *Commentary and Cases on the Law of Trusts and Equitable Remedies* (10th edn 1996), p. 754 with further references.

[387] *Re Berkeley Applegate Ltd* [1989] Ch 32 at 50, *per* Edward Nugee QC.

[388] *Re Duke of Norfolk's Settlement Trusts* [1982] Ch 61 at 79, *per* Fox J.

is *Foster v Spencer*,[389] in which it took two trustees of a cricket club twenty years of 'vigorous effort' to secure the sale of the club's ground. Paul Baker QC, sitting as a judge of the High Court, accepted that the services rendered by the trustees were 'wholly outside their contemplation when appointed'. 'I have no doubt', he said, 'that if they had realised what they were in for, they would have declined to act unless remunerated in some way'.[390] Both trustees were awarded remuneration for the services they had rendered. Even where the trust instrument includes a clause allowing the trustee remuneration, a court can use its inherent jurisdiction to increase the amount by which he or she is remunerated.[391] Also, the court can use its jurisdiction for the benefit of express and constructive trustees alike.[392]

Given that the underlying considerations of the above doctrine are 'he who seeks equity must do equity' and 'the promotion of the good administration of trusts', we might ask ourselves whether the same considerations could justify an extension of this doctrine to parties other than trustees. This question was considered by the Chancery Division in *Re Berkeley Applegate Ltd*.[393] Berkeley Applegate Ltd, a company of investment consultants, went into voluntary liquidation. Amongst its assets were 1.2 million pounds in the clients' accounts plus interest of 29,509 pounds, as well as some 10.2 million pounds worth of loans made by the company and secured by mortgages. These assets, said the court, were held by the company on trust for its investors. In the course of making an inventory of the company's other assets, it became clear to the liquidator that these other assets would not suffice to cover his expenses and remuneration. The liquidator applied to the court for the determination of the question whether any part of his expenses and remuneration could be paid out of the trust assets. For the company's investors and creditors it was argued – *inter alia* – that the liquidator was a stranger to the trust, and therefore could not invoke the rules allowing a trustee expenses and/or remuneration. Edward Nugee QC, sitting as deputy High Court judge, rejected this argument as being 'based upon too narrow a view of the principles on which a court acts'.[394] While it is true that the liquidator was not a trustee, the investors still needed the assistance of a court of equity to assert their equitable interest. And, since he who seeks equity must do equity, the court could here exercise its discretion to ensure that a proper allowance was made to the liquidator.[395] The deputy judge went on to formulate the following general principle:

> Where a person seeks to enforce a claim to an equitable interest in property, the court has a discretion to require as a condition of giving effect to that equitable interest that an allowance be made for costs incurred and for skill and labour expended in connection with the administration of the property.[396]

This is of course not to say that the court's discretion will automatically be exercised. Among the factors that persuaded the deputy judge to exercise his discretion

389 [1996] 2 All ER 672. 390 *Ibid.* at 681.
391 *Re Duke of Norfolk's Settlement Trusts* [1982] Ch 61.
392 *Boardman v Phipps* [1967] 2 AC 46. Cf. *Guiness Plc v Saunders* [1990] 1 All ER 652.
393 [1989] Ch 32.
394 [1989] Ch 32, at 50. 395 *Ibid.* 396 *Ibid.*

in this case was the fact that if the work were not done by the liquidator, it would have to be done by a paid receiver. Also, the liquidator's work was of substantial benefit to the equitable interest of the investors.[397] Finally, the deputy judge mentioned that in his view the situation that existed immediately before the winding up of the company 'could fairly be called an emergency'.[398]

The possible scope of application of the principle enunciated by Edward Nugee QC is wide, some would say too wide.[399] On the face of it, anyone who voluntarily intervenes in the 'administration' of another's equitable interest – in any case in a situation of emergency – could be granted reimbursement or remuneration by the court. However, there is no authority for this broad a principle. As the deputy judge himself acknowledged, all the cases in point involved interveners who were, like the liquidator in the present case, subject to fiduciary duties.[400] The fulfilment of these duties, one might argue, entitles fiduciaries to a 'correlative right' to reimbursement or, in the appropriate case, remuneration.[401] If the equitable principle is indeed limited to fiduciaries,[402] it does not assist the intervener who is a complete stranger to the equitable interest.

Following a 1999 Law Commission report,[403] the old presumption that a trustee performed his duties gratuitously has been abolished. The Trustee Act 2000 includes a statutory charging clause for trustees who act in a professional capacity.[404] Naturally, the introduction of this provision will reduce the likelihood of the courts being called upon by trustees to exercise their inherent jurisdiction. However, there does not appear to be any reason why the courts could not continue to use their discretion to reimburse or remunerate persons other than trustees, in cases in which equity demands it.

11.9 Maritime Salvage

An investigation into the position of English law in respect of voluntary intervention would not be complete without some discussion of the law of salvage.[405] For

[397] [1989] Ch 32, at 50–51.

[398] *Ibid.* at 52. This observation has been criticized: A. Burrows, *The Law of Restitution* (2nd edn 2002), pp. 312–313 and Lord Goff of Chieveley and G. Jones, *The Law of Restitution* (6th edn 2002), p. 453, footnote 57.

[399] *E.g.* D.J. Hayton, *Underhill and Hayton, Law Relating to Trusts and Trustees* (15th edn 1995), p. 645.

[400] *Re Berkeley Applegate Ltd* [1989] Ch 32 at 52.

[401] Cf. *China Pacific S.A. v Food Corporation of India* (HoL) [1982] AC 939 at 960, *per* Lord Diplock.

[402] Cf. J.E. Martin, *Hanbury & Martin; Modern Equity* (16th edn 2001), p. 604.

[403] Law Commission Report No. 260, *Trustees' Powers and Duties* (1999), pp. 72–74 (para. 7.1–7).

[404] Trustee Act 2000, s. 29. See for more detail Chr. Whitehouse and N. Hassall, *Trusts of Land, Trustee Delegation and the Trustee Act 2000* (2nd edn 2001), pp. 274–281.

[405] The area covered by the law of salvage is vast, and it is here only intended to convey some of the most basic principles of the law of salvage. For a detailed survey, see G. Brice, *Maritime Law of Salvage* (3rd edn 1999) and F.D. Rose, *Kennedy and Rose; The Law of Salvage* (6th edn 2002).

once, we are dealing with an area of the law in which there is no doubt that the intervener is entitled to some form of a claim:

It is what the law calls *jus liquidissimum*, the clearest general right that they who have saved lives and property at sea should be rewarded for such salutary exertions; (. . .)[406]

The basis of this ancient doctrine is twofold. On the one hand, salvage has a close affinity with the law of unjust enrichment, in that it introduces a right to be paid where benefits have been conferred.[407] Where there has been no benefit conferred – *i.e.* where the salvage operation was unsuccessful[408] – the salvors will not be entitled to a reward. 'Upon general principles', Dr Lushington once said, 'a mere attempt to save the vessel and cargo, however meritorious that attempt may be, or whatever degree of risk or danger may have been incurred, if unsuccessful, can never be considered in this Court as furnishing any title to a salvage reward. The reason is obvious, viz., that salvage reward is for benefits actually conferred, not for a service attempted to be rendered'.[409] However, whether the doctrine is in fact based upon unjust enrichment is doubtful.[410] While the benefit to the defendant is a material factor in the assessment of the award, reversal of enrichment does not seem to be its main function. Instead, the primary purpose of the reward appears to be to encourage necessitous intervention in emergencies on the high seas.[411] As we have seen in Section 10.1 of Part II, a similar policy underlay the Roman doctrine of *negotiorum gestio*. However, the present policy goes beyond the Roman in two respects. Firstly, where the Roman doctrine merely served to remove the existing disincentives against intervention – providing the intervener with a claim for expenses incurred – the law of salvage aims to provide a positive incentive as well. Accordingly, the salvage reward – perhaps we should say 'award' – incorporates elements of reimbursement, remuneration and reward.[412] Secondly, maritime law not only aims to encourage salvage in general, but aims to encourage the development of a salvage industry.[413] It is for that reason that the courts have been more generous in rewarding professional salvors. After all, if a salvage industry is to survive, the sum of the rewards will need to cover

406 *The Waterloo* (1820) 2 Dods 433, 165 ER 1537 at 435–436, *per* Sir William Scott.

407 F.D. Rose, *Kennedy and Rose; The Law of Salvage* (6th edn 2002), pp. 13–20 with further references.

408 Although some might argue that the service itself, regardless of its outcome, would constitute a benefit. See below, Section 12.2.

409 *The Zephyrus* (1842) 1 W Rob 329, 166 ER 596 at 330–331.

410 P.B.H. Birks, *An Introduction to the Law of Restitution* (1985), p. 307 and F.D. Rose, 'Restitution and Maritime Law' in E.J.H. Schrage, *Unjust Enrichment and the Law of Contract* (2001), pp. 367–380.

411 *Contra*: M. McInnes, 'Life Rescue in Maritime Law' (1994) 25 JMLC 451–484 at 454–455, where it is stated that the policy consideration is 'subordinate', and 'alone . . . cannot provide the basis for liability'. 'No matter how heroic or skilled, an attempt to provide salvage services will go uncompensated if it fails to produce a benefit'. However, if the policy underlying the law of salvage is not just one of encouraging rescue, but one of encouraging *successful* rescue, it can on its own serve as a basis for the doctrine.

412 F.D. Rose, 'Restitution and Maritime Law' in E.J.H. Schrage, *Unjust Enrichment and the Law of Contract* (2001), pp. 367–380 at p. 378.

413 F.D. Rose, *Kennedy and Rose; The Law of Salvage* (6th edn 2002), pp. 23–27.

the cost of keeping a professional salvage fleet on 'standby'[414] as well as the cost of all the unsuccessful salvage operations.[415]

When a person is in danger of being lost at sea, the law promotes intervention through the imposition of penal sanctions for failure to render assistance.[416] Yet paradoxically, the law of salvage is reluctant to reward the rescue of human life. Originally, it was concerned only with the preservation of property. As Dr Lushington explained:

> One of the reasons for this state of the law was, that no property could be arrested applicable to the purpose. There could be no proceeding *in rem*, the ancient foundation of the salvage suit.[417]

Indeed, in the early days of maritime law the reward was assessed by direct reference to the value of the property saved, and often at a percentage thereof.[418] With its focus being on property, maritime law did not reward the salvage of life as such. Yet, the courts were willing to grant more liberal rewards to those who had saved lives as well as property.[419] However, the maximum amount awarded was – and still is – the value of the salved property.[420]

The law's ungenerous attitude towards the saving of life has been somewhat softened by statute. Since the introduction of the Merchant Shipping Act 1854, a right to a share in the reward has been available to 'independent life salvors',[421] that is, salvors who save lives while property is salved in the same salvage operation (though not by the same salvors).[422] Naturally, this share of the reward – along with the rest of it – is to be paid by the owners of the salved property, not by those whose lives are saved.[423] It follows that where life alone is saved, no salvage reward

414 *The Glengyle* [1898] P 97 at 109, *per* Smith LJ.

415 *The City of Chester* (1884) 9 PD 182 at 202–203, *per* Lindley LJ.

416 First introduced into English law in the Maritime Conventions Act 1911, s. 6(1); see now Merchant Shipping Act 1995, Sch. 11, Pt I (International Convention on Salvage 1989), art. 10 and Pt II, § 3(1). It is doubtful whether there is a parallel duty in private law: *The 'Ogopogo'* [1970] 1 Lloyd's Rep 257 at 261, *per* Schroeder JA.

417 *The Fusilier* (1865) 3 Moore NS 51, 16 ER 19 at 55.

418 G. Brice, *Maritime Law of Salvage* (3rd edn 1999), p. 152. Cf. W. Ashburner (ed.), *The Rhodian Sea Law* (1909), pp. 288–290 (*cap.* 45–47). This practice has long been abandoned. In *The Aquilia* (1798) 1 C Rob 37, 165 ER 87 at 40, the King's Advocate suggested that no traces of this practice could be discovered later than the times of Charles II.

419 G. St Clair Pilcher and O.L. Bateson, *Maclachlan on Merchant Shipping* (7th edn 1932), p. 539 and *The Fusilier* (1865) 3 Moore NS 51, 16 ER 19 at 74, *per* Lord Chelmsford.

420 *The Tojo Maru* [1972] AC 242 at 293, *per* Lord Diplock and Merchant Shipping Act 1995, s. 224(2) and Sch. 11, Pt I (International Convention on Salvage 1989), art. 13.3.

421 Merchant Shipping Act 1854, s. 458. This provision applied only to salvage operations within British waters, but was extended to apply also to salvage of British ships in foreign waters by the Admiralty Court Jurisdiction Act 1861, s. 9. Cf. Merchant Shipping Act 1894, s. 544(1) and Merchant Shipping Act 1995, s. 224(2) and Sch. 11, Pt I (International Convention on Salvage 1989), art. 16.2.

422 M. McInnes, 'Life Rescue in Maritime Law' (1994) 25 JMLC 451–484 at 456.

423 Merchant Shipping Act 1995, s. 224(2) and Sch. 11, Pt I (International Convention on Salvage 1989), art. 16.1.

is payable.[424] True, the Secretary of State has been given a discretionary power to award the 'pure' life salvor a sum out of public funds,[425] but there appear to have been no recorded instances of its exercise in over fifty years.[426] Thus, there remains a stark contrast in the law's approach towards lifesaving that 'piggybacks' onto property salvage and pure life salvage.

The incentive offered by the salvage reward, is intended only for situations of true danger.[427] 'Danger', it has been said, 'is the very foundation of [the] claim to salvage'.[428] While the danger need not be absolute – a 'state of difficulty and reasonable apprehension' will suffice[429] – the danger must be *real*. An honest but mistaken belief that a ship is in danger and in need of assistance will not do.[430]

Furthermore, the salvor must have rendered his services voluntarily. He is not regarded as a volunteer if he was bound to intervene by a pre-existing legal duty, such as a contractual or a public duty. After all, as Goff and Jones put it, 'a person bound by duty should not (. . .) need the bait of a prospective reward to induce him to intervene'.[431] Thus, the master and the crew of a ship in distress are not normally entitled to a salvage reward, because they are under a contractual duty to protect the ship.[432] Similarly, no reward is payable where a publicly owned fire-fighting vessel renders its services in the ordinary performance of its public duties.[433] However, the voluntariness of the salvor's intervention is not negated merely because he acted in the performance of his statutory duty to render assistance to a person in danger of being lost at sea.[434] Nor does it matter that he was ordered to intervene by a third party. In *The Sarpen* the master of a tug was instructed by the naval authorities to give assistance to a stranded ship. The defendants refused to pay its owners, master and crew salvage, arguing that the service had not been rendered voluntarily. The Court of Appeal rejected this argument, Pickford LJ stating:

> The test of voluntariness is only applicable as between the salvor and salved, and if the services be voluntary in relation to the salved, *i.e.*, not rendered by reason of any obligation

[424] M. McInnes, 'Life Rescue in Maritime Law' (1994) 25 JMLC 451–484 at 466 and F.D. Rose, *Kennedy and Rose; The Law of Salvage* (6th edn 2002), p. 344. Both Birks and Goff and Jones suggest that the right to a salvage reward is now available even in cases of 'pure life salvage'. It can only be assumed that these authors rely on an erroneous interpretation of Merchant Shipping Act 1894, s. 544 and Merchant Shipping (Salvage and Pollution) Act 1994, Sch. 1, Pt II, § 5 respectively. See P.B.H. Birks, *An Introduction to the Law of Restitution* (1985), p. 304 and Lord Goff of Chieveley and G. Jones, *The Law of Restitution* (6th edn 2002), p. 472.

[425] Merchant Shipping Act 1995, s. 224(2) and Sch. 11, Pt II, § 5.

[426] F.D. Rose, *Kennedy and Rose; The Law of Salvage* (6th edn 2002), p. 150 footnote 81.

[427] *Nicholson v Chapman* (1793) 2 H Bl 254, 126 ER 536 at 257, *per* Eyre CJ.

[428] *The Wilhelmine* (1842) 1 NoC 376 at 378, *per* Dr Lushington.

[429] *The Phantom* (1866) LR 1 A & E 58 at 60, *per* Dr Lushington.

[430] *The Ranger* (1845) 3 NoC 589.

[431] Lord Goff of Chieveley and G. Jones, *The Law of Restitution* (6th edn 2002), p. 473.

[432] *The Neptune* (1824) 1 Hagg 227, 166 ER 81 at 236–237, *per* Lord Stowell. See also Merchant Shipping Act 1995, s. 224(2) and Sch. 11, Pt I (International Convention on Salvage 1989), art. 17.

[433] G. Brice, *Maritime Law of Salvage* (3rd edn 1999), p. 76.

[434] Merchant Shipping Act 1995, s. 224(2) and Sch. 11, Pt II, § 3(2). Cf. Maritime Conventions Act 1911, s. 6(2) and *The Tower Bridge* [1936] P 30 at 35, *per* Sir Boyd Merriman.

towards him, it is quite immaterial that the salvor has been ordered by some one who has control of his movements to render them.[435]

It is uncertain whether an intervention can be called 'voluntary' where the salvor was motivated by self-preservation. It could be argued that interventions that are in the interest of the intervener do not require promotion by the law.[436] Accordingly, it is stated in *Kennedy and Rose on Salvage* that a salvor is 'not permitted to found a title to salvage reward upon exertions to which he is driven *solely* by self-interest (. . .) although they may be at the same time incidentally beneficial to other interests.[437] Later on in the same book, it is said that 'the mere presence of the interest of self-preservation, if it is not the sole interest, does not take the services outside the scope of voluntariness'.[438] In practice, there is no more than a thin dividing line between interventions that are undertaken solely in the interest of self-preservation and those that are only partly so undertaken. The leading case of *The Lomonosoff* illustrates this vividly. A group of British and Belgian soldiers were in Murmansk when the town fell into the hands of the Bolsheviks. To avoid capture and probable execution, they decided to take a Russian ship called *Lomonosoff* and managed to escape under heavy fire. When they eventually reached Tromso, the defendant owners of the ship refused to pay the soldiers salvage arguing, *inter alia*, that the soldiers' sole object was to save themselves. Hill J rejected this defence, observing that the plaintiffs could also have escaped Murmansk by sleigh:

(. . .) and where in a case like the present the salvor has two means of saving himself and elects one which also saves maritime property I have no doubt that qua that property he is a volunteer.[439]

Relying mainly on this decision, Brice concluded that the salvor's motive, including self-preservation, is 'irrelevant';[440] a conclusion that received judicial confirmation in 1995 in *The Sava Star*.[441] However, it remains questionable whether a claim would be upheld in a case in which it could be established that the salvor intervened solely for reasons of self-preservation.

As was observed earlier in this section, the salvage 'reward' serves to compensate, reimburse, remunerate, and reward the salvor. In practice, the court or, more often, the arbitrator, awards one single sum of money. However, that the reward performs all of these functions can be seen from the factors that are taken into account when assessing this reward. The relevant factors were identified in the International Convention on Salvage and include the expenses and losses incurred

[435] *The Sarpen* [1916] P 306 at 315.
[436] Lord Goff of Chieveley and G. Jones, *The Law of Restitution* (6th edn 2002), p. 473.
[437] F.D. Rose, *Kennedy and Rose; The Law of Salvage* (6th edn 2002), p. 245 (emphasis added).
[438] *Ibid.* at 263. [439] *The Lomonosoff* [1921] P 97 at 103.
[440] G. Brice, *Maritime Law of Salvage* (3rd edn 1999), p. 66.
[441] [1995] 2 Lloyd's Rep 134 at 144, *per* Clarke J.

by the salvors (reimbursement and compensation), the time they used and their skill and efforts (remuneration) and the measure of success obtained (reward).[442]

Originally, the salvor's action for a reward was *in rem*, but he can now also claim *in personam*.[443] His claim is supported by a maritime lien, that is, 'a true charge on the ship and freight of a proprietary kind in favour of the privileged creditor'.[444] This maritime lien enables the salvor to retain possession of the salved property until sufficient security has been given or, if he is not in possession, to have the property arrested by the court.[445]

The law of salvage has been extended by statute to cover aircraft as well as hovercraft.[446]

442 Merchant Shipping Act 1995, s. 224(2) and Sch. 11, Pt I (International Convention on Salvage 1989), art. 13.1

443 *Five Steel Barges* (1890) 15 PD 142 and F.D. Rose, *Kennedy and Rose; The Law of Salvage* (6th edn 2002), p. 563.

444 *The Tolten* [1946] P 135 at 150, *per* Scott LJ. See for more detail D.R. Thomas, *Maritime Liens* (1980), pp. 10–11.

445 Supreme Court Act 1981, s. 21(3) and F.D. Rose, *Kennedy and Rose; The Law of Salvage* (6th edn 2002), p. 578 with further references.

446 Hovercraft Act 1968, s. 1(h); Hovercraft (Application of Enactments) Order 1972, SI 1972/971, art. 8(1); Merchant Shipping Act 1995, s. 310 and Civil Aviation Act 1982, s. 87.

12

Towards a General Principle: Using the Existing Doctrines?

The picture that emerges from the previous chapter is that this is a 'patchwork' area of the law. Throughout the centuries, the courts' attitude towards necessitous interveners has been ambiguous. There are numerous *obiter dicta* that oppose the granting of a claim to the intervener. Yet, there is an ever-growing list of cases in which the courts have granted a claim to the voluntary intervener. Regrettably, in granting such claims, the courts have resorted to a variety of doctrines.

Meanwhile, the difference in the courts' attitude towards interveners does not appear to be based on any sound distinction. No reason is offered as to why the intervener who has buried another, salvaged a ship, *etc.* should recover, yet the good Samaritan should not.[1] Indeed, the policy considerations underlying many of the decisions that have been favourable to the intervener apply with equal force to other cases of beneficial intervention. Consistency, therefore, requires a reconsideration of the present state of the law: either we develop a general principle allowing the voluntary intervener a claim, or we deny him this claim across the board. There is no point in pretending that this is an easy choice to make. Yet, Birks has argued that the law has already, albeit implicitly, decided in favour of the former option. 'It is', Birks writes, 'tolerably clear that the old proposition denying the intervener reimbursement has been swallowed by its numerous so-called exceptions'.[2] While it cannot be denied that there are numerous exceptions to the principle of no recovery, it is perhaps too early to conclude that these exceptions have now become the rule. Notwithstanding, it would indeed be preferable for the law to abandon the proposition denying the intervener a right to recover. The justifications for this choice have been discussed in Chapter 9. It was there explained that the very nature of emergencies denies both the intervener and the person assisted the power of self-determination in its true sense. Any position the law adopts, including the present one, would on occasion go against the wishes of one or indeed both of the parties. Given that this is the case, it was agreed with Dagan that the law should aim to develop a rule that represents the interest of the majority of interveners and persons assisted. Such a rule, it was concluded, would

[1] See also A. Burrows, *The Law of Restitution* (2nd edn 2002), p. 317.
[2] P.B.H. Birks, *Unjust Enrichment* (2003), p. 22.

grant the intervener a claim, not deny it. However, in reaching this conclusion, reliance had to be placed on a second justification, namely that to grant a claim would encourage voluntary intervention. After all, the majority of persons assisted would only have agreed to pay the intervener, if it was believed that payment would increase the likelihood of intervention. It was submitted that to grant the intervener a claim would indeed serve as a stimulus to some who would not intervene under the present system. In the previous chapter we have seen that this justification was at the heart of many of the decisions that were favourable to the intervener. In the context of burial, the courts were eager to promote the 'common principles of decency and humanity'.[3] When it came to shipmasters, it was stressed that they should act 'for the safety of the cargo'.[4] The law of tort was used to encourage potential rescuers to react to the 'cry of distress',[5] and the courts of equity ensured the 'good administration of trusts'.[6] If necessary, an additional and rather pragmatic argument can be drawn from the mere fact that virtually all of the European continental systems have adopted a general principle of voluntary intervention in some form or other. In *The Goring*, Sir John Donaldson MR suggested that one of the reasons for adopting the doctrine of salvage had been to ensure uniformity in the maritime laws of nations, 'because of the international character of the carriage of goods by sea'.[7] With its citizens moving freely between the member states of the European Union, there is something to be said for bringing the legal principles of these states – if only on a general level – closer together, too.

By contrast, the arguments against the granting of a claim appeared unable to withstand scrutiny. Most notably, it was agreed with Dagan that the libertarian argument ignores the interest of a majority of both interveners and persons assisted. To leave the law as it is, is to undermine the preferences of the majority of beneficiaries solely to protect the presumed wishes of the minority. Therefore, it is here suggested that the law ought to work towards a general principle allowing voluntary interveners to recover. The logical first step in this process is to investigate whether any of the existing doctrines can be extended so as to incorporate such a general principle. Some of these doctrines can be dismissed out of hand. The law of contract is the first amongst these. Of course, the implied contract theory could have been employed to develop a general principle, equivalent to the Roman doctrine of *negotiorum gestio*. Indeed, Lord Bankton had argued as much in 1751.[8] However, as we saw in the previous chapter, the implied contract theory has now been abandoned by all but a small minority of academics, and for the reasons discussed there does not provide a solid basis for the development of a general

[3] *Rogers v Price* (1829) 3 Y & J 28, 148 ER 1080 at 34.

[4] *Cargo ex Argos* (1873) LR 5 PC 134 at 165, *per* Sir Montague Smith.

[5] *Wagner v International Rly Company* 232 NY 176, 133 NE 437 (Ct of App. of NY, 1921), *per* Cardozo J.

[6] *Re Duke of Norfolk's Settlement Trusts* [1982] Ch 61 at 79, *per* Fox J.

[7] *The Goring* (CA) [1987] 2 QB 687 at 705.

[8] Lord Bankton, *An Institute of the Laws of Scotland in Civil Rights*, Vol I (1751), p. 241.

principle of necessity. Neither does the law of tort require further discussion here. As it is concerned only with wrongdoing, the law of tort will be of no assistance in cases in which the emergency that prompted the intervention was not the result of anyone's wrongdoing. The law of bailment is also too narrow a basis, affecting only those who intervene to preserve goods. At its broadest, it might allow finders to claim reimbursement of their expenses.

Of the remaining doctrines, only three are serious candidates: agency of necessity, unjust enrichment and salvage. Upon these doctrines, a general principle allowing the necessitous intervener to recover could conceivably be based. 'Conceivably', because it shall here be argued that none of the three doctrines is ideally suited for the purpose.

12.1 Agency of Necessity

On a practical level, the main obstacle for any intervener who attempts to rely on agency of necessity, is the fact that – barring one or two exceptions – the courts have been willing to label an intervener as 'agent of necessity' for the person assisted only if there was some pre-existing relationship between the two parties. If this were the only obstacle, it could be left to the courts to circumvent it and develop a general principle of necessitous intervention upon this doctrinal basis. However, the more potent objections against any such development are of a dogmatic nature. For one thing, the doctrine itself is built upon shaky foundations. The criticism levelled against the implied contract theory would seem to apply with equal force to agency of necessity. The term 'authority by operation of the law' is just as fictitious and misleading as the notion of requests and promises 'implied in law'.[9] The principal has either authorized the intervention – or made a representation to that effect – or he has not. And, as Reynolds has pointed out, application of the modern rules on implied and apparent authority will often lead to the desired result without a need to resort to the old necessity rules.[10]

Moreover, even if we assume that the present doctrine deserves a place in modern law, it is doubtful whether it provides a good basis for the intervener's claim. The true agency question that arises in cases of 'agency of necessity' is whether the intervener, when confronted with a situation of 'necessity', can create a legal relationship between his 'principal' and a third party. Whether he can be reimbursed for the expenses he incurred in acting on behalf of his 'principal' is a different matter. That is not to say that the issues are not related. But they are distinct.[11] Already in 1968, under the heading of 'Agency of Necessity', Reynolds distinguished between 'cases of true agency' and 'cases where a person acts for another in circumstances of

[9] See J.S. Ewart's review of the 14th edition of Anson's *Principles of the Law of Contracts*, (1920) 33 Harvard LR 626–629 at 626–627.

[10] F.M.B. Reynolds, *Bowstead and Reynolds on Agency* (17th edn 2001), pp. 130–131.

[11] R. Powell, *The Law of Agency* (2nd edn 1961), p. 410.

necessity and seeks reimbursement'.[12] In the latter category of case, he said, 'the "agent" does not affect the relations of the principal with third parties'.[13] And in a later edition of his book he added: 'if this is an example of agency reasoning, it involves only the internal relationship between principal and agent'.[14] In the past, the distinction between these two classes of cases has not been drawn sufficiently clearly. Many cases that were only concerned with the internal issue of reimbursement – cases of Reynolds's 'second category' – involve an inappropriate use of agency reasoning. Conversely, cases that did address the agency issue were misinterpreted as being concerned with the issue of reimbursement.

In the 1976 case of *White v Troups Transport*,[15] the defendant's lorry became jammed under a bridge over a busy road. The police were unable to contact the defendant, and asked the plaintiff, a crane hirer, to pull the lorry out. The County Court of Stockton-on-Tees allowed the plaintiff to recover his usual fees from the defendant. While the report in the Current Law Year Book is rather brief, the Court's reasoning is clear: 'an agency of necessity ha[d] been created by the police giving an order on behalf of [the defendant]'.[16] The plaintiff could recover his usual fees, as would have been the case if the police had actually been the defendant's agent. Confusingly, however, a rather different reading of the case was put forward by Goff and Jones. In a footnote in the second edition of their *The Law of Restitution*, the authors suggested that it was the crane hire firm, not the police, who had acted as agents of necessity.[17] This not only contradicts the Year Book report, but also fails to explain why the plaintiffs were allowed to recover more than their expenses. With respect, it is here submitted that Goff and Jones's reading of the case must be erroneous.

A case with rather similar facts was put before the Court of Appeal in *Surrey Breakdown Ltd v Knight*.[18] The police found a car on the edge of a pond in Sanderstead, Surrey. It emerged that the car had been stolen from a Mr Knight, the defendant, who could not be contacted because he did not have a telephone. The police instructed the plaintiff company to remove the car. When the defendant turned up at the plaintiff's premises to retrieve his car, he was required to pay 130 pounds for recovery and storage. He first agreed to pay, but later changed his mind. The car was left at the plaintiff's premises for what appears to have been over a year, after which the plaintiff company issued a claim for 3,600 pounds in recovery and storage fees. At first instance, judgment was given for the plaintiff, albeit for a much lesser sum. On appeal it was argued on behalf of the plaintiff, that the police had acted as agents of necessity for the owners.[19] Sir Christopher Staughton, giving judgment for the Court of Appeal, 'investigated' the boundaries

[12] F.M.B. Reynolds, *Bowstead on Agency* (13th edn 1968), pp. 29 and 32. [13] *Ibid.* at p. 32.
[14] F.M.B. Reynolds, *Bowstead and Reynolds on Agency* (16th edn 1996), p. 149. Cf. F.M.B. Reynolds, *Bowstead and Reynolds on Agency* (17th edn 2001), p. 128. [15] [1976] CLY 33.
[16] *Ibid.*
[17] R. Goff and G. Jones, *The Law of Restitution* (2nd edn 1978), p. 270, footnote 68. Cf. p. 470, footnote 81 of the current edition. [18] [1999] RTR 84.
[19] *Ibid.* at 87.

of this doctrine, and concluded that 'the modern view is to be found (. . .) in Goff & Jones, *The Law of Restitution*'.[20] His Lordship then cited a passage from that book, in which it is stated that necessity must have compelled the intervention. At this point, the judgment becomes strangely confused. For instead of discussing the necessity of the action taken by the police, his Lordship proceeded to discuss the necessity of the intervention by the plaintiff company:

> It seems to me that it cannot reasonably be said that Surrey Breakdown Ltd in taking the car out of the pond at 4.35 in the morning were doing so because necessity compelled them to do so without the authority of Mr Knight, the owner. Plainly, they were doing it because the police invited them to do it. (. . .) in my judgment, it was not a common law case of agency of necessity.[21]

This clearly misses the point. As in *White v Troups Transport*, the plaintiff had argued that *the police*, acting as agents of necessity, had instructed them on behalf of the defendant. Accordingly, their claim was for their usual contractual fees, not reimbursement of expenses. Whether or not they themselves had acted out of necessity was, or should have been, completely irrelevant. The question that should have been addressed by the Court was whether *the police* had in the present case met all the requirements to establish an agency of necessity.[22] Given the fact that there was no pre-existing relationship between the police and the defendant, it would have been interesting to hear the Court's answer.[23] Regrettably however, Sir Christopher Staughton approached the case as if it was concerned with reimbursement – or indeed remuneration – for benefits voluntarily conferred.

Thus, the use of agency reasoning in cases concerned with interveners' claims has proven to be both unhelpful and confusing. The solution is straightforward. In future, cases of Reynolds's first and second category must be separated more carefully. Lord Diplock already suggested as much in *China Pacific S.A. v Food Corporation of India*.[24] In his Lordship's view, use of the term 'agent of necessity' should not be extended to:

> (. . .) cases where the only relevant question is whether a person who without obtaining instructions from the owner of goods incurs expense in taking steps that are reasonably necessary for their preservation is in law entitled to recover from the owner of the goods the reasonable expenses incurred by him in taking those steps.[25]

This is not to say that the fact that there was an agency relationship between a particular intervener and the beneficiary of his intervention should have no bearing whatsoever on cases of this type. An agent's duty to look after the interests of his principal may well provide a justification to grant him a correlative right to reimbursement. Indeed, where the pre-existing agency relationship is contractual, the

20 [1999] RTR 84 at 88.
21 *Ibid.* at 88. See also *Lambert v Fry* [2000] CLY 113.
22 S. O'Doherty, 'Parking and Paying', (2001) 165 JP 4–5 at 5.
23 See above, Part II, Section 11.4.
24 [1982] AC 939.
25 *Ibid.* at 958. Cf. *ibid.* at 965, *per* Lord Simon.

intervener is usually entitled to reimbursement upon an implied term. Where the agency is not contractual, however, the doctrinal basis of a right to recovery must be sought outside of the law of agency.[26]

12.2 Unjust Enrichment

With regard to American law it has been argued that 'if the ideas at work in [*negotiorum*] *gestio* are to find a room of their own (. . .), it must be in our law of restitution'.[27] Accordingly, the *Restatement of the Law of Restitution* includes a chapter on 'benefits voluntarily conferred without mistake, coercion or request'.[28] It might be argued that in English law the doctrine of unjust enrichment can be expanded upon to incorporate all cases of necessitous intervention. However, a first difficulty occurs when we try to establish what exactly it was that made the enrichment on the part of the person assisted 'unjust'. The most elaborate attempt at identification of the so-called 'unjust factor' has probably been by Birks. In his *Introduction to the Law of Restitution*, Birks grouped together many of the cases discussed in the previous chapter under the heading of 'moral compulsion'.[29] As we have seen earlier in this book,[30] this unjust factor does not distinguish sufficiently clearly between necessitous intervention and charitable donations. An additional problem is that not all necessitous interveners are in truth motivated by moral compulsion. Professional interveners, for example, are unlikely to have acted because they felt morally compelled.[31]

By way of alternative, Professor Burrows has suggested that the unjust factor rests on a policy encouraging intervention, or at least a policy of removing the existing disincentives.[32] We have already established that such a policy can provide a legitimate reason for granting the intervener a remedy, but does it translate into an 'unjust factor'? If so, this particular unjust factor would encourage the very enrichment that it seeks to reverse. To the question: 'why was the wounded man by the side of the road to Jericho *unjustly* enriched?' the answer would be: 'because the law encourages those in the position of the good Samaritan to confer an enrichment.' The logical inference would be, that the law in these cases encourages unjust enrichment, which it then reverses for the same reason.[33]

[26] F.M.B. Reynolds, *Bowstead and Reynolds on Agency* (17th edn 2001), pp. 274–275.

[27] J.P. Dawson, '*Negotiorum Gestio*: the Altruistic Intermeddler' (1961) 74 Harvard LR 817–865 and 1073–1129 at 1094.

[28] American Law Institute, *Restatement of the Law of Restitution* (1937), chapter 5.

[29] P.B.H. Birks, *An Introduction to the Law of Restitution* (1985), pp. 193–202.

[30] Part II, Section 9.2.

[31] A. Burrows, *The Law of Restitution* (2nd edn 2002), p. 315.

[32] *Ibid.*, p. 243. See also A. Burrows and E. McKendrick, *Cases and Materials on the Law of Restitution* (1997), p. 474; G. Virgo, *The Principles of the Law of Restitution* (1999), pp. 302–303 and P.B.H. Birks and C. Mitchell, 'Unjust Enrichment' in P.B.H. Birks (ed.), *English Private Law*, Vol II (2000), pp. 525–635 at p. 580.

[33] The same objection can be levelled against 'legal compulsion' as an unjust factor.

Semantics aside, and assuming that the said policy can constitute an unjust factor, it is doubtful whether the law of unjust enrichment can actually achieve the goals set by that policy. To remove the disincentives existing under the present law, one would need to render necessitous interventions *ex ante* 'cost-neutral'. In other words, one would need to assure the potential intervener that all his expenses would be covered. The law of unjust enrichment, however, focuses primarily on the defendant's enrichment rather than the intervener's expenditure. This means that an intervener will only recover in as far as his expenditure has resulted in an enrichment on the part of the person assisted.

The nature of 'enrichment' is a notoriously difficult issue. This is particularly true where the alleged enrichment consists of services, as is often the case with necessitous intervention. Most would agree that the good Samaritan conferred a *benefit*. But is it an *enrichment*? And if so, how does one value this enrichment? The starting point must be that the person assisted can only be regarded as 'enriched' if he has actually received a benefit. This follows from the nature of restitutionary remedies.[34] Yet, the difficulty lies in establishing when a benefit has been received. Of course, a clearly discernible increase in the defendant's wealth would constitute an enrichment. However, even when there is no such increase, one can be enriched. This is true where the defendant has avoided an expense that he would otherwise have incurred. Sometimes an expense avoided can be qualified as a positive enrichment. The clearest example involves the payment of another's debt. If one accepts that wealth is measured by subtracting someone's negative assets (debts) from his positive assets, payment of another's debt can be seen as positively increasing the latter's wealth.[35] Similar, although not always as easily quantifiable, is the enrichment in cases involving the performance of another's legal duty. Where a married woman is provided with necessaries, a legal duty of her husband has been performed and – it could be argued – he has thus been positively enriched. However, even where the defendant was under no duty to incur expenses it is sometimes possible to conclude that he has been enriched. For despite the fact that he is under no duty to incur expenses, we sometimes know that the defendant would have incurred expenses if it had not been for the intervention. Whether that is so, depends on the facts. But where it is established that the defendant has avoided an expense that he otherwise would have incurred, we regard him as having been enriched – not positively, because there is no immediate increase in his wealth, but negatively. For, as Burrows put it, 'to save someone an expense of £100 is as valuable to him as the receipt of a realisable gain of £100'.[36] An illustration can be drawn from *Craven-Ellis v Canons Ltd*,[37] where the

[34] G. Virgo, *The Principles of the Law of Restitution* (1999), p. 63 and A. Burrows, *The Law of Restitution* (2nd edn 2002), pp. 16–17 and G.A. Muir, 'Unjust Sacrifice and the Officious Intervener' in P.D. Finn (ed.), *Essays on Restitution* (1990), pp. 297–351 at p. 299.

[35] *Contra*: G.A. Muir, 'Unjust Sacrifice and the Officious Intervener' in P.D. Finn (ed.), *Essays on Restitution* (1990), pp. 297–351 at p. 303.

[36] A. Burrows, *The Law of Restitution* (2nd edn 2002), p. 16.

[37] [1936] 2 KB 403.

plaintiff successfully claimed for *quantum meruit*, after having worked as a managing director for the defendant company in the mistaken belief that he was working under a valid contract. It could be said that the company had received a negative enrichment because it was established on the facts of the case that the company, if it had not been for the plaintiff acting as managing director, would have employed someone else to provide the same services.[38] Similarly, it is at least arguable that the friendly intervener who makes emergency repairs to the roof on his neighbour's house thereby enriches his neighbour. After all, a reasonable person makes emergency repairs to their house, so on the facts it is likely that this neighbour has avoided an expense. To put it differently: 'but for' his neighbour's intervention, the owner of the damaged house would have incurred the expense of repairing his roof. However, the parable of the good Samaritan illustrates that this negative enrichment analysis does not fit all cases of necessitous intervention. 'But for' the good Samaritan's intervention, the man stripped of his raiment would not have incurred much expenditure. On the balance of probability he would have died. At most one could argue that his estate has been saved the expense of having to bury him.

In order to bring also the latter type of case within the scope of the law of restitution, Birks has advocated a broader notion of negative enrichment, which includes what one might term 'expenses hypothetically avoided'. In his view, negative enrichment not only includes expenditure that the defendant would *in fact* have incurred, but also expenditure that he would have incurred 'if he had not been deprived of the opportunity (as by absence or disability)'.[39] However, it is doubtful whether this leap from the actual to the hypothetical avoidance of expenses can be made.[40] There is little authority to support it. Indeed, it would appear that Birks's approach would result in an artificially broad notion of enrichment, as can be seen most clearly in cases of unsuccessful rescue. For even in cases of unsuccessful rescue, it can usually be argued that the defendant would have agreed to pay for the rescue services, had he been given the opportunity. Following Birks's view, one would have to conclude that unsuccessful rescue services constitute an actual enrichment on the part of the intended rescuee. A rare example that may be said to support this view is the Canadian case of *Matheson v Smiley*.[41] There, the plaintiff surgeon unsuccessfully attempted to save the life of Mr Smiley, who had shot himself in a suicide bid. The Manitoba Court of Appeal allowed the surgeon to recover the value of the services rendered, employing

38 *Ibid.* at 412, *per* Greer LJ. See P.B.H. Birks, '*Negotiorum Gestio* and the Common Law' (1971) 24 CLP 110–132 at 122.

39 P.B.H. Birks, *An Introduction to the Law of Restitution* (1985), p. 117.

40 An analogy can be drawn from the law of tort. Negligence is primarily concerned with the opposite of an enrichment, namely a decrease in wealth. However, the courts are also willing to take into account profits foregone – the reverse of expenses avoided – provided that it is established at trial that the claimant would have made those profits 'but for' the defendant's wrongdoing (*e.g.* loss of earnings). Yet, there is no recognized 'reverse equivalent' of Birks's expenses hypothetically avoided.

41 [1932] 2 DLR 787 (Manitoba CA).

implied contract reasoning. With the implied contract theory now almost universally rejected, a different analysis is required. Perhaps the case is best viewed as involving liability for loss wrongfully caused.[42] Or maybe the case involves a rare example of true *negotiorum gestio* reasoning in a common law court. But to argue that the defendant had been enriched – as Birks has done – would seem counter-intuitive and has been almost universally rejected by other writers on the subject.[43] True, Goff and Jones have conceded that, while in their view an unsuccessful rescuee does not receive an actual benefit, he may by way of exception be 'deemed to have benefited'.[44] But they, too, feel uncomfortable with this legal fiction, adding:

> But the recognition of this claim (. . .) may simply reflect society's concern to encourage intervention in an emergency rather than its desire to deprive a defendant of an unjust benefit.[45]

However, even if we do assume that costs hypothetically avoided qualify as 'enrichment' the problem remains that the primary focus here lies on the defendant's enrichment, rather than the plaintiff's expenses. And, as Birks too would have agreed, the cost avoided by the defendant is not necessarily the same as the cost incurred by the plaintiff. The defendant might have a friend who is a builder and who would fix his roof for a very favourable price. If the plaintiff intervener then arranges for the defendant's roof to be repaired at the going rate, his expenses would be considerably higher than the cost avoided by the defendant. In such cases, one might want to argue that the defendant's enrichment should be valued at the market rate for the type of service he provides.[46] But even this does not solve the problem. For those potential interveners who would – for whatever reason – not be able to provide the required service at the market rate would continue to be discouraged from intervention. I may, for example, be on my way to the airport when I see a wounded man by the side of the road. If I decide to drive him to the nearest hospital, the going rate for a similar ride in a taxi will be little consolation if as a result of my intervention I missed my plane and – say – one day of holiday or the opportunity to conclude a big business deal.

It follows that the law of unjust enrichment does not provide the required tools to remove the existing disincentives against necessitous intervention. The law of unjust enrichment focuses on the beneficiary's enrichment, whereas a doctrine of

[42] A. Burrows, *The Law of Restitution* (2nd edn 2002), p. 320, footnote 13. This view is somewhat problematic, because Dr Matheson only suffered economic loss.

[43] A. Burrows, *ibid.*; G. Jones, 'Restitutionary Claims for Services Rendered' (1977) 93 LQR 273–295 at 284; G. Virgo, *The Principles of the Law of Restitution* (1999), p. 92 and E. McKendrick, 'Taxonomy: does it matter?' in D. Johnston and R. Zimmermann, *Unjustified Enrichment: Key Issues in Comparative Perspective* (2002), pp. 627–657 at p. 653, footnote 127.

[44] Lord Goff of Chieveley and G. Jones, *The Law of Restitution* (6th edn 2002), p. 27.

[45] *Ibid.* at p. 26.

[46] American Law Institute, *Restatement of the Law of Restitution* (1937), pp. 473–474, comment g) and J.P. Dawson, '*Negotiorum Gestio*: the Altruistic Intermeddler' (1961) 74 Harvard LR 817–865 and 1073–1129 at 1116. Cf. American Law Institute, *Restatement of the Law of Restitution* (1937), p. 490, comment d).

necessitous intervention would inevitably focus on the intervener's impoverishment. Eventually Birks, too, acknowledged that his attempt to explain cases of necessitous intervention in terms of unjust enrichment had not been successful. Indeed, in *Unjust Enrichment* he omitted the subject altogether:

'The interesting condition of the modern law on this subject cannot be explored here because it does not belong within unjust enrichment. There is no doubt that the intervener's right to reimbursement turns on the utility of the intervention, not on its success. There is no inquiry into the enrichment of the beneficiary. The measure of recovery is not gain-based.'[47]

12.3 Salvage

For present purposes the clear advantage held by the law of salvage over the law of unjust enrichment is that its main aim is to encourage beneficial intervention, rather than reverse unjust enrichment. True, one could argue that the salvor's claim has restitutionary characteristics in that it takes account of the benefit conferred, because it is dependent upon a successful outcome.[48] Yet, the negative effect that this requirement might have on potential interveners is more than made up for by the fact that – if successful – they will receive a reward, rather than mere reimbursement of expenses. However, herein lies also a disadvantage of this particular doctrine. For as we have seen in Section 9.1, the introduction of a reward might cause potential interveners to think of intervention as a commercial commodity. This accords with one of the aims of the law of salvage, which is to promote the development of a salvage industry. Given the variety of emergency services operating on land, there is not the same need here for such an industry.[49] Instead, the main purpose of granting a claim here is to encourage intervention by individuals who happen to be confronted with a situation of emergency.[50] In this context, the introduction of a claim for reward might have the unwanted side-effect of undermining the intrinsic motivation of potential interveners.[51] Also, the risk of abuse increases as interventions become more profitable.[52] Depending on the weight that one attaches to these considerations, one may decide that necessitous interveners should receive reimbursement, compensation and perhaps

47 P.B.H. Birks, *Unjust Enrichment* (2003), pp. 21–22.

48 *E.g.* P.B.H. Birks and C. Mitchell, 'Unjust Enrichment' in P.B.H. Birks (ed.), *English Private Law*, Vol II (2000), pp. 525–635 at p. 581.

49 Lord Goff of Chieveley and G. Jones, *The Law of Restitution* (6th edn 2002), p. 458. Cf. *The Goring* (CA) [1987] 2 QB 687 at 710, *per* Ralph Gibson LJ.

50 F.D. Rose, 'Restitution for the Rescuer' (1989) 9 OJLS 167–204 at 192.

51 See above, Part II, Section 9.1.

52 See above, Part II, Section 8.4. Dagan adds that rewards do not have the same effect on the 'garden-variety bystander' as on professional rescuers, because the former is not 'self-insured against failed transactions'. Even if this is true, this problem could probably be remedied by giving private individuals higher rewards for their successful interventions. H. Dagan, 'In Defense of the Good Samaritan' (1999) 97 Michigan LR 1152–1200 at 1182.

remuneration, but not reward. Yet, even for those who do hold that the intervener should be rewarded, the law of salvage may not prove to be the right vehicle. For, as we have seen,[53] the salvor is in law entitled to a lien on the salvaged goods. In respect of land interventions, however, there is clear authority that no such liens are available.[54] Thus, if one were to argue that the good Samaritan should be rewarded, it might be preferable to develop a separate doctrine to that effect, rather than attempt to apply the law of salvage by analogy to land.

[53] Above, Part II, Section 11.9.

[54] *Binstead v Buck* (1776) 2 Black W 1117, 96 ER 660; *Nicholson v Chapman* (1793) 2 H Bl 254, 126 ER 536; *Falcke v Scottish Imperial Insurance Co.* (1886) 34 Ch D 234 and *The Goring* (HoL), [1988] 1 AC 831, all discussed in Part II, Section 11.1, above.

13

Towards a New General Principle

13.1 Requirements for the Intervener's Claim

With none of the existing doctrines possessing the right tools for the development of a general principle allowing the intervener to recover, the alternative is to develop a separate doctrine.[1] In doing so we can partly draw upon our own experience with cases in which interveners have been granted a claim under English law. In addition, it may be helpful to see what can be learned from the continental systems discussed in Chapter 10. Whatever the exact nature of the principle we develop, the true touchstone shall be provided by the theoretical foundations it is built on. If the submissions in Chapter 9 are accepted, our doctrine must achieve two aims. First and foremost, it must succeed in removing the existing disincentives against voluntary intervention. To the potential intervener, the intervention must therefore at least appear cost-neutral. On the other hand, however, the doctrine must interfere no more than is strictly necessary with the right of self-determination of both parties involved. As we observed in Chapter 9, self-determination is impossible in emergencies in which parties cannot negotiate or, more generally, communicate their will. In such situations, it was argued, the law should intervene to provide what is in accordance with the interest of a majority of interveners and persons assisted. Yet, when it is possible for the parties to communicate, it is difficult to see why the law should interfere. So here we have our first requirement:

a) It must have been impossible for the intervener and the beneficiary to communicate
This requirement is not new to English law. We have already encountered it when discussing the shipmaster's agency of necessity. We observed there, that while some courts required that communication between shipmaster and ship- or cargo owner was absolutely impossible, the predominant opinion is that it suffices that communication was practically or commercially impossible.[2] In Germany, the doctrine of *Geschäftsführung ohne Auftrag* has been applied in cases where the

[1] This is of course not to say that this separate doctrine could not, for purposes of taxonomy, be grouped together with other – existing – doctrines, such as salvage and general average. Cf. F.D. Rose, *General Average* (1997), pp. 6, 7 and 9.

[2] *Springer v Great Western Rly Co.* [1921] 1 KB 257 at 265, *per* Bankes LJ and at 268, *per* Scrutton LJ and *The Choko Star* [1990] 1 Lloyd's Rep 516 at 525, *per* Slade LJ.

interveners paid off the defendant's contractual debt, despite the fact that it was possible for the intervener to communicate with the principal debtor.[3] Whether this takes the German doctrine beyond its natural limits is a question that shall here remain unanswered. What is submitted here, though, is that such a decision could not be based on the doctrine here proposed. If English law is generally to allow those who pay off debts to recover against the principal debtor it shall have to be on a different doctrinal basis.[4]

b) The intervention must have been necessary In the absence of necessity, the intervener is under no real pressure to intervene. Nor is there the same need for the law to encourage interventions that are merely useful, not necessary. Where in the context of agency of necessity it was merely required that the measures taken were 'in a mercantile sense' necessary,[5] it may be preferable to adopt a more restrictive approach in other cases. The pre-existing relationship in agency of necessity cases is almost invariably a commercial one, so practically any intervention that makes good business sense can be assumed to be in accordance with the wishes of the beneficiary. The same is not necessarily true where there is no such relationship. If someone's horse breaks a leg during his absence, it may make good business sense for a passer-by to sell the horse to an abattoir. Indeed, 'in a mercantile sense' it may even be necessary to do so.[6] However, unlike the shipmaster, the passer-by does not know whether the person whose property he is saving regards this property as a commercial commodity. The owner of the horse may have bought it for his children, who may in turn be emotionally attached to it. In a case like this – and in the absence of any further information – the intervener should not be encouraged to do more than is strictly necessary, *e.g.* to call for a vet to determine whether it is necessary in the circumstances to put the animal out of its misery.

A difficult issue is whether actual necessity should be required, or whether a reasonably perceived situation of necessity should suffice. In Part II, Section 11.9, we saw that the law of salvage has adopted the former position. This means that the risk of mistakenly identifying a situation as one of necessity remains with the salvor. Thus, the requirement that there be a real situation of necessity constitutes a disincentive – albeit in most cases a minor one – to potential interveners. In the context of salvage this might not pose a problem. After all, the generous reward offered to successful salvors will in most cases outweigh the cost of potential misinterpretation of the situation. However, the same cannot be said if we decide that the intervener should merely be granted a right to reimbursement and/or compensation. On the other hand, if we hold that any reasonably perceived necessity should suffice, an action will lie even in cases in which we can establish from an

[3] *E.g. BGH* 20 April 1967, *BGHZ* 47, 370 and *MünchKomm*-Seiler (1997) § 683, *RdNr* 6 with further references.

[4] Cf. J.P. Dawson, '*Negotiorum Gestio*: the Altruistic Intermeddler' (1961) 74 Harvard LR 817–865 and 1073–1129 at 862, where it is stated that *negotiorum gestio* would seem 'at first sight so obviously suited' for this class of cases.

[5] *Australasian Steam Navigation Co. v Morse* (1872) LR 4 PC 222, *per* Sir Montague Smith.

[6] Cf. *ibid.*

objective viewpoint that the person 'assisted' would not have desired the intervention. The issue is aptly illustrated by the German example of the mountain rescue operation launched to find a skier who turned out to be safe and sound in a fellow skier's hotel room.[7] Should the rescue team be allowed to claim even though it is obvious that the supposed rescuee – or indeed any reasonable person in the same position – would not have agreed to pay for the intervention had negotiation been possible? Perhaps the better solution is to allow a claim only if both a reasonable intervener and a reasonable beneficiary would have perceived the situation as one of necessity. This would deny the unfortunate mountain rescue team, but would make a claim available in cases in which there is an objective appearance of danger, which subsequently turns out to have been non-existent.[8] Imposition of liability in the latter case could be justified on the basis that both parties would probably have agreed to the intervention if given the opportunity.

c) Must the intervener have acted without being obliged to act by a pre-existing duty? As we have seen in Part II, Chapter 10, the French and the German doctrines of *negotiorum gestio* required that the intervener acted voluntarily, that is, without being obliged to intervene by contract or by law. A similar requirement could be discerned in the English law of salvage.[9]

It was for this reason that, for example, a public fire brigade could not successfully claim against its rescuees. The underlying consideration in this case was, it was suggested by Goff and Jones, that a person bound by duty should not need any further encouragement to intervene.[10] Yet in both French and German law the intervener who acts in the performance of his criminal law duty – and in French law, private law duty – is allowed to recover.[11] Similarly, the shipmaster who undertakes a rescue in pursuance of his duty to assist persons in danger of being lost at sea will be granted salvage, provided, of course, that all the other requirements of the law of salvage are satisfied.[12] Yet, it is rarely articulated why these duties do not bar a claim in *negotiorum gestio* or salvage. Why would life rescuers in France, Germany or on the high seas need the additional bait of a right to reimbursement or a reward if a refusal to go to the rescue might land them in prison and, at least in France, render them liable in tort? What is so different about these duties that they do not preclude the right to recover? The answer has been hinted at in Part I, Section 3.5: some affirmative obligations do, and some do not have – as Friedmann put it – 'a "built-in" element that justifies their imposition'.[13] This built-in element, it was suggested, is most often a *quid pro quo*. Looking first at the intervener who was under a contractual duty to intervene, it is obvious that this duty does contain the

[7] See above, Part II, Section 10.3.
[8] Cf. *The Wilhelmine* (1842) 1 NoC 376 and *The Ranger* (1845) 3 NoC 589.
[9] See above, p. 161.
[10] Lord Goff of Chieveley and G. Jones, *The Law of Restitution* (6th edn 2002), p. 473.
[11] See above, pp. 105 and 107 respectively. [12] See above, p. 161.
[13] D. Friedmann, 'Valid, Voidable, Qualified and Non-existing Obligations: An Alternative Perspective on the Law of Restitution' in A. Burrows (ed.), *Essays on the Law of Restitution* (1991), pp. 247–278 at 253.

built-in element. In entering upon the contract, this intervener has determined his rights and duties and has had a chance to negotiate a *quid pro quo*. If in retrospect it becomes apparent that he has made a bad deal, then he has only himself to blame. Not altogether dissimilar is the position of the public emergency services. The state could have decided to fund its emergency services by charging anyone who received its services, but instead it decided to charge the taxpayer. In return, the state assumed a duty towards all its citizens. The situation is different, however, for the duty-bound shipmaster and the continental Samaritans. They found themselves under a duty to which they could not avoid being subjected, and they were unable to negotiate for any *quid pro quo*. This duty, therefore, does not contain the built-in element that justifies its imposition. In cases like these, therefore, the existence of a pre-existing duty may provide a positive reason to allow the intervener to recover. For it is one thing to require the priest and the Levite to intervene, but quite another to also require them to financially support the wounded man.[14]

Hence, the condition that the intervener was under no pre-existing duty to intervene is not sufficiently specific to include in our list of requirements. Yet, it is by no means easy to formulate an alternative requirement that is specific enough to allow us to distinguish correctly between contract-bound interveners, emergency services *etc.* and the mere bystander, such as the good Samaritan. Perhaps the best way of putting it is by saying that the intervener must not have received, or have had the opportunity to freely determine, whether he would receive a *quid pro quo*. This would not only exclude the contract-bound intervener and the emergency services, but also the intervener who made a positive decision that he intended the cost of his services to be a gift. However, the burden of proving such an intention should be on the beneficiary. Otherwise, the policy of encouraging intervention would be jeopardized.[15] If the experience in France and Germany are anything to go by, this burden would in practice be difficult to discharge.[16]

d) Must the intervention be successful? A claim in salvage will only lie if the intervention was successful. By contrast, the continental doctrines of *negotiorum gestio* do not require success. There are both advantages and disadvantages to such a requirement. On the positive side, it might prevent interveners from becoming too easily disheartened halfway through an intervention.[17] Also, the imposition of an obligation is more obviously justified where the obligee receives an actual benefit in return.

On the other hand, if they had had the opportunity, most persons assisted would probably have agreed to pay for any attempt at a necessitous intervention that was *ex ante* cost beneficial.[18] After all, to insist on success would provide a

[14] *Ibid.* at 255.

[15] Lord Goff of Chieveley and G. Jones, *The Law of Restitution* (6th edn 2002), pp. 457 and 460.

[16] See above pp. 106 and 109 respectively.

[17] F.D. Rose, 'Restitution for the Rescuer' (1989) 9 OJLS 167–204 at 198 and A. Burrows, *The Law of Restitution* (2nd edn 2002), pp. 319–320.

[18] Lord Goff of Chieveley and G. Jones, *The Law of Restitution* (6th edn 2002), p. 458 and H. Dagan, 'In Defense of the Good Samaritan' (1999) 97 Michigan LR 1152–1200 at 1182. Cf. A. Burrows, *The Law of Restitution* (2nd edn 2002), p. 319, footnote 10.

disincentive to potential interveners.[19] In the law of salvage this disincentive is neutralized by the prospect of a generous reward if the intervention is brought to a successful conclusion. But without this neutralizing factor, the requirement of success would adversely affect the policy of encouraging intervention.

Hence, whether or not success should be required largely depends on the measure of recovery we allow the intervener. If we decide merely to grant him a right to reimbursement and/or compensation, success should not be required. If we also grant him a reward, we could insist that the intervention must be brought to a successful completion. If, however, instead of reward we remunerate the intervener, it may depend on the type of service provided whether we should require success. In some lines of work, one is generally only paid for a result, not an effort. Roof contractors, for example, will not normally receive full payment unless they successfully complete the building or repair work according to specifications. Then to allow the intervening roof contractor full remuneration even where no success has been achieved, would be to grant him more rights than he would have had if he had had the opportunity to negotiate with the defendant. Most contracts for professional services, however, require the application of best endeavours, not results. A physician, for example, is normally paid even if his treatment is not successful.[20] Then to make his remuneration in cases of necessitous intervention dependent upon success would have the undesired effect of discouraging him from intervening in the first place. For unlike the roof contractor, the physician's usual level of remuneration does not incorporate an allowance for losses suffered because services occasionally fail to achieve their desired result.

13.2 The Measure of Recovery: Reimbursement, Compensation, Remuneration, and/or Reward?

The issue on which the doctrines investigated in Part II of this book differ most, is without doubt the measure of recovery. The French doctrine of *gestion d' affaires* entitles the *gérant* to reimbursement and compensation; not, it was decided after some hesitation, to remuneration.[21] German law, by contrast, does grant remuneration to those who intervened in the course of their profession. And whilst most of the English doctrines discussed in Chapter 11 merely allowed claims for reimbursement of expenses and/or compensation of loss, the salvage cases formed an obvious exception, and so did some cases in equity, where trustees were on occasion remunerated for services voluntarily rendered.[22]

In choosing which of these various measures to adopt, our starting point must again be the policy of removing the existing disincentives against intervention. This policy leaves us with one of two general approaches. Either we render all

[19] See above, Part II, Section 9.1.

[20] F.D. Rose, 'Restitution for the Rescuer' (1989) 9 OJLS 167–204 at 198.

[21] See above, pp. 103–104.

[22] See above, pp. 156–158.

FOREMAN'S HEROISM IN THAMES WORKS TRAGEDY

interventions that meet our criteria cost-neutral, or we allow unsuccessful interventions to leave the intervener worse off, but provide a counter-balance by making successful interventions positively lucrative. With some hesitation, it was concluded in the previous chapter that the latter approach is not here preferred. The reasons there mentioned were that any approach that makes an intervention profitable is at risk of undermining the intervener's intrinsic motivation, and is more prone to abuse.

The former approach is, broadly speaking, that of the continental doctrine of *negotiorum gestio*. Accordingly, the *gérant* and the *Geschäftsführer* are entitled to both reimbursement of expenses reasonably incurred and compensation of loss suffered. As we have seen, it is inherent in this approach that success is not a requirement. In most cases, this approach works out reasonably well. The intervener gains nothing by his intervention but gratitude and perhaps – in rescue cases – public acclaim for his bravery, but at least he is not left worse off. Again, in most cases the person assisted will not be shortchanged: a lost dog is reunited with its owner, who will owe the intervener the cost of a week's worth of dog food and perhaps one or two phone calls to the police station; the man saved from an otherwise certain death by drowning will owe his brave rescuer the cost of dry-cleaning her dress *etc.* Occasionally, however, this approach leads to results that leave one with a distinct feeling of unease, especially when the intervention ends up being both unsuccessful and very costly. Consider for example the tragic fate of librettist and poet W.S. Gilbert – most famous for his collaboration with A.S. Sullivan – who died of a heart attack while attempting to rescue a woman from drowning; or the nightmare scenario that was reported on the front page of *The Illustrated Police News*, 30 July 1931 (see opposite page). While working at a Ford plant in Dagenham docks in a giant cylinder fifteen feet below the surface, four workmen were overcome by a 'mysterious gas'. Their foreman, William O'Donnell, noticed that his men failed to signal and immediately went to the rescue. However, he himself was also overcome by the gas and all five men died. Unless the accident was caused by negligence,[23] English law would not grant O'Donnell's dependents a claim. However, provided that O'Donnell's intervention was reasonable, both French and German law would hold the estates of the four workmen liable to O'Donnell's dependents for the loss suffered as a result of his death. Esmein has suggested that such a result is 'severe' ('*rigoureuse*') and would pose problems for any judge confronted with such a case.[24] Dawson has called it 'grossly unjust'.[25] However, it is doubtful whether this injustice is anything more than perceived. True, it would be unfortunate if any defendant were obliged to pay a large amount of money without receiving any benefit, but that is a contingency of every approach that does not insist on success. Moreover, it is difficult to see how the law's approach could be adjusted so as to lead to a different result. Lord Goff and Professor Jones have suggested that the intervener's right to compensation should be denied altogether, granting him a claim for reimbursement only.[26] However, this would leave in place one of the existing disincentives against intervention, and thus be contrary to our policy aim. Moreover, even reasonable expenditure can on occasion reach very high levels. If a high level of expenditure is incurred but success is not achieved, are we not again faced with a situation of (perceived) injustice? Indeed, it is questionable whether it is possible to draw a clear distinction between loss suffered and expenses incurred. As was argued earlier in this book, expenses are in truth a subcategory of loss, albeit loss voluntarily suffered.[27] Professor Jones has opined that one can nevertheless distinguish, by looking at the purpose for which the loss was incurred. The example he gives is that of a man who – like W.S. Gilbert – dives into a lake to save a drowning woman. In the course of the intervention, he binds her wounds with his necktie. His suit is ruined and by a stroke of bad fortune his gold watch chain irretrievably sinks to the bottom of the lake. In the view of Jones, only the use of the necktie represents a true

23 See *Baker v T.E. Hopkins & Son Ltd* [1959] 3 All ER 225.

24 P. Esmein, comment on *Civ.* 16 November 1955, *JCP* 1956, 9087.

25 J.P. Dawson, '*Negotiorum Gestio*: the Altruistic Intermeddler' (1961) 74 Harvard LR 817–865 and 1073–1129 at 1114.

26 Lord Goff of Chieveley and G. Jones, *The Law of Restitution* (6th edn 2002), p. 458–459.

27 Part II, Chapter 7.

expense. The suit and the watch chain, however, were lost rather than expended.[28] In *The Law of Restitution*, Goff and Jones further clarify this distinction by stating that expenses include the cost of 'materials that have been *used* in [the intervention]'.[29] Apparently, only materials that have been purposefully used in the intervention can be said to have been expended. Yet, no justification is given for this narrow definition of expenditure. Considering that there was probably not much time to get to the drowning woman, it may have been necessary for the man to dive after her fully clothed. Why should it matter that the necktie was purposefully used in binding the woman's wounds, if the suit was just as purposefully sacrificed? Again, the only difference between the watch chain and the suit is that there was merely a risk of losing the watch chain, as opposed to the certainty that the suit would be ruined. Surely, the distinction between expenses and loss cannot turn upon the degree of certainty with which we know that they will be incurred or suffered?

For these reasons it is here submitted that if we decide to adopt the first approach of aiming to neutralize the cost of intervention, we must entitle the intervener to compensation as well as reimbursement. There is no viable escape from the unfortunate consequences that this approach will have in extreme cases where the intervention proves to be unsuccessful as well as costly.[30] Meanwhile, we could, of course, decide to supplement the intervener's rights to reimbursement and compensation with a right to remuneration. As we have seen, German law confers such a right upon professional interveners. The strongest argument in favour of granting remuneration is that the time spent on the intervention in a sense also represents a loss of the opportunity to spend one's time otherwise, and earn money thereby. Therefore, if we are truly committed to rendering the intervention cost-neutral, we should probably remunerate the intervener.[31] Indeed, Dagan has argued that there is no reason to distinguish between interveners who render a professional service and other interveners. A passer-by lawyer who comes upon the wounded man stripped of his raiment will by intervening lose the opportunity to spend his time more profitably, just as the passing physician would do.[32] From this point of view, the level of remuneration would have to be the hourly rate of this particular lawyer, not the value of the service itself.[33]

While Dagan's argument is a powerful one, there is at least one objection to the approach he suggests. By remunerating the non-professional intervener at his usual level of remuneration, we run the risk of undermining his intrinsic motivation.[34]

[28] G. Jones, *Restitution in Public and Private Law* (1991), pp. 164–165.

[29] *Ibid.* at 472 (emphasis added).

[30] Unless one accepts Dagan's defence of the Israeli system, which gives the court a discretionary power to award compensation for property loss, and provides compensation for bodily injuries out of public funds. See H. Dagan, 'In Defense of the Good Samaritan' (1999) 97 Michigan LR 1152–1200 at 1195–1199.

[31] H. Dagan, 'In Defense of the Good Samaritan' (1999) 97 Michigan LR 1152–1200, p. 1188.

[32] *Ibid.* at 1190. [33] *Ibid.* at 1191–1192 and footnote 154.

[34] See Part II, Section 9.1.

Remuneration invariably incorporates an element of profit. This fact cannot be disguised by requalifying the payment as compensation for a lost opportunity. When the lawyer performs his everyday job, he may attribute his efforts at least in part to the extrinsic motivation offered by his salary. It is only logical, then, to assume that his intrinsic motivation to assist the wounded man is at risk of being undermined if he receives for his efforts the exact same hourly rate as he usually does for his legal services. However, the same risk does not occur, or at least not to the same extent, where professional interveners are concerned. Unlike the non-professional intervener, the professional intervener provides the required services on a daily basis, and normally receives payment for it. It would be of no surprise, therefore, if he already attributes most of his professional conduct to extrinsic motivation. Yet, in as far as he has been able to maintain intrinsic motivation, it is unlikely that this will be undermined by awarding him the level of remuneration he usually receives.

If and when it is decided that remuneration should be awarded, it must not be forgotten, however, that in virtually all professions and businesses the fee that is charged already includes an allowance for the risk of loss suffered. Would it not be inconsistent, then, if the professional intervener were allowed to claim his usual fee as well as compensation for losses suffered?[35] Perhaps it is necessary to draw a distinction between interventions that are within the usual scope of the intervener's profession or business, and interventions that go beyond that. A physician, for example, will regularly use syringes. The risk of any accidents with these devices is normally borne by him. Therefore, if he accidentally harms himself with a syringe during an intervention that takes place in unexceptional circumstances, he should not be allowed to claim compensation as well as remuneration. To allow him to do so would be inconsistent with the position that would have resulted if the parties had been able to negotiate. Yet, the situation may be different if professionals have to intervene in circumstances with which they would not normally be confronted. Especially if they are asked to perform their services in dangerous circumstances – as was true in respect of the many physicians who were called to the scene of the September 11 attack – they might not have agreed to do so at their usual fee.

13.3 Remaining Issues

a) To what extent is the actual will of the person assisted relevant? If properly applied, the rule here proposed will in most cases be in accordance with the will of both parties at the time of the intervention. What, however, if it can be positively established that the person assisted did not in fact desire the intervention? Of course, if the intervener is aware of his contrary wishes, a claim should in principle be denied. This follows – albeit somewhat indirectly – from the requirement that

[35] R.A. Albert, 'Restitutionary Recovery for Rescuers of Human Life' (1986) 74 Cal LR 85–125 at 118.

it must have been impossible for the parties to communicate their will. However, as we saw in Part II, Section 10.3, German law in principle denies the intervener a claim even if he did not know, nor should have known that he acted contrary to the wishes of the person assisted. This rule constitutes a considerable disincentive for potential interveners, and must therefore be rejected. If our general principle is to have its desired effect, the idiosyncratic wishes of the few will have to yield to the interest of the majority. Hence, the physician who intervenes to treat an elderly man who, as it later turns out, had privately expressed his wishes not to be resuscitated, should nevertheless be able to recover. The same is true if I repair my neighbour's roof, and it later emerges that my neighbour had decided to let it fall into decay. This may seem harsh on the elderly man and the neighbour, but if we were to decide otherwise we would jeopardize the effectiveness of our policy. In future, the elderly man should perhaps be advised to carry with him a declaration stating that he does not wish to be resuscitated, and my neighbour should consider putting up a sign in the front garden.

The German scholar Kohler has suggested a subsidiary rule that might alleviate some of the more severe consequences of ignoring the actual will of the person assisted. In Kohler's view, the owner of property improved by the intervener should be allowed to escape liability by giving up the property altogether to the intervener.[36] After all, if the intervener thought that it was worth preserving, then why not let him keep the property himself? In certain cases, a similar adjustment to our general rule would undoubtedly lead to an equitable result. However, there are at least two drawbacks to Kohler's proposition. Firstly, it obviously cannot be applied in cases involving intervention for the preservation of life or in cases involving the performance of another person's duty. More importantly, however, the proposition disregards the fact that it may be perfectly reasonable for the intervener to assume that certain property is of value to its owner, even though he would not wish to own it himself. If, for example, the occupant of a small city apartment stumbles upon a wounded horse, he might think twice about rescuing it if his claim for expenses could be defeated by his receiving the poor animal instead. Thus, Kohler's proposed adjustment would constitute a disincentive to potential interveners where the property at risk is of significantly lower value to the intervener than it would normally be to the owner. Consequently, if this adjustment is to be accepted at all, the better option is perhaps to grant the courts a discretionary power to order the transfer of the property upon request by its owner.

b) Should the intervener be denied a claim merely because a third party asked him to intervene? It was demonstrated earlier in this book, that the Court of Appeal in *Surrey Breakdown Ltd v Knight* misconceived the essence of the agency question put to it.[37] Consequently, much of the reasoning in that case cannot be safely

[36] J. Kohler, '*Die Menschenhülfe im Privatrecht*', (1887) 25 *Jahrbücher für die Dogmatik des heutigen römischen und deutschen Privatrechts* 1–141 at 56–57. See also J.P. Dawson, '*Negotiorum Gestio*: the Altruistic Intermeddler' (1961) 74 Harvard LR 817–865 and 1073–1129 at 1093.

[37] See above, Part II, Section 12.1, pp. 167–168.

relied on. Nevertheless, Sir Christopher Staughton's judgment does contain an interesting submission in relation to the meaning of 'necessity'. In his Lordship's view, the breakdown service could not be said to have acted out of necessity 'because the police invited them to do it'.[38] In this respect, the position of the breakdown service bears some resemblance to that of Mr Chapman in *Nicholson v Chapman*. Chapman, it may be remembered, recovered Nicholson's timber after having been requested to do so by the bailiff of the manor of Wimbledon.[39] Yet, why exactly should the mere fact that their services were rendered upon invitation by a third party affect the rights of Chapman or Surrey Breakdown Ltd? Surely, a mere request cannot suffice to negate the intervener's claim.[40] Otherwise, how would we deal with a situation in which one intervener asks assistance from a bystander because he cannot successfully complete the intervention on his own? Say, a brave woman who dives after a drowning man needs assistance to pull him out of the water. Of course, if the woman comes to a contractual agreement with the bystander – though it is difficult to see how in these circumstances – the latter will be able to recover against her, and she in turn can claim reimbursement from the person assisted. But in the absence of a contract between the 'primary' and the 'secondary' intervener, it is difficult to see why the latter should not be able to claim directly from the person assisted. Indeed, both of the theoretical foundations of the general principle here proposed suggest that he should be able to: the secondary intervention was necessary for the preservation of a life and should not be discouraged. Also, to allow a claim to the secondary intervener is in accordance with the interest of the person assisted. Both French and German courts have allowed the claims brought by breakdown services that were requested by police to intervene under the heading of their respective variants of *negotiorum gestio*.[41] However, the *Cour d'Appel* of Paris did indicate that it might have decided differently if the request amounted to a public command. It is here suggested that even the intervener who acted upon a public command ought not necessarily to be denied a remedy. Whether or not that is so should depend on the type of duty to which this public command gives rise. If, as often will be the case, it is a duty which the intervener could not have avoided being subjected to, and for the performance of which he does not already receive a *quid pro quo*, he should be entitled to recover under the doctrine here proposed.[42]

c) Should the intervener have authority to bind the person assisted? The final question that shall be addressed here is whether the law should enable the intervener to act as the agent of the person assisted. In other words, should the intervener be granted authority 'by operation of the law'. As we have seen, French law answers this question affirmatively.[43] German law, however, denies the intervener authority to act as an agent for the person assisted.[44] In the German view, it is simply not

[38] *Surrey Breakdown Ltd v Knight* [1999] RTR 84 at 88. [39] See above p. 111.
[40] See also *The Sarpen* [1916] P 306 at 315, *per* Pickford LJ, cited above in Part II, Section 11.9.
[41] See above, pp. 104–5 and 109 respectively. [42] See above, pp. 177–178.
[43] Art. 1375 *C.civ.* [44] See above, p. 110.

necessary to confer such authority.[45] After all, how would the mere fact that he does not have authority constitute a disincentive to a potential intervener? However, the German position does overlook one important consideration. While the intervener may not be discouraged from intervention by a lack of authority to bind the beneficiary, he may nevertheless find that successful intervention is impossible, because he does not have the required means. As has become particularly clear in shipping cases, necessary interventions can occasionally be very costly. It is doubtful whether a lender would have been willing to accept the personal credit of a shipmaster for any substantial amount of money. The risk of insolvency would simply have been too great. It is exactly for this reason that shipmasters were given authority to pledge the credit of the ship- and cargo owners. While interventions on land will rarely involve a similarly high level of costs, it would not be prudent to exclude the possibility altogether. It is therefore submitted that in cases in which it is a necessary prerequisite for a successful outcome of the intervention that the intervener be allowed to bind the person assisted, the law should provide the required authority.

[45] Staudinger/Wittmann (1995), *Vorbem. zu* §§ 677 ff., *RdNr* 60. Cf. A. Ernst, *Schuldrecht, Besonderer Teil* (1999), pp. 245–246.

EPILOGUE

Epilogue

This book commenced with the biblical parable of the good Samaritan. This parable, it was observed, raises two private law issues: firstly, whether those who are in the position of the priest and the Levite have a legal duty to aid the wounded man and, secondly, whether those who do intervene – like the Samaritan did – have in law a claim against the beneficiary of their intervention. Both issues were addressed separately. Part I was concerned with the former issue, and established that in English law there is no general duty to intervene for the benefit of another where a reasonable person would do so. In this respect, it turned out, English law is different from both French and German law. French law not only imposes penal sanctions for failure to intervene in certain circumstances, but when it comes to claims in negligence it treats misfeasance and nonfeasance, broadly speaking, alike. The German criminal code also includes a provision that penalizes failure to intervene in an emergency, but there the courts have been more reluctant than their French counterparts to recognize corresponding duties in private law.

In Part II the second issue was addressed. Again, it emerged that the approach taken by the English courts is fundamentally different from the position in civilian jurisdictions. Where English law in principle denies the good Samaritan a claim – and then proceeds to formulate exceptions to this principle – French and German law contain a general rule that does grant the intervener a right to be reimbursed for expenses incurred and to be compensated for loss suffered.

Thus, it appears that English law discourages beneficial intervention on two levels. It threatens those who do intervene with liability in negligence if they display carelessness in the course of the intervention, while it rewards those who refuse to intervene with immunity against such liability. Again, intervention is discouraged when the courts deny interveners a claim, thereby forcing them to risk having to bear all the cost of the intervention themselves. By contrast, French and German law encourage intervention on roughly the same two levels. Those who refuse to intervene where a reasonable person would do so risk incurring criminal sanctions and – at least in France – risk having to compensate the victims of their apathy. Meanwhile, the doctrine of *negotiorum gestio* neutralizes the cost of the intervention to potential interveners, by allowing them to claim reimbursement and compensation from the beneficiary.

Clearly there is, in the words of Levmore, 'some evidence of symmetry, or of balance, between carrots and sticks'.[1] The systems that penalize non-intervention offer at least reimbursement and compensation to necessitous interveners. By contrast, the system that does not penalize non-intervention – the English system – generally denies the necessitous intervener a claim against the beneficiary of his intervention. This symmetry could, of course, be purely coincidental. However, it is here suggested that the two issues, while not perfectly symmetrical, are indeed connected. We have encountered traces of this connection earlier in this book; most prominently, of course, when we discussed Lord Hoffmann's defence of the rule of no liability for nonfeasance in *Stovin v Wise*. One of the grounds on which his Lordship justified this rule, was that English law does not in principle grant a claim to the voluntary intervener. 'So there must be some special reason why he should have to put his hand in his pocket'.[2] Conversely, in *China Pacific S.A. v Food Corporation of India*, the existence of an affirmative duty was one of the factors that persuaded the House of Lords to grant the appellants a claim for expenses incurred. Having established that even a gratuitous bailee owes his bailor a duty to take care of the bailed goods, Lord Diplock concluded that if the bailor fulfils that duty, he should have 'a *correlative* right to charge the owner of the goods with the expenses reasonably incurred in doing so'.[3]

The question we must ask ourselves is to what extent the two issues discussed in this book are correlated. If the views expressed at the end of Part I are accepted – and if the rigid distinction between misfeasance and nonfeasance were to be abandoned – how would this affect our answer to the question whether the good Samaritan ought to be granted a claim? Conversely, if interveners were to be granted a claim, would this add force to the argument in favour of abandoning the misfeasance/nonfeasance distinction? Or, as Levmore might put it, if we provide sticks, should we also provide carrots, and *vice versa*?[4] In part, this question has already been answered. In Part I, Section 3.5 it was observed that the law does not generally impose duties without giving something in return. A general duty to act, however, would not have a built-in *quid pro quo*.[5] It would be somewhat unjust, we concluded, to require the priest and the Levite to intervene without ensuring that for them the intervention would at least be cost-neutral.[6] Hence, our answer to the question that was addressed in the first part of this book depends to some extent on how we answer the question that was advanced in the second part.

[1] S. Levmore, 'Waiting for Rescue: An Essay on the Evolution and Incentive Structure of the Law of Affirmative Obligations', (1986) 72 Virginia LR 879–941.

[2] *Stovin v Wise* [1996] 3 All ER 801 at 819, quoted above, Part I, Section 3.1.

[3] *China Pacific S.A. v Food Corporation of India* (HoL) [1982] AC 939 at 960 (emphasis added).

[4] S. Levmore, 'Waiting for Rescue: An Essay on the Evolution and Incentive Structure of the Law of Affirmative Obligations', (1986) 72 Virginia LR 879–941.

[5] Cf. D. Friedmann, 'Valid, Voidable, Qualified and Non-existing Obligations: An Alternative Perspective on the Law of Restitution' in A. Burrows (ed.), *Essays on the Law of Restitution* (1991), pp. 247–278 at 253.

[6] See Part II, Section 13.1 (c), above.

Liability for omissions, it could be argued, should not be imposed unless the law also grants the intervener a remedy: 'no sticks without carrots'.[7]

A similar dependency, however, does not affect the second part of this book. At this point it becomes apparent that the relation between the two issues is not one of perfect symmetry. There is no reason why the law could not grant interveners a remedy, without at the same time forcing them to intervene. This is recognized also in civilian jurisdictions. For example, neither French nor German law requires a person to risk his own safety to rescue a fellow human being. Nevertheless, both jurisdictions allow the brave intervener who does put his own life on the line for another reimbursement of expenses and compensation of loss suffered.[8] Unlike the first part, therefore, the argument developed in the second part of this book can stand entirely on its own.

In summary, it is here recommended that English law abandon the rigid distinction between misfeasance and nonfeasance in favour of a test that treats negligent acts and omissions alike, but takes account of the defendant's personal circumstances in cases in which the defendant could not avoid being subjected to the affirmative duty in question. Secondly, it is here suggested that the courts should aim to develop a general principle allowing necessitous interveners to claim reimbursement of expenses as well as compensation for loss suffered in the course of the intervention, subject to the various requirements set out in Part II, Chapter 13. Arguably, the first recommendation stands or falls with the second: 'no sticks without carrots'. The reverse is not true: even if the use of sticks is rejected, the argument in favour of introducing carrots loses nothing of its validity. In this book, however, I have advocated the use of both sticks and carrots.

[7] Cf. A. Burrows, *The Law of Restitution* (2nd edn 2002), p. 318.
[8] Provided, of course, that the intervention was reasonable.

Select Bibliography

Abbott, J.H. (ed.), *A Treatise of the Law Relative to Merchant Ships and Seamen* (5th edn 1827).

Allen, C.K., 'Legal Duties' (1931) 40 Yale LJ 331–380, reprinted in C.K. Allen, *Legal Duties and Other Essays in Jurisprudence* (1931), pp. 156–220.

Aitken, L.J.W., 'Negotiorum gestio and the Common Law: A Jurisdictional Approach', (1988) 11 Sydney LR 566–598.

Albert, R.A., 'Restitutionary Recovery for Rescuers of Human Life' (1986) 74 Cal LR 85–125.

American Law Institute, *Restatement of the Law of Restitution* (1937).

Ames, J.B., *Lectures on Legal History* (1913).

Austin, J., *Lectures on Jurisprudence* (1863).

Bacon, M., *A New Abridgment of the Law* (1736–1740).

Bagshaw, R., 'Proximity's Siren Song: Negligence Liability of Fire Brigades in England', (1998) 6 Tort L Rev 109–113.

—— 'The duties of care of emergency service providers' [1999] LMCLQ 71–92.

Baker, J.H., and S.F.C. Milsom, *Sources of English Legal History* (1986).

—— 'The Use of Assumpsit for Restitutionary Money Claims' in E.J.H. Schrage, *Unjust Enrichment* (2nd edn 1999), pp. 31–57.

—— *An Introduction to English Legal History* (4th edn 2002).

Bar, C. von, *Verkehrspflichten: richterliche Gefahrensteuerungsgebote im deutschen Deliktsrecht* (1980).

—— *The Common European Law of Torts* (1998–2000).

Barker, K., 'Unreliable Assumptions in the Modern Law of Negligence' (1993) 109 LQR 461–484.

Batson, C.D., 'Altruism and Prosocial Behaviour' in D.T. Gilbert, S.T. Fiske and G. Lindzey (eds), *The Handbook of Social Psychology*, Vol. 2 (4th edn 1998).

Beinart, B., '*Culpa in Omittendo*' [1949] THRHR 141–169.

Bell, J., S. Boyron, and S. Whittaker, *Principles of French Law* (1998).

Bentham, J., *An Introduction to the Principles of Morals and Legislation* (J.H. Burns and H.L.A. Hart, eds, 1970).

Bertzel, K., '*Der Notgeschäftsführer als Repräsentant des Geschäftsherrn*' (1959) 158 *AcP* 107–150.

Birks, P.B.H., '*Negotiorum Gestio* and the Common Law' (1971) 24 CLP 110–132.

—— 'Restitution for Services' (1974) 27 CLP 13–36.

—— and J. Beatson, 'Unrequested Payment of Another's Debt' (1976) 92 LQR 188–212.

—— *An Introduction to the Law of Restitution* (1985).

—— 'Doing and causing to be done' in A.D.E. Lewis and D.J. Ibbetson, *The Roman Law Tradition* (1994), pp. 32–54.

—— and Ch. Mitchell, 'Unjust Enrichment' in P.B.H. Birks (ed.), *English Private Law*, Vol II (2000), pp. 525–635.

—— *Unjust Enrichment* (2003).

Birnbacher, D., *Tun und Unterlassen* (1995).
Bohlen, F.H., 'The Moral Duty to Aid Others as a Basis of Liability' [1908] 56 U.Pa.LR 217.
Bout, R., *Juris-Classeur Civil, Quasi-contrats, Gestion d'Affaires, artt.* 1372–1375 *C.civ.* (1996).
Brice, G., *Maritime Law of Salvage* (3rd edn 1999).
Buckland W.W., and A.D. McNair, *Roman Law and Common Law* (1936).
Burrows, A., *The Law of Restitution* (2nd edn 2002).
—— and E. McKendrick, *Cases and Materials on the Law of Restitution* (1997).
Cane, P., 'Negligent Solicitors and Disappointed Beneficiaries' (1980) 96 LQR 182–185.
—— *The Anatomy of Tort Law* (1997).
—— *Atiyah's Accidents, Compensation and the Law* (6th edn 1999).
Carnegie, A.R , 'Bailment and Contract in English Law Today', (1966) 3 Adel LR 7.
Comyns, J., *A Digest of the Laws of England* (5th edn 1822).
Cornish W.R., 'Interveners and Unjust Enrichment' (1975) 38 MLR 563–566.
Dagan, H., 'In Defense of the Good Samaritan' (1999) 97 Michigan LR 1152–1200.
Dam, C.C. van, *Aansprakelijkheid voor nalaten*, Preadvies voor de Nederlandse Vereniging voor Rechtsvergelijking (1995).
Dawson, J.P., '*Negotiorum Gestio*: the Altruistic Intermeddler' (1961) 74 Harvard LR 817–865 and 1073–1129.
—— 'The Self-Serving Intermeddler', (1974) 87 Harvard LR 1409–1458.
Deci, E.L., R.M. Ryan and R. Koestner, 'A Meta-Analytic Review of Experiments Examining the Effects of Extrinsic Rewards on Intrinsic Motivation', (1999) 125 Psychological Bulletin 627–668.
Degeling, S.E., *Victims and Carers; Liabilities in Tort and Unjust Enrichment* (1998) (Unpublished thesis, University of Oxford).
Delvilani, A-F, *La Responsabilité Civile pour Omission ou Abstention* (1978).
Domat, J., *Les loix civiles dans leur ordre naturel* (rev. edn 1745).
Dovidio, J.F., J.A. Piliavin, S.L. Gaertner, D.A. Schroeder and R.D. Clark, 'The Arousal: Cost–Reward Model and the Process of Intervention' in M.S. Clark, *Prosocial Behavior* (1991), pp. 86–118.
Dütz, W., '*Zur privatrechtlichen Bedeutung unterlassener Hilfeleistung (§ 330c StGB)*', (1970) 23 *NJW* 1822–1826.
Eisenberger R., and J. Cameron, 'Detrimental Effects of Reward: Reality or Myth?', (1996) 51 American Psychologist 1153–1166.
Eldredge, L.H., *Modern Tort Problems* (1941).
Epstein, R.A., 'A Theory of Strict Liability', (1973) 2 J.Leg.Stud. 151.
Fifoot, C.H.S., *History and Sources of the Common Law* (1949).
Finch, H., *Law, or a Discourse Thereof* (1678 edn).
Fischer, D.A., 'Causation in Fact in Omission Cases' [1992] Utah LR 1335.
Fleming, D., 'Knights Errant and the Law' (1982) 41 CLJ 33–36.
Fleming, J.G., *The Law of Torts* (9th edn 1998).
Frey B.S., and L. Goette, 'Does Pay Motivate Volunteers?' (1999).
Friedmann, D., 'Valid, Voidable, Qualified and Non-existing Obligations: An Alternative Perspective on the Law of Restitution' in A. Burrows (ed.), *Essays on the Law of Restitution* (1991), pp. 247–278.
Galligan, T.C., 'Aiding and Altruism: a Mythopsycholegal Analysis' (1994) 27 Univ. of Michigan Journal of Law Reform 439–520.

Gerven, W. van, J. Lever and P. Larouche, *Cases, Materials and Text on National, Supranational and International Tort Law* (2000).

Glover, J., *Causing Death and Saving Lives* (1977).

Goff, Lord, of Chieveley and G. Jones, *The Law of Restitution* (6th edn 2002).

Goodhart, A.L., 'Rescue and Voluntary Assumption of Risk', (1934) 5 CLJ 192–203.

Gray, N., and J. Edelman, 'Developing the Law of Omissions: a Common Law Duty to Rescue?' (1998) 6 TLJ 240–259.

Gregory, Ch. O., 'Gratuitous Undertakings and the Duty of Care', 1 De Paul LR 30 (1951).

Hadden, T., 'Larceny by Finding – How Not to Reform the Law', [1965] CLJ 173–175.

Hager, J., *J. von Staudingers Kommentar zum Bürgerlichen Gesetzbuch* (13th edn 1999), § 823 (hereafter: Staudinger/Hager (1999)).

Halsbury, the Earl of, *The Laws of England* (1907–1914).

Harris, J.W., *Legal Philosophies* (2nd edn 1997).

Hart, H.L.A., and A.M. Honoré, *Causation in the Law* (2nd edn 1985).

Hartshorne, J., 'The Liability in Negligence of the Fire Service – the Court of Appeal Decides', (1997) 13 PN 53–58.

Hedley, S., *Restitution: Its Division and Ordering* (2001).

Hoffmann, H-J, *Die Abstufung der Fahrlässigkeit in der Rechtsgeschichte* (1986).

Honoré, A.M., 'Are Omissions Less Culpable?' in P. Cane and J. Stapleton (eds), *Essays for Patrick Atiyah* (1991).

—— 'Law, Morals and Rescue' in J.M. Ratcliffe (ed.), *The Good Samaritan and the Law* (1966), pp. 225 ff., reprinted and expanded in A.M. Honoré, *Making Law Bind, Essays Legal and Philosophical* (1987), pp. 256 ff.

Hocquet-Berg, S., '*Remarques sur la Prétendue Convention d'Assistance*' *Gaz Pal* 1996 (*Doctrine*), 32–40.

Holdsworth, W.S., *A History of English Law*, Vol. III (3rd edn 1923).

—— *A History of English Law*, Vol. VIII (1903).

Holmes, O.W., *The Common Law* (1881).

Hope, E.W., 'Officiousness', (1929–30) 15 Cornell LQ 25–53 and 205–242.

Hoyano, L.C.H., 'The Dutiful Tortfeasor in the House of Lords' (1995) 3 Tort LR 63–75.

Ibbetson, D.J., *A Historical Introduction to the Law of Obligations* (1999).

Jackson, R.M., *The History of Quasi-Contract in English Law* (1936).

Jaffey, P., *The Nature and Scope of Restitution* (2000).

Jones, G., 'Restitutionary Claims for Services Rendered' (1977) 93 LQR 273–295.

—— *Restitution in Public and Private Law* (1991).

Jones, W., *An Essay on the Law of Bailments* (1781).

Kant, I., *The Metaphysics of Morals*, translated by M. Gregor (1991).

Keener, W.A., *A Treatise on the Law of Quasi-Contracts* (1893).

Keeton, W. Page (ed.), *Prosser and Keeton on the Law of Torts* (5th edn 1984).

Kemp, D., 'Voluntary Services Provided by Tortfeasor to his Victim' (1994) 10 LQR 524–526.

Kemp, K.J., 'The Duty to Rescue – Compulsion or Laissez faire?', (1985) XVIII CILSA 163–186.

—— *Delictual Liability for Omissions* (1978) (Unpublished thesis, University of Port Elizabeth, South Africa).

Kohler, J., '*Die Menschenhülfe im Privatrecht*', (1887) 25 *Jahrbücher für die Dogmatik des heutigen römischen und deutschen Privatrechts* 1–141.

Krupp, E., '*Kameradschaftspflichten und Rechtspflichten*', (1938) 8 *DR* 465.
Kunda Z., and S.H. Schwartz, 'Undermining Intrinsic Moral Motivation: External Reward and Self-Presentation', (1983) 45 Journal of Personality and Social Psychology 763–771.
Landes W.M., and R.A. Posner, 'Salvors, Finders, Good Samaritans, and Other Rescuers: an Economic Study of Law and Altruism', (1978) 7 J.Leg.Stud. 83–128.
Lawson, F.H., *Negligence in the Civil Law* (1950).
—— and B.S. Markesinis, *Tortious Liability for Unintentional Harm in the Common Law and the Civil Law*, Vols I & II (1982).
Levmore, S., 'Waiting for Rescue: An Essay on the Evolution and Incentive Structure of the Law of Affirmative Obligations', (1986) 72 Virginia LR 879–941.
Linden, A.M., 'Rescuers and Good Samaritans' (1971) MLR 241.
Lowndes, R., *The Law of General Average* (1873).
Luntz, H., 'Torts Turnaround Downunder' (2001) 1 OUCLJ 95–106.
Marasinghe, M.L., 'The Place of Negotiorum Gestio in English Law', (1976) 8 Ottowa LR 573–587.
Markesinis, B.S., 'Negligence, Nuisance and Affirmative Duties of Action' (1989) 105 LQR 104.
—— W. Lorenz and G. Dannemann, *The German Law of Obligations*, Vol. I (1997).
—— and H. Unberath, *The German Law of Torts* (4th edn 2002).
Matthaeus, A., *De Criminibus* (1644).
Matthews P., and M. Lunney, 'A Tortfeasor's Lot is not a Happy One?' (1995) 58 MLR 395–404.
Mazeaud, H., L. Mazeaud and A. Tunc, *Traité Théorique et Pratique de la Responsabilité Civile* (6th edn 1965).
McInnes, M., 'Life Rescue in Maritime Law' (1994) 25 JMLC 451–484.
McKendrick, E., 'Taxonomy: Does it Matter?' in D. Johnston and R. Zimmermann, *Unjustified Enrichment: Key Issues in Comparative Perspective* (2002), pp. 627–657.
Mill, J.S., *On Liberty* (G. Himmelfarb, ed., 1974).
Milsom, S.F.C., 'Not Doing is No Trespass' (1954) 12 CLJ 105–117.
Mitchell, C., *The Law of Subrogation* (1994).
Mitchell, P., 'A Ratio Decidendi for Upton-on-Severn Rural District Council v Powell', (1997) 12 Journal of Contract Law 76–86.
Moore, S.A., *A History of the Foreshore and the Law Relating Thereto* (3rd edn 1888).
Muir, G.A., 'Unjust Sacrifice and the Officious Intervener' in P.D. Finn (ed.), *Essays on Restitution* (1990), pp. 297–351.
Munkman, J.H., *The Law of Quasi-Contracts* (1950).
Oechsler, J., *J. von Staudingers Kommentar zum Bürgerlichen Gesetzbuch* (13th, rev. edn 2003), § 826 (hereafter: Staudinger/Oechsler (2003)).
Palmer, G.E., 'History of Restitution in Anglo-American Law' in P. Schlechtriem (ed.), *International Encyclopedia of Comparative Law*, Vol. X, 'Restitution – Unjust Enrichment and Negotiorum Gestio' (1989), ch. 3.
Palmer, N.E., *Bailment* (2nd edn 1991).
Partsch, J., *Studien zur Negotiorum Gestio I* (1913).
Pernice, A., *Zur Lehre von den Sachbeschädigungen nach Römischem Rechte* (1867).
Picard, M., '*La Gestion d'Affaires dans la Jurisprudence Contemporaine*', *Rev.trim.dr.civ.* 1921, 419–467.

Piliavin, J.A., J.F. Dovidio, S.L. Gaertner, and R.D. Clark, *Emergency Intervention* (1981).
Plucknett, Th.F.T., *A Concise History of the Common Law* (5th edn 1956).
Pollock, F., *Principles of Contract* (1876).
—— *The Law of Torts* (1887).
—— and F.W. Maitland, *The History of English Law before the Time of Edward I*, Vol. II (2nd edn 1898).
Posner, R.A., *Economic Analysis of Law* (5th edn 1998).
Pothier, R.J., *Traité du Contrat de Mandat* (edn 1821).
Powell, R., *The Law of Agency* (2nd edn 1961).
Prosser, W.L., *Selected Topics on the Law of Torts* (1953).
Pufendorf, S. von, *De Jure Naturae et Gentium* (edn 1688).
Pyle, A. (ed.), *Liberty: Contemporary Responses to John Stuart Mill* (1994).
Ratcliffe, J.M. (ed.), *The Good Samaritan and the Law* (1966).
Reckseen, D., 'The Duty to Rescue' (1972) Indiana LJ 321.
Reed, A., 'A Commentary on *Hunt v Severs*' (1995) 15 OJLS 133–140.
Reynolds, F.M.B., *Bowstead and Reynolds on Agency* (17th edn 2001).
Richards, D.A.J., 'Kantian Ethics and the Harm Principle: a Reply to John Finnis' (1987) 87 Columbia LR 457–471.
Riou, M., 'L'Acte de Dévouement', *Rev.trim.dr.civ.* 1957, 221–245.
Rose, F.D., 'Restitution for Inland Salvage' (1986) 102 LQR 185–191.
—— 'Restitution for the Rescuer' (1989) 9 OJLS 167–204.
—— *General Average* (1997).
—— *Kennedy and Rose: the Law of Salvage* (6th edn 2002).
Ruhstrat, E., '*Beiträge zur Lehre von der Negotiorum Gestio*' (1849) 32 *AcP* 173–199.
Saxoferrato, Bartolus de, *Super prima parte ff. vetus* (edn 1489) *ad D.* 7.1.13.2.
Schäfer, K., *J. von Staudingers Kommentar zum Bürgerlichen Gesetzbuch* (12th edn 1985) (hereafter: Staudinger/Schäfer (1985)).
Schlechtriem, P., *Schuldrecht, Besonderer Teil* (5th edn 1998).
Schoordijk, H.C.F., *De verbintenis uit en de verplichting tot altruisme* (1987).
Schubert, W., '*Der Tatbestand der Geschäftsführung ohne Auftrag*' (1978) 178 *AcP* 425–455.
Schulz, F., '*Nachklassische Quaestionen in den justinianischen Reformgesetzen des Codex Justinianus*', (1930) 50 *ZSS* 212–248.
—— *Classical Roman Law* (1951).
Seavey, W.A., 'Reliance on Gratuitous Promises or Other Conduct' [1951] 64 Harvard LR 913.
Seiler, H.H., *Der Tatbestand der Negotiorum Gestio im römischen Recht* (1968).
—— in H.P. Westermann (ed.), *Münchener Kommentar zum Bürgerlichen Gesetzbuch*, Vol. 4 (3rd edn 1997) (hereafter: *MünchKomm* – Seiler (1997)).
Smith J.C., and P. Burns, 'Donoghue v. Stevenson – the Not So Golden Anniversary' (1983) 46 MLR 147.
Smith, L.D., 'The Province of the Law of Restitution' (1992) 71 Can BR 672–699.
Smits, J.M., *The Good Samaritan in European Private Law* (2000).
Staub, E., D. BarTal, J. Karylowski and J. Reykowski (eds), *The Development and Maintenance of Prosocial Behaviour* (1982).
Steele, R.D., *The National Assistance Act 1948* (1949).
St. German, Chr., *Doctor and Student* (T.F.T. Plucknett and J.L. Barton, eds, 1974).

Stoljar, S.J., 'Negotiorum Gestio' in E. von Caemmerer and P. Schlechtriem (eds), *International Encyclopedia of Comparative Law*, Vol. X, 'Restitution – Unjust Enrichment and Negotiorum Gestio' (1984), ch. 17.

—— *The Law of Quasi-Contract* (2nd edn 1989).

Stoll, H., '*Rechtsfragen bei Hilfeleistung in vermeintlicher Not*' in H. Ehmann, W. Hefermehl and A. Laufs (eds), *Privatautonomie, Eigentum und Verantwortung* (1980), pp. 411–430.

Story, J., *Commentaries on the Law of Agency* (1839).

—— *Commentaries on the Law of Bailments* (4th edn 1846).

Thomas, J.A.C., *Textbook of Roman Law* (1976).

Titmuss, R.M., *The Gift Relationship* (original ed. with new chapters, A. Oakley and J. Ashton, eds, 1997).

Treitel, G.H., 'Agency of Necessity', (1954) 3 Univ of Western Australia LR 1–12.

Tunc, A., 'The Volunteer and the Good Samaritan' in J.M. Ratcliffe, (ed.), *The Good Samaritan and the Law* (1966), pp. 43–62.

Virgo, G., *The Principles of the Law of Restitution* (1999).

Voet, J., *Commentarius ad Pandectas*, Vol. I (6th edn 1731).

Wächter, C.G. von, '*Beiträge zur Lehre von der Negotiorum Gestio*' (1837) 20 *AcP* 333–361.

Watson, A., *The Law of Obligations in the Later Roman Republic* (1965).

—— *Contract of Mandate in Roman Law* (1961).

Watts, P., 'Guarantees Undertaken Without the Request of the Debtor', [1989] LMCLQ 7–10.

Weimar, W.. '*Besteht eine Schadensersatzpflicht eines Krankenhauses bei Abweisung Schwerverletzter?*' *JR* 1975, 145.

—— '*Schadensersatzpflicht bei Schädigungen durch Unterlassen*', (1937) 7 *DR* 77.

Weinrib, E.J., 'The Case for a Duty to Rescue', (1980) 90 Yale LJ 247–293.

—— 'Law as a Kantian Idea of Reason' (1987) 87 Columbia LR 472–508.

—— *The Idea of Private Law* (1995).

Weir, J.A., 'Doing Good by Mistake – Restitution and Remedies' (1973) 71 CLJ 23–28.

Wellmann, R., *Der Aufwendungsersatz des Geschäftsführers ohne Auftrag in der Rechtsprechung der anglo-amerikanischen Gerichte* (1959).

Welzel, H., '*Zur Dogmatik der echten Unterlassungsdelikte, insbesondere des § 330c StGB*', *NJW* 1953, 327.

Williams, G.L., *Liability for Animals* (1939).

—— 'Some Reforms in the Law of Tort' (1961) 24 MLR 101–115.

Williams, K., 'Medical Samaritans: Is there a Duty to Treat?' (2001) 21 OJLS 393–413.

Williston, W.B., 'Agency of Necessity' [1944] 22 Can Bar Rev 492–508.

Windscheid B., and Th. Kipp, *Lehrbuch des Pandektenrechts*, Vol. 2 (9th edn 1906).

Winfield, P.H., *The Province of the Law of Tort* (1931).

—— *The Law of Quasi-Contracts* (1952).

Wittmann, R., *Begriff und Funktionen der Geschäftsführung ohne Auftrag* (1981).

—— in *J. von Staudingers Kommentar zum Bürgerlichen Gesetzbuch* (13th edn 1995) (hereafter: Staudinger/Wittmann (1995)).

Wlassak, M., *Zur Geschichte der Negotiorum Gestio* (1879).

Wollschläger, Chr., *Geschäftsführung ohne Auftrag im öffentlichen Recht und Erstattungsanspruch* (1977).

Woodward, F.C., *The Law of Quasi Contracts* (1913).
Zimmermann, E., *Die Lehre von der Stellvertretenden Negotiorum Gestio* (1876).
Zimmermann, R., '*Der Selbstmort als Gefährdungssachverhalt*' (1979) *FamRZ* 103–110.
—— *The Law of Obligations: Roman Foundations of the Civilian Tradition* (1996).
Zyl, D.H. van, *Negotiorum Gestio in South African Law* (1985).

Index